THE SCANDALS OF TRANSLATION

'*The Scandals of Translation* is one of the most provocative and far-reaching books to be published in the field of Translation Studies in recent years. Lawrence Venuti has proved himself a cultural commentator of the very first order. This book should be required reading for all those engaged in the humanities.'

Terry Hale, Performance Translation Centre, University of Hull

'Venuti proposes a radical reformulation of what constitutes a valid translation . . . I find everything he says intellectually stimulating. If a good book makes the reader want to enter into a personal dialogue with the author, this is a very good book.'

Michael Henry Heim, University of California at Los Angeles

Translation remains on the margins of society. Stigmatized as a form of authorship, discouraged by copyright law, depreciated by the academy, exploited by publishers and corporations, governments and religious organisations. Lawrence Venuti argues that translation is in this predicament because it reveals the contradictions and exclusions of dominant cultural values and institutions and thereby calls their authority into question.

Venuti exposes what he refers to as the 'scandals of translation' by looking at the relationship between translation and the practices which at once need and marginalize it. The book moves between different languages, cultures, periods, disciplines and institutions and is richly illustrated by numerous case studies including: Bible translation in the early Christian Church; translations of poetry and philosophy from classical Greek and German (Homer, Plato, Aristotle, Wittgenstein, Heidegger); translations of the modern Japanese novel; the translation of bestsellers, advertisements and business journalism; and the author's own translation of the Italian writer, I.U. Tarchetti.

The Scandals of Translation advances current thinking about translation, as Venuti works towards the formulation of an ethics that enables translations to be written, read and evaluated with greater respect for linguistic and cultural differences.

Lawrence Venuti is professor of English at Temple University, Philadelphia. He is a professional translator and the author of *The Translator's Invisibility: A history of translation* (Routledge, 1995).

THE SCANDALS OF TRANSLATION

Towards an ethics of difference

Lawrence Venuti

London and New York

First published 1998
by Routledge
11 New Fetter Lane, London EC4P 4EE

Simultaneously published in the USA and Canada
by Routledge
29 West 35th Street, New York, NY 10001

Reprinted 1999

Transferred to Digital Printing 2003

Routledge is an imprint of the Taylor & Francis Group

© 1998 Lawrence Venuti

Typeset in Bembo by
The Florence Group, Stoodleigh, Devon

British Library Cataloguing in Publication Data
A catalogue record for this book is available from the British Library.

Library of Congress Cataloging in Publication Data
Venuti, Lawrence
The scandals of translation: towards an ethics of difference /
Lawrence Venuti.
Includes bibliographical references and index.
1. Translating and interpreting – Moral and ethical aspects.
2. Intercultural communication. I. Title.
P306.2.V45   1998.
418'.02 – dc21   98-9530

ISBN 0–415–16929–1 (hbk)
ISBN 0–415–16930–5 (pbk)

FOR GEMMA LEIGH VENUTI

*C'è un amore più grande
di te e di me, me e voi nella specie,
acqua su acqua.*

CONTENTS

Introduction 1

1 Heterogeneity 8

2 Authorship 31

3 Copyright 47

4 The formation of cultural identities 67

5 The pedagogy of literature 88

6 Philosophy 106

7 The bestseller 124

8 Globalization 158

Acknowledgements 190
Bibliography 193
Index 206

INTRODUCTION

scandal. A grossly discreditable circumstance, event, or condition of things.

Oxford English Dictionary

The scandals of translation are cultural, economic, and political. They are revealed when one asks why translation today remains in the margins of research, commentary, and debate, especially (although not exclusively) in English. Any description of these margins risks seeming a mere litany of abuse, the premise of an incredible victimology of translation and the victims it leaves in its wake. Translation is stigmatized as a form of writing, discouraged by copyright law, depreciated by the academy, exploited by publishers and corporations, governments and religious organizations. Translation is treated so disadvantageously, I want to suggest, partly because it occasions revelations that question the authority of dominant cultural values and institutions. And like every challenge to established reputations, it provokes their efforts at damage control, their various policing functions, all designed to shore up the questioned values and institutions by mystifying their uses of translation.

My project is, first, to expose these scandals by enquiring into the relationships between translation and a range of categories and practices that contribute to its current marginal status. This enquiry must begin with the emergent discipline of translation studies. Translation research and translator training have been impeded by the prevalence of linguistics-oriented approaches that offer a truncated view of the empirical data they collect. Because such approaches promote scientific models for research, they remain reluctant to take into account the social values that enter into translating as well as the study of it. Research thus becomes scientistic, claiming to be objective or value-free, ignoring the fact that translation, like any cultural practice, entails the creative reproduction of values. As a result, translation studies get reduced to the formulation of general theories and the description of textual features and strategies. These lines of research are not only limited in their explanatory power, but directed primarily to other academic specialists in linguistics, instead of translators or readers of translations or even specialists in other humanistic disciplines. In the end, translation suffers from an institutional isolation, divorced from the contemporary cultural developments and debates that invest it with significance.

By far the greatest hindrances to translation, however, exist outside the discipline itself. Translation is degraded by prevalent concepts of authorship, especially in literature and in literary scholarship, and these concepts underwrite its unfavorable definition in copyright law, not only the codes of specific national jurisdictions, but the major international treaties. Translation lies deeply repressed in the cultural identities that are constructed by academic, religious, and political institutions; in the pedagogy of foreign literatures, notably the "Great Books," the canonical texts of Western culture; and in the discipline of philosophy, the academic study of philosophical concepts and traditions. Translation figures hugely in the corporate world, in the international publishing of bestsellers and the unequal patterns of cross-cultural commerce between the hegemonic Northern and Western countries and their others in Africa, Asia, and South America. Translation powers the global cultural economy, enabling transnational corporations to dominate the print and electronic media in the so-called developing countries by capitalizing on the marketability of translations from the major languages, preeminently English. "Developing" here means no more than a backward relation to world capitalism. Translation embarrasses the institutions that house these categories and practices because it calls attention to their questionable conditions and effects, the contradictions and exclusions that make them possible – and discredit them.

The scandals may appear where we least expect them. The April 1990 issue of the *Courier*, a monthly magazine published by UNESCO to promote intercultural understanding, ran an article – in its Spanish and English editions – that presented a history of Mexican peoples. The English translation is extraordinary for its ideological slanting against pre-Columbian Mexicans, whose oral culture is represented as inferior, especially as a repository of the past (Mason 1994; cf. Hatim and Mason 1997: 153–159). Thus, "antiguos mexicanos" ("ancient Mexicans") is rendered as "Indians," distinguishing them sharply from their Spanish colonizers; "sabios" ("wise men") as "diviners," opposing them to European rationalism; and "testimonias" ("testimonies") as "written records," subtly privileging literary over oral traditions. The most recurrent term in the Spanish text, "memoria," a crucial faculty for the oral transmission of culture, is translated variously as "history" and "knowledge of the past," as well as "memory." In the following sentence, the translation has edited the Spanish, diminishing the indigenous culture by simplifying the syntax and deleting another key term, "mitos" ("myths"):

> Los mitos y leyendas, la tradición oral y el gran conjunto de inscripciones perpetuaron la memoria de tales aconteceres.

2

The memory of these events lives on in the thousands of inscrip-
tions and the legends of oral tradition.

As Mason observed, we do not need to attribute a deliberate intention to
the translator in order to perceive the skewed representation in the translation (Mason 1994: 33). The ideological slanting against the indigenous
population is inscribed in specific discursive choices which work both to
create a subordinate identity and to make it seem natural or obvious – as
it must have seemed to the translator and the magazine editors. Or perhaps
they were guided by a translation strategy that prizes the utmost clarity, easy
readability, so that the most familiar language turned out to be the most
prejudicial, but unconsciously so. What does seem obvious is that the thinking
about translation at UNESCO – an institution that is utterly dependent on
translating and interpreting for its operation – is not incisive enough to vet
a translated text that compromises its basic principles and goals.

Despite the magnitude of this particular example, the exposures that translation enables here will seek to avoid the sensationalism inherent in any
simple muckraking. I want instead to initiate a productive rethinking of the
questioned values and institutions, although through their anxious relationships with translation. I want to explore the ways in which translation
redefines authorship in literature and in law, creates identities receptive to
cultural difference, requires different approaches to teaching literature and
to doing philosophy, and recommends new policies for publishers and corporations. In the process translation will be conceived anew on the basis of
detailed case studies, resulting in a set of theoretical concepts that carry practical consequences.

Specific cases, past and present, are invaluable for the light they shed not
only on the current marginality of translation, but on the meanings and
functions it can support if greater attention were paid to its diverse motives
and effects. Translations are produced for many reasons, literary and commercial, pedagogical and technical, propagandistic and diplomatic. Yet no
translator or institutional initiator of a translation can hope to control or
even be aware of every condition of its production. And no agent of a
translation can hope to anticipate its every consequence, the uses to which
it is put, the interests served, the values it comes to convey. Nonetheless,
it is these conditions and consequences that offer the most compelling
reasons for discriminating among the stakes involved in translating and reading
translations.

My chapters present a series of cultural studies that aim to advance current
thinking about translation. They move between several different languages,
cultures, periods, disciplines, and institutions in an effort to describe and
evaluate the social effects of translated texts, to expand the possibilities for
translation projects, to establish translation more firmly as an area of research
in the academy, and to win for translators greater cultural authority and a

more favorable legal status, especially (although not exclusively) in the United States and the United Kingdom.

The authority I wish to achieve for translators and translations isn't a mere aggrandizement. It doesn't trade on the cultural prestige now enjoyed by original authors and compositions – novelists, say, or poets – or on the official nature of the institutions in which their prestige is maintained. On the contrary, because translating is intercultural, it involves a distinct kind of authorship, secondary to the foreign text and in the service of different communities, foreign as well as domestic. The only authority that translation can expect depends on its remaining derivative, distinguishable from the original compositions that it tries to communicate, and collective, remaining open to the other agents who influence it, especially domestic readerships. Hence, the only prestige that a translator can gain comes from practicing translation, not as a form of personal expression, but as a collaboration between divergent groups, motivated by an acknowledgement of the linguistic and cultural differences that translation necessarily rewrites and reorders. Translating, like any writing, is usually practiced in solitary conditions. But it links multitudes, often in the most unexpected groupings.

The focus on the marginality of translation is strategic. It assumes that a study of the periphery in any culture can illuminate and ultimately revise the center. Yet in the case of translation, of cross-cultural exchange, the peripheries are multiple, domestic and foreign at once. They take the form of marginal cultures, so defined by their position in national or global frameworks, situated in relation to hegemonic languages, a standard dialect at home and English generally, still the most translated language worldwide. The overriding assumption of this book is perhaps the greatest scandal of translation: asymmetries, inequities, relations of domination and dependence exist in every act of translating, of putting the translated in the service of the translating culture. Translators are complicit in the institutional exploitation of foreign texts and cultures. But there have also been translators who acted just as dubiously on their own, not in the employ of any bureaucracy.

Between 1967 and 1972, the American translator Norman Thomas di Giovanni worked closely with the Argentine writer Jorge Luis Borges, publishing several English-language volumes of Borges's fiction and poetry, acting as his literary agent, helping him gain the canonical status he enjoys today (Rostagno 1997: 117–120). Yet di Giovanni's editing and translating aggressively revised the Spanish texts to increase their accessibility to an American readership: he assimilated them to American stylistic canons, adhering to current standard usage, smoothing out the abrupt transitions in Borges's prose, avoiding abstractions in favor of concrete diction, even correcting quotations that the writer made from memory (Howard 1997). Of his work with Borges, di Giovanni said: "I liken it to cleaning a painting: you could see the bright colors and the sharp outlines underneath where you couldn't before" (ibid.: 49). Di Giovanni felt he was advocating a writerly approach to translation, opposed to "professors and pseudoscholars who look at writing through microscopes, placing too much emphasis on single words and abstractions" (ibid.: 44). But he was himself enforcing a discursive regime that sought to repress the literary peculiarities of Borges's innovative writing, practicing an anti-intellectualism in the translation of a most intellectual writer. After four years Borges abruptly ended their collaboration.

Authors have in turn exploited translators, but few have publicly denounced the translations of their writing. The Czech novelist Milan Kundera seems unique not only in scrutinizing and correcting the foreign-language versions of his books, but in asserting his preferred translation practice in wittily pointed essays and prefaces. The most notorious case involves the different English versions of his novel *The Joke* (1967). The first in 1969 appalled Kundera because it edited, excised, and rearranged chapters; the second in 1982 was "unacceptable" because he judged it "not my text," a "translation–adaptation (adaptation to the taste of the time and of the country for which it is intended, to the taste, in the final analysis, of the translator)" (Kundera 1992: x).

Kundera is rightly suspicious of domesticating translations that assimilate foreign literary texts too forcefully to dominant values at home, erasing the sense of foreignnness that was likely to have invited translation in the first place (see Kundera 1988: 129–130). Yet how can any foreignness be registered in a translation except through another language – i.e., through the taste of another time and country? Kundera's thinking about translating is remarkably naive for a writer so finely attuned to stylistic effects. He assumes that the meaning of the foreign text can avoid change in translation, that the foreign writer's intention can travel unadulterated across a linguistic and cultural divide. A translation always communicates an interpretation, a foreign text that is partial and altered, supplemented with features peculiar to the translating language, no longer inscrutably foreign but made comprehensible in a distinctively domestic style. Translations, in other words, inevitably perform a work of domestication. Those that work best, the most powerful in recreating cultural values and the most responsible in accounting for that power, usually engage readers in domestic terms that have been defamiliarized to some extent, made fascinating by a revisionary encounter with a foreign text.

Kundera, in effect, wishes to control the interpretations put forward by French and English translators – but on the basis of the author's sheer disagreement with them. That a translation was well received in French or English, important for achieving an international readership for the author, doesn't matter to Kundera (whose own writing has acquired considerable cultural and economic capital through translations). He wishes only to evaluate the relationship between the translation and the foreign text as if his access to the latter were direct and unmediated. With Kafka, he criticizes the French use of "marcher" ("walk") to translate "gehen" ("go, walk") because the resulting effect "is surely not what Kafka wanted here" (Kundera 1995: 105). But a translation can't give what a foreign writer would want if he were alive and writing in the translating language and culture. What Kafka would write in French can be no more than another French interpretation, not a rendering more faithful or adequate to the German text. The fact that the author is the interpreter doesn't make the interpretation unmediated by target-language values.

Kundera doesn't want to recognize the linguistic and cultural differences that a translation must negotiate; he rather wants to preside over them by selecting the ones he most prefers. Thus, he produced a third English version of his novel *The Joke*, which he cobbled together not just from his own English and French renderings, but also from the "many fine solutions" and the "great many faithful renderings and good formulations" in the previous translations (Kundera 1992: x). Whether the translators consented to Kundera's handling of their work remains unclear; the title page of his revision does not list their names.

Copyright law permits Kundera to get away with his questionable uses of translation by giving him an exclusive right in works derived from his. The law underwrites his view that the author should be the sole arbiter of all interpretations of his writing. And that turns out to mean that he can be arbitrary as well. Kundera's "definitive" English version of *The Joke* actually revises the 1967 Czech text: it omits more than fifty passages, making the novel more intelligible to the Anglo-American reader, removing references to Czech history but also altering characters (Stanger 1997). Kundera's preface passed silently over these revisions. In fact, he concluded his version with the misleading notation, "completed December 5, 1965," as if he had merely translated the unabridged original text. When the author is the translator, apparently, he is not above the domestications that he attacked in previous English versions.

Translation clearly raises ethical questions that have yet to be sorted out. The mere identification of a translation scandal is an act of judgment: here it presupposes an ethics that recognizes and seeks to remedy the asymmetries in translating, a theory of good and bad methods for practicing and studying translation. And the ethics at issue must be theorized as contingent, an ideal grounded in the specific cultural situations in which foreign texts are chosen and translated or in which translations and the act of translating are made the objects of research. I articulate these ethical responsibilities first in terms of my own work, beginning with a discussion of the choices I confront as an American translator of literary texts. The issue of a translation ethics is addressed subsequently in other pertinent contexts, particularly when the power of translation to form identities and qualify agents is examined. The ethical stance I advocate urges that translations be written, read, and evaluated with greater respect for linguistic and cultural differences.

Insofar as translation involves an intercultural collaboration, my aim extends to the global reach of my topic: to address translators and users of translations throughout the world, but with an attentiveness to their different locations that influences the terms of address. The more detailed the case studies, the more historically and locally specified, the more deeply they interrogate and shape the theoretical concepts derived from them. This critical give-and-take seems essential for studying the many dimensions of cross-cultural exchange. For translation looms large among the cultural practices that at once join and separate us.

1

HETEROGENEITY

Although the growth of the discipline called "translation studies" has been described as "a success story of the 1980s" (Bassnett and Lefevere 1992: xi), the study of the history and theory of translation remains a backwater in the academy. Among the English-speaking countries, this is perhaps most true of the United States, where only a handful of graduate programs in translator training and translation research have been instituted, and foreign-language departments continue to assign greater priority to the study of literature (literary history, theory, and criticism) than to translating, whether literary or technical (see Park 1993). Yet elsewhere as well, despite the recent proliferation of centers and programs throughout the world (see Caminade and Pym 1995), translation studies can only be described as emergent, not quite a discipline in its own right, more an interdiscipline that straddles a range of fields depending on its particular institutional setting: linguistics, foreign languages, comparative literature, anthropology, among others.

This fragmentation might suggest that translation research is pursued with a great deal of scholarly openness and resistance against rigidly compart-mentalized thinking. But it has produced just the opposite effect. Indeed, translation hasn't become an academic success because it is beset by a frag-mentary array of theories, methodologies, and pedagogies, which, far from being commensurate, still submit to the institutional compartments of intel-lectual labor (now adjusted to admit translation). The prevalent approaches can be divided – loosely but without too much conceptual violence – into a linguistics-based orientation, aiming to construct an empirical science, and an aesthetics-based orientation that emphasizes the cultural and political values informing translation practice and research (see Baker 1996; cf. Robyns 1994: 424–425).

This theoretical division is reflected, for example, in Routledge's recent publishing in translation studies. In the early 1990s, these books were published in two different areas, each with its own commissioning editor, catalogue, and audience: "linguistics and language studies" and "literary and cultural studies." The potential market seemed so divided that Routledge cut back its translation studies series (whose general editors then left to initiate a similar series with Multilingual Matters Ltd). Currently, Routledge shrewdly aims to counter the fragmentation of the field by assigning the commissioning responsibilities to the linguistics editor, who is pursuing more interdisciplinary projects. Yet this international publisher, at once academic and commercial, remains unique. In English, and no doubt in other languages, translation studies tend to be published by small presses, whether trade or university, for a limited, primarily academic readership, with most sales made to research libraries. Splintered into narrow constituencies by disciplinary boundaries, translation is hardly starting new trends in scholarly publishing or setting agendas in scholarly debate.

This current predicament embarrasses translation studies by suggesting that it is suffering, to some extent, from a self-inflicted marginality. With rare exceptions, scholars have been reluctant to negotiate areas of agreement and to engage more deeply with the cultural, political, and institutional problems posed by translation (for an exception see Hatim and Mason 1997). And so a critical assessment of the competing theoretical orientations, an account of their advances and limitations, seems in order. As a translator and student of translation, I can evaluate them only as an interested party, one who has found cultural studies a most productive approach, but who remains unwilling to abandon the archive and the collection of empirical data (how could studies be cultural without them?). My main interest in the theories lies in their impact on the methodological fragmentation that characterizes trans-lation research and keeps translation in the margins of cultural discourse, both in and out of the academy. The question that most concerns me is whether theorists are capable of bringing translation to the attention of a larger audience – larger, that is, than the relatively limited ones to which the competing theories seem addressed. This question of audience in fact guides my own theory and practice of translation, which are premised on the irreducible heterogeneity of linguistic and cultural situations. To assess the current state of the discipline, then, and to make intelligible my assess-ment, I must begin with a manifesto of sorts, a statement of why and how I translate.

Writing a minor literature

As an American translator of literary texts I devise and execute my projects with a distinctive set of theoretical assumptions about language and textuality. Perhaps the most crucial is that language is never simply an instrument of com-munication employed by an individual according to a system of rules – even if communication is undoubtedly among the functions that language can perform. Following Deleuze and Guattari (1987), I rather see language as a collective force, an assemblage of forms that constitute a semiotic regime. Circulating among diverse cultural constituencies and social institutions, these forms are positioned hierarchically, with the standard dialect in dominance but subject to constant variation from regional or group dialects, jargons, clichés and slogans, stylistic innovations, nonce words, and the sheer accumulation of previous uses. Any language use is thus a site of power relationships because a language, at any historical moment, is a specific conjuncture of a major form holding sway over minor variables. Lecercle (1990) calls them the "remainder." The linguistic variations released by the remainder do not merely exceed any communicative act, but frustrate any effort to formulate systematic rules. The remainder subverts the major form by revealing it to be socially and historically situated, by staging "the return within language of the contradictions and struggles that make up the social" and by containing as well "the anticipation of future ones" (Lecercle 1990: 182).

A literary text, then, can never simply express the author's intended meaning in a personal style. It rather puts to work collective forms in which the author may indeed have a psychological investment, but which by their very nature depersonalize and destabilize meaning. Although literature can be defined as writing created especially to release the remainder, it is the stylistically innovative text that makes the most striking intervention into a linguistic conjuncture by exposing the contradictory conditions of the standard dialect, the literary canon, the dominant culture, the major language. Because ordinary language is always a multiplicity of past and present forms, a "diachrony-within-synchrony" (Lecercle 1990: 201–208), a text can be no more than "a synchronic unity of structurally contradictory or heterogeneous elements, generic patterns and discourses" (Jameson 1981: 141). Certain literary texts increase this radical heterogeneity by submitting the major language to constant variation, forcing it to become minor, delegitimizing, deterritorializing, alienating it. For Deleuze and Guattari such texts compose a minor literature, whose "authors are foreigners in their own tongue" (1987: 105). In releasing the remainder, a minor literature indicates where the major language is foreign to itself.

It is this evocation of the foreign that attracts me to minor literatures in my translation projects. I prefer to translate foreign texts that possess minority status in their cultures, a marginal position in their native canons – or that, in translation, can be useful in minoritizing the standard dialect and dominant cultural forms in American English. This preference stems partly from a political agenda that is broadly democratic: an opposition to the global hegemony of English. The economic and political ascendancy of the United States has reduced foreign languages and cultures to minorities in relation to its language and culture. English is the most translated language worldwide, but one of the least translated into (Venuti 1995a: 12–14), a situation that identifies translating as a potential site of variation.

To shake the regime of English, a translator must be strategic both in selecting foreign texts and in developing discourses to translate them. Foreign texts can be chosen to redress patterns of unequal cultural exchange and to restore foreign literatures excluded by the standard dialect, by literary canons, or by ethnic stereotypes in the United States (or in the other major English-speaking country, the United Kingdom). At the same time, translation discourses can be developed to exploit the multiplicity and polychrony of American English, "conquer[ing] the major language in order to delineate in it as yet unknown minor languages" (Deleuze and Guattari 1987: 105). Foreign texts that are stylistically innovative invite the English-language translator to create sociolects striated with various dialects, registers and styles, inventing a collective assemblage that questions the seeming unity of standard English. The aim of minoritizing translation is "never to acquire the majority," never to erect a new standard or to establish a new canon, but rather to promote cultural innovation as well as the understanding of cultural difference by proliferating the variables within English: "the minority is the becoming of everybody" (ibid.: 106, 105).

My preference for minoritizing translation also issues from an ethical stance that recognizes the asymmetrical relations in any translation project. Translating can never simply be communication between equals because it is fundamentally ethnocentric. Most literary projects are initiated in the domestic culture, where a foreign text is selected to satisfy different tastes from those that motivated its composition and reception in its native culture. And the very function of translating is assimilation, the inscription of a foreign text with domestic intelligibilities and interests. I follow Berman (1992: 4–5; cf. his revision in 1995: 93–94) in suspecting any literary translation that mystifies this inevitable domestication as an untroubled communicative act. Good translation is demystifying: it manifests in its own language the foreignness of the foreign text (Berman 1985: 89).

This manifestation can occur through the selection of a text whose form and theme deviate from domestic literary canons. But its most decisive occurrence depends on introducing variations that alienate the domestic language and, since they are domestic, reveal the translation to be in fact a translation, distinct from the text it replaces. Good translation is minoritizing: it releases the remainder by cultivating a heterogeneous discourse, opening up the standard dialect and literary canons to what is foreign to themselves, to the substandard and the marginal. This does not mean conceiving of a minor language as merely a dialect, which might wind up regionalizing or ghetto-izing the foreign text, identifying it too narrowly with a specific cultural constituency – even though certain foreign texts and domestic conjunctures might well call for a narrow social focus (e.g. Québec during the 1960s and 1970s, when canonical European drama was translated into *joual*, the working-class dialect, to create a national Québecois theater: see Brisset 1990). The point is rather to use a number of minority elements whereby "one invents a specific, unforeseen, autonomous becoming" (Deleuze and Guattari 1987: 106). This translation ethics does not so much prevent the assimilation of the foreign text as aim to signify the autonomous existence of that text behind (yet by means of) the assimilative process of the translation.

Insofar as minoritizing translation relies on discursive hetereogeneity, it pursues an experimentalism that would seem to narrow its audience and contradict the democratic agenda I have sketched. Experimental form demands a high aesthetic mode of appreciation, the critical detachment and educated competence associated with the cultural elite, whereas the communicative function of language is emphasized by the popular aesthetic, which demands that literary form be not only immediately intelligible, needing no special cultural expertise, but also transparent, sufficiently realistic to invite vicarious participation (Bourdieu 1984: 4–5, 32–33; cf. Cawelti 1976, Radway 1984, Dudovitz 1990).

Yet translation that takes a popular approach to the foreign text isn't necessarily democratic. The popular aesthetic requires fluent translations that produce the illusory effect of transparency, and this means adhering to the current standard dialect while avoiding any dialect, register, or style that calls attention to words as words and therefore preempts the reader's identification. As a result, fluent translation may enable a foreign text to engage a mass readership, even a text from an excluded foreign literature, and thereby initiate a significant canon reformation. But such a translation simultaneously reinforces the major language and its many other linguistic and cultural exclusions while masking the inscription of domestic values. Fluency is assimilationist, presenting to domestic readers a realistic representation inflected with their own codes and ideologies as if it were an immediate encounter with a foreign text and culture.

The heterogeneous discourse of minoritizing translation resists this assimilationist ethic by signifying the linguistic and cultural differences of the text – within the major language. The heterogeneity needn't be so alienating as to frustrate a popular approach completely; if the remainder is released at significant points in a translation that is generally readable, the reader's participation will be disrupted only momentarily. Moreover, a strategic use of minority elements can remain intelligible to a wide range of readers and so increase the possibility that the translation will cross the boundaries between cultural constituencies, even if it comes to signify different meanings in different groups. A minoritizing translator can draw on the conventionalized language of popular culture, "the patter of comedians, of radio announcers, of disc jockeys" (Lecercle 1988: 37), to render a foreign text that might be regarded as elite literature in a seamlessly fluent translation. This strategy would address both popular and elite readerships by defamiliarizing the domestic mass media as well as the domestic canon for the foreign literature. Minoritizing translation can thus be considered an intervention into the contemporary public sphere, in which electronic forms of communication driven by economic interest have fragmented cultural consumption and debate. If "the public is split apart into minorities of specialists who put their reason to use non-publicly and the great mass of consumers whose receptiveness is public but uncritical" (Habermas 1989: 175), then translating should seek to invent a minor language that cuts across cultural divisions and hierarchies. The goal is ultimately to alter reading patterns, compelling a not unpleasurable recognition of translation among constituencies who, while possessing different cultural values, nonetheless share a long-standing unwillingness to recognize it.

A minoritizing project

I was able to explore and test these theoretical assumptions in recent translations involving the nineteenth-century Italian writer I.U. Tarchetti (1839–69). From the start the attraction was his minority status, both in his own time and now. A member of a Milanese bohemian subculture called the "scapigliatura" (from "scapigliato," meaning "dishevelled"), Tarchetti sought to unsettle the standard Tuscan dialect by using it to write in marginal literary genres: whereas the dominant fictional discourse in Italy was the sentimental realism of Alessandro Manzoni's historical novel, *I promessi sposi* (*The Betrothed*), Tarchetti favored the Gothic tale and the experimental realism of French novelists like Flaubert and Zola (Venuti 1995a: 160–161). The Italian standards against which Tarchetti revolted were not just linguistic and literary, but moral and political as well: whereas Manzoni posited a Christian providentialism, recommending conjugal love and resigned submission before the status quo, Tarchetti aimed to shock the Italian bourgeoisie, rejecting good sense and decency to explore dream and insanity, violence and aberrant sexuality, flouting social convention and imagining fantastic worlds where social inequity was exposed and challenged. He was admired by his contemporaries and, amid the cultural nationalism that characterized newly unified Italy, was soon admitted to the canon of the national literature. Yet even if canonical he has remained a minor figure: he receives abbreviated, sometimes dismissive treatment in the standard manuals of literary history, and his work fails to resurface in the most provocative debates in Italian writing today.

A translation project involving Tarchetti, I realized, would have a minoritizing impact in English. His writing was capable of unsettling reigning domestic values by moving between cultural constituencies. In *Fantastic Tales* (1992) I chose to translate a selection of his work in the Gothic, a genre that has both elite and popular traditions. Initially a middlebrow literature in Britain (Ann Radcliffe), the Gothic was adopted by many canonical writers (E.T.A. Hoffmann, Edgar Allan Poe, Théophile Gautier) and has since undergone various revivals, some satisfying a highbrow interest in formal refinement (Eudora Welty, Patrick McGrath), others offering the popular pleasure of sympathetic identification (Anne Rice, Stephen King). Importing Tarchetti would cast these traditions and trends in a new light. It would also challenge the canon of nineteenth-century Italian fiction in English, long dominated by Manzoni and Giuseppe Verga, the two major realists. Although Italy is a recurrent motif in the Gothic, *Fantastic Tales* was the first appearance in English of the first Gothic writer in Italian.

Tarchetti wrote other texts that were equally flexible in their potential appeal. Under the title *Passion* (1994) I translated his novel *Fosca*, which mixes romantic melodrama with realism in an experiment variously suggestive of *Madame Bovary* and *Thérèse Raquin*. In English *Fosca* promised to straddle readerships as a rediscovered classic and as a historical romance, a foreign wrinkle on the bodice ripper. Yet as I was translating the Italian text I also learned that Tarchetti's novel had metamorphosed into a "tie-in," the source of an adaptation in a popular form: Stephen Sondheim and James Lapine's Broadway musical *Passion* (1994). Suddenly, a canonical Italian text, which in English might be expected to interest mainly an elite audience, was destined to have a much wider circulation.

What especially attracted me to Tarchetti's writing was its impact on the very act of translating: it invited the development of a translation discourse that submitted the standard dialect of English to continual variation. From the beginning I determined that archaism would be useful in indicating the temporal remoteness of the Italian texts, their emergence in a different cultural situation at a different historical moment. Yet any archaism had of course to be drawn from the history of English, had to signify in a current English-language situation, and would therefore release a distinctive literary remainder. With *Fantastic Tales* I assimilated the Italian texts to the Gothic tradition in British and American literature, modeling my syntax and lexicon on the prose of such writers as Mary Shelley and Poe, ransacking their works for words and phrases that might be incorporated in the translation. This is not to say that accuracy was sacrificed for readability and literary effect, but that insofar as any translating produces a domestic remainder, adding effects that work only in the domestic language and literature, I made an effort to focus them on a specific genre in English literary history. In minoritizing translation, the choice of strategies depends on the period, genre, and style of the foreign text in relation to the domestic literature and the domestic readerships for which the translation is written (cf. the translation ethic of "respect" in Berman 1995: 92–94).

My version in fact follows the Italian quite closely, often resorting to calque renderings to secure a suitably archaic form of English. This excerpt from Tarchetti's tale, "Un osso di morto" ("A Dead Man's Bone"), is typical:

Nel 1855, domiciliatomi a Pavia, m'era allo studio del disegno inuna scuola privata di quella città; e dopo alcuni mesi di soggiorno aveva stretto relazione con certo Federico M. che era professore di patologia e di clinica per l'insegnamento universitario, e che morì di apoplessia fulminante pochi mesi dopo che lo aveva conosciuto. Era un uomo amantissimo delle scienze, della sua in particolare – aveva virtù e doti di mente non comuni – senonché, come tutti gli

anatomisti ed i clinici in genere, era scettico profondamente e inguari-
bilmente – lo era per convinzione, né io potei mai indurlo alle mie
credenze, per quanto mi vi adoprassi nelle discussioni appassionate
e calorose che avevamo ogni giorno a questo riguardo.

(Tarchetti 1977: 65)

In 1855, having taken up residence at Pavia, I devoted myself to
the study of drawing at a private school in that city; and several
months into my sojourn, I developed a close friendship with a
certain Federico M., a professor of pathology and clinical medicine
who taught at the university and died of severe apoplexy a few
months after I became acquainted with him. He was very fond of
the sciences and of his own in particular – he was gifted with extraordinary mental powers – except that, like all anatomists and doctors
generally, he was profoundly and incurably skeptical. He was so by
conviction, nor could I ever induce him to accept my beliefs, no
matter how much I endeavored in the impassioned, heated discus-
sions we had every day on this point.

(Venuti 1992: 79)

The archaism in the English passage is partly a result of its close adherence to
the Italian, to Tarchetti's suspended sentence construction and his period diction ("soggiorno," "apoplessia," "indurlo" are calqued: "sojourn," "apoplexy,"
"induce him"). In other cases, when a choice presented itself I took the
archaism over current usage: for "né io potei mai," I used the inverted construction "nor could I ever" instead of the more fluent "and I could never"; for
"per quanto mi vi adoprassi," I preferred the slightly antique formality of "no
matter how much I endeavored" instead of a modern colloquialism, "no matter
how hard I tried."

The translation discourse of *Fantastic Tales* deviates noticeably from current
standard English, yet not so much as to be incomprehensible to most contemporary readers. This was evident in the reception. I tried to shape readers'
responses in an introductory essay that alerted them to the minoritizing
strategy. The reviews made clear, however, that the archaism also registered
in the reading experience, and not only by situating Tarchetti's tales in the
remote past, but by implicitly comparing them to English-language Gothic
and thus establishing their uniqueness. Most importantly, the archaism called
attention to the translation as a translation without unpleasurably disrupting
the reading experience. The *Village Voice* noticed the "atmospheric wording
of the translations" (Shulman 1992), while *The New Yorker* remarked that
the "translation distills a gothic style never heard before, a mixture of
Northern shadows and Southern shimmer" (1992: 119).

Such reviews suggest that the formal experiment in the translation was
most keenly appreciated by the cultural elite, readers with a literary education,

if not academics with a specialist's interest. Yet *Fantastic Tales* also appealed to other constituencies, including fans of horror writing who are widely read in the Gothic tradition. A reviewer for the popular Gothic magazine, *Necrofile*, concluded that the book "is not so very esoteric that it has nothing to offer the casual reader," adding that "the connoisseur will undoubtedly be grateful for 'Bouvard' and 'The Fated,'" two tales that he felt distinguished Tarchetti as a "contributor to the rich tradition of nineteenth-century fantasy" (Stableford 1993: 6).

Tarchetti's *Fosca* encouraged a more heterogeneous translation discourse because he pushed his peculiar romanticism to an alienating extreme, making the novel at once serious and parodic, participatory and subversive. The plot hinges on a triangle of erotic intrigue: the narrator Giorgio, a military officer engaged in an adulterous affair with the robust Clara, develops a pathological obsession with his commander's cousin, the repulsively emaciated Fosca, a hysteric who falls desperately in love with him. The themes of illicit love, disease, female beauty and ugliness, the pairing of the bourgeois ideal of domesticated femininity with the vampire-like femme fatale – these familiar conventions of the romantic macabre again prompted me to assimilate the Italian text to nineteenth-century British literature, and I fashioned an English style from related novels like Emily Brontë's *Wuthering Heights* (1847) and Bram Stoker's *Dracula* (1897). Yet to match the emotional extravagance of Tarchetti's novel, I made the strain of archaism more extensive and denser, still comprehensible to a wide spectrum of contemporary American readers yet undoubtedly enhancing the strangeness of the translation. The theoretical point here is that the strategies developed in minoritizing translation depend fundamentally on the translator's interpretation of the foreign text. And this interpretation always looks in two directions, since it is both attuned to the specifically literary qualities of that text and constrained by an assessment of the domestic readerships the translator hopes to reach, a sense of their expectations and knowledge (of linguistic forms, literary traditions, cultural references).

I imagined my readership as primarily American, so the effect of strangeness could also be obtained through Britishisms. I used British spellings ("demeanour," "enamoured," "apologised," "offence," "ensure"), even a British pronunciation: "a herb" instead of the American "an herb," a choice that provoked an exasperated query from the publisher's copyeditor, "What can you mean by this?" (Venuti 1994: 33, 95, 108, 157, 188, 22). Some archaisms resulted from calque renderings: "in tal guisa" became "in such guise"; "voler far le beffe della mia sconfitta," which in modern English might be translated as "wanting to make fun of my defeat," became "wanting to jest at my discomfiture"; "addio" became "adieu" instead of "goodbye"; and where Tarchetti's Rousseau-influenced thinking led him to write "amor proprio," I reverted to the French: "amour propre" (Tarchetti 1971: 140, 151, 148, 60; Venuti 1994: 146, 157, 154, 60). I adopted syntactical inversions characteristic of nineteenth-century English: "Mi basta di segnare qui alcune epoche" ("It was enough for me to note down a few periods [of my life] here") became "Suffice it for me to record a few episodes" (Tarchetti 1971: 122; Venuti 1994: 128). And I seized every opportunity to insert an antique word or phrase: "abbandonato" ("abandoned") became "forsaken"; "da cui" ("from which") became "whence"; "dirò quasi" ("I should almost say") became "I daresay"; "fingere" ("deceive") became "dissemble"; "fu indarno" ("it was useless") became "my efforts were unavailing," a sentence lifted directly from Stoker's *Dracula* (Tarchetti 1971: 31, 90, 108, 134; Venuti 1994: 31, 92, 109, 140).

The more excessive archaism worked to historicize the translation, signaling the nineteenth-century origins of the Italian text. Yet to indicate the element of near-parody in Tarchetti's romanticism, I increased the heterogeneity of the translation discourse by mixing more recent usages, both standard and colloquial, some distinctly American. Occasionally, the various lexicons appeared in the same sentence. I translated "Egli non è altro che un barattiere, un cavaliere d'industria, una cattivo soggetto" ("He is nothing more than a swindler, an adventurer, a bad person") as "He is nothing but an embezzler, a con artist, a scapegrace," combining a modern American colloquialism ("con artist") with a British archaism ("scapegrace") that was used in novels by Sir Walter Scott, William Thackeray, George Meredith (Tarchetti 1971: 106; Venuti 1994: 110; *OED*). This technique immerses the reader in a world that is noticeably distant in time, but nonetheless affecting in contemporary terms – and without losing the awareness that the prose is over the top.

At a few points, I made the combination of various lexicons more jarring to remind the reader that he or she is reading a translation in the present. One such passage occurred during a decisive scene in which Giorgio spends an entire night with the ecstatic but ailing Fosca, who is dying for love of him:

> Suonarono le due ore all'orologio.
> – Come passa presto la notte; il tempo vola quando si è felici – diss'ella.
>
> (Tarchetti 1971: 82)

> The clock struck two.
> "How quickly the night passes; time flies when you're having fun," she said.
>
> (Venuti 1994: 83)

The adage-like expression, "time flies when you're having fun," is actually a close rendering of the Italian (literally, "time flies when one is happy"). Yet in current American English it has acquired the conventionality of a cliché, used most often with irony, and with this remainder it can have multiple effects. On the one hand, the cliché is characteristic of Fosca, who both favors pithy statements of romantic commonplaces and is inclined to be ironic in her conversation; on the other hand, the abrupt appearance of a contemporary expression in an archaic context breaks the realist illusion of the narrative, interrupting the reader's participation in the characters' drama and calling attention to the moment in which the reading is being done. And when this moment is brought to mind, the reader comes to realize that the text is not Tarchetti's Italian, but an English translation.

Another opportunity to produce these effects occurred in one of Giorgio's introspective passages. When he describes his tendency toward extreme psychological states, he rationalizes, "Perché non mirare agli ultimi limiti?" ("Why not aim for the utmost bounds?"), which I translated as "Why not shoot for the outer limits?" (Tarchetti 1971: 18; Venuti 1994: 18). This rendering, also quite close to the Italian, nonetheless releases an American remainder: it alludes to space travel and, more specifically, to *The Outer Limits*, a 1960s television series devoted to science fiction themes. It too disrupts the engrossed reader by suddenly foregrounding the domestic culture where the reading experience is situated, introducing a contemporary popular code in what might otherwise be taken for an archaic literary text. But the allusion can simultaneously be absorbed into a highbrow interpretation: it is appropriate to the character, since it points to the fantastic nature of Giorgio's romanticism.

The discursive heterogeneity of my translation deviated not only from the standard dialect of English, but from the realism that has long dominated Anglo-American fiction. As a result, the reception varied according to the readership. The translation discourse found more favor with elite readers who were accustomed to formal experiments, as I gathered from interviews with colleagues, university-level teachers of British and American literature. Among readers who took the popular approach, responses depended on the degree of interest in Tarchetti's narrative. In an unsolicited letter, a member of an informal reading group in southern California complimented the publisher "on a lovely book," expressing particular appreciation for the "chilling drama of [Fosca's] death" (Heinbockel 1995). For other popular readers, sympathetic identification did not come readily, so they wanted greater fluency to support it. The review service, Kirkus, praised *Passion* precisely because it offered a thrilling experience: "Tarchetti's striking novel," the reviewer wrote, "has it all – obsession, deception, sex, death, and passion," noting as well that "both unwilling lover and disapproving reader are woven into [Fosca's] spell" (Kirkus Reviews 1994). The translation, however, was judged to be "sometimes stiff, with an occasional jarring phrase."

The nonfiction writer Barbara Grizzuti Harrison, who reviewed the book for the *New York Times*, went further by questioning Tarchetti's narrative altogether. And this led to a critique of my minoritizing project. For Harrison, the problems began with the Italian text. It frustrated her popular expectation for the participatory experience typically provided by melodramatic romance. But, interestingly, it also exposed her investment in an ethnic stereotype, the equation of "Italian" with intense emotion:

> What a strange book this is! You would think that a novel called *Passion* – by an Italian writer – would ensnare your emotions. Well, it does and it doesn't. What it does not do is affect you viscerally, notwithstanding that blood and convulsive sex and death are the stuff of it. It is a kind of literary, intellectual twister, and it poses a puzzle (which does nothing to encourage the suspension of dis-belief): Is this guy for real?
>
> (Harrison 1994: 8)

For Harrison any novel that cast doubt on the realist illusion was itself suspect: it demanded the sort of critically detached response that relegated it to elite culture ("literary, intellectual twister") and preempted the pleasures of participation.

In this case, however, she was also confronted by a recalcitrant translation:

> I am obliged to wonder if some of the problems presented by *Passion* have to do with the determination of the translator, Lawrence Venuti, to use contemporary clichés, and his failure to use 20th-century colloquialisms convincingly. Surely 19th-century Italian romantics didn't have "siblings" (detestable word), and they didn't get into anything resembling a "funk"; nor was a woman of lyrical violence capable of saying, on the eve of her rapture, "Time flies when you're having fun."
>
> (ibid.)

The exaggerated effect I sought worked with this reviewer. Yet she refused to understand it according to the explanation presented in my introduction: there I stated my intention to use clichés and colloquialisms *unconvincingly*, deviating from the archaic context to mimic the characters' overheated romanticism. Harrison's refusal points to a deeper impatience with formal experiments that complicate the communicative function of language. Since the popular aesthetic prizes the illusion of reality in literary representations, erasing the distinction between art and life, she preferred the translation to be immediately intelligible so as to seem transparent, untranslated, or simply nonexistent, creating the illusion of originality. Hence her insistence that archaisms like "funk" should be omitted because Italian romantics didn't use them. This makes the naive assumption that the English version ("the funk wherein I fell") could somehow be – or be perfectly equivalent to – the Italian text ("l'abbandono in cui ero caduto"). The fact is that Italian romantics would not have used most of the words in my translation because they wrote in Italian, not English. Harrison's preference for transparency entails a mystifying concealment of translation by privileging the English dialect that is the most familiar and so the most invisible: the current standard dialect. Here is evidence that in translation the popular aesthetic reinforces the major language, the dominant narrative form (realism), even a prevalent ethnic stereotype (the passionate Italian).

My project was minoritizing, however, and *Passion* did in fact manage to reach different constituencies. This was due in large part to the serendipitous tie-in with a popular form, a Broadway musical by a leading contemporary composer. The publisher capitalized on this connection by using Sondheim and Lapine's title for the translation and by designing a striking cover to suggest the artwork that appeared in the poster and advertisements for the musical. Reviewers were drawn to the translation by the musical, which was routinely cited in reviews. Copies were sold in the lobby of the theater at performances, which continued for nearly a year. Within four months of publication, 6,500 copies were in print; within two years, 4,000 copies had been sold. The translation did not make the bestseller list, but it was widely circulated for a marginal Italian novel that had previously been unknown to English-language readers.

The tie-in undoubtedly benefited the translation more than the musical. Yet because the musical was itself a minoritizing project within the American theater, the tie-in also limited the circulation of the translation. The similarity in their strategies is striking. Working not only from the novel but from Ettore Scola's film adaptation, *Passione d'amore* (1981), Sondheim and Lapine incorporated cultural materials that were elite and Italian into a form that was popular and American, whereas I incorporated popular materials into an elite literary form, working from a novel known only to academic specialists while inscribing it with popular genres, codes, allusions.

And like the translation the musical provoked a mixed response. Some reviewers sought greater assimilation to the spectacle and sentimentality that currently dominate musical theater on Broadway. Thus the *New York Times* complained that the Sondheim–Lapine production "leads the audience right up to the moment of transcendence but is unable in the end to provide the lift that would elevate the material above the disturbing" (Richards 1994: B1). Other reviewers faulted the musical for conceding too much to Broadway, failing to develop the ironies of the narrative. To the *New Yorker* "it is just as commercially compromised as the musicals it pretends to be in rebellion against – it's forced, presumably for box-office reasons, to claim a triumph of love at the finale" (Lahr 1994: 92). Sondheim and Lapine's *Passion* submitted the musical form to sufficient variation to divide audiences, so that it inevitably sustained the divided responses that greeted the translation and helped to prevent it from being a bestseller.

But, finally, my aim was cultural, not commercial, to create a work of minor literature within the major language. And this, I believe, was accomplished.

The limitations of linguistics

My translation theory and practice have led me to question the linguistics-oriented approaches that began emerging in translation studies during the 1960s and currently constitute a prevalent trend, influencing both research and training throughout the world. These approaches, usually based on text linguistics and pragmatics, set out from diametrically opposed assumptions about language and textuality which are often deliberately limited in their explanatory power and, in certain formulations, repressive in their normative principles. From my particular standpoint as a translator, they project a conservative model of translation that would unduly restrict its role in cultural innovation and social change. Nonetheless, I don't wish to suggest that such approaches be abandoned, but rather that they be reconsidered from a different theoretical and practical orientation – one that will in turn be forced to rethink itself.

The key assumption in the linguistics-oriented approaches is that language is an instrument of communication employed by an individual according to a system of rules. Translation is then theorized on the model of Gricean conversation, in which the translator communicates the foreign text by co-operating with the domestic reader according to four "maxims": "quantity" of information, "quality" or truthfulness, "relevance" or consistency of context, and "manner" or clarity (Grice 1989: 26–27; cf. Hatim and Mason 1990: 62–65, 95–100; Baker 1992: 225–254; Neubert and Shreve 1992: 75–84).

Grice interestingly admits that language is much more than cooperative communication when he proceeds to argue that the maxims are routinely "flouted" in conversation, "exploited" by interlocutors to open up a substratum of "implicature," such as irony (Grice 1989: 30–31; Lecercle 1990: 43). In the case of translation, linguistics-oriented theorists have construed implicature as a feature of the foreign text that reveals a difference between the foreign and domestic cultures, usually a gap in the domestic reader's knowledge for which the translator must somehow compensate. Yet communication (or even compensation) doesn't quite describe the translator's remedy, which seems more like ventriloquism, a rewriting of the foreign text according to domestic intelligibilities and interests. As one commentator describes the remedy, *"information essential to the success of conversational implicatures should be included in the text* if the translation is to be coherent and sensible" (Thomson 1982: 30; his emphasis).

The problem is not this rewriting, which translators do routinely, myself included, but rather the way it is understood. Neither the conversational maxims nor implicature can account for the working of the remainder in any translation; on the contrary, they effectively repress it. The domestic linguistic forms that are added to the foreign text to make it "coherent and sensible" in the domestic culture inevitably exceed any intention to convey a message (and so violate the maxim of quantity) because these forms are at once collective and variable in significance, sedimented with the different functions they perform in different constituencies and institutions. If according to Gricean implicature translation is a process of exploiting the maxims of the domestic linguistic community (Baker 1992: 238), the remainder exposes the fact that maxims can differ within any community, and a translation discourse, even when cooperatively described in an introductory statement, can divide readerships. To compensate for an implicature in the foreign text, a translator may add footnotes or incorporate the supplementary material in the body of the translation, but either choice adheres to a different maxim of quantity that addresses a different constituency: adding footnotes to the translation can narrow the domestic audience to a cultural elite since footnotes are an academic convention.

The remainder likewise threatens other Gricean maxims. It violates the maxim of truth, or the "virtual reality" created in the translation (Neubert and Shreve 1992: 79), because the variables it contains can introduce a competing truth or break the realist illusion. Furthermore, insofar as the remainder is heterogeneous, any translation is likely to contain shifts between dialects, codes, registers, and styles that violate the maxims of relevance and manner by deviating from contexts and risking multiple meanings and obscurity. In repressing the remainder, a translation theory based on Gricean conversation leads to fluent strategies that mystify their domestication of the foreign text while reinforcing dominant domestic values – notably the major language, the standard dialect, but possibly other cultural discourses (literary canons, ethnic stereotypes, an elite or a popular aesthetic) inscribed in the translation to render a foreign implicature.

Linguistics-oriented approaches, then, would seem to block the ethical and political agenda I envisaged for minoritizing translation. Grice's cooperative principle assumes an ideal speech situation in which the interlocutors are on an equal footing, autonomous from cultural differences and social divisions. Yet the remainder, the possibility for variation in any linguistic conjuncture, means that the translator works in an asymmetrical relationship, always cooperating more with the domestic than the foreign culture and usually with one constituency among others. In the shift from conversation to translation, as one linguistics-oriented theorist has incisively observed, the cooperative principle itself is thrown into contradiction, shown to be exclusionary: "Grice's maxims seem to reflect directly notions which are known to be valued in the English-speaking world, for instance sincerity, brevity, and relevance" (Baker 1992: 237).

More, when made the basis of literary translating, the conversational maxims require that the translator not frustrate domestic expectations in the choice of foreign texts and in the development of discourses to translate them. An American literary translator will thus be inclined to maintain existing canons for domestic and foreign literatures and cultivate a homogeneous discourse by excluding what is foreign to it, the substandard and the marginal. Yet to redress the global hegemony of English, to interrogate American cultural and political values, to evoke the foreignnness of the foreign text, an American literary translator must not be cooperative, but challenging, not simply communicative, but provocative as well. Grice's pacific maxims encourage translation that strengthens current reading patterns, both elite and popular, whereas Deleuze and Guattari's agonistic concept of language encourages translation that seeks to revise those patterns by crossing the cultural boundaries between them.

The limitations of linguistics-oriented approaches are perhaps most clear with literary translation in the broad sense, not only literature but texts in the various genres and disciplines that constitute the human sciences, both fiction and nonfiction, and in electronic as well as print media. The minoritizing translator, motivated to release the domestic remainder by working with a stylistically innovative text, will not abide by the cooperative principle. Nor will a majoritarian reader who strongly resists any discursive heterogeneity that makes a reading experience less participatory and more critically detached – or, in other words, that aims to modulate between an elite and popular aesthetic. The Gricean model of translation holds out the hope that "readers' versions of reality, their expectations, and their preferences can be challenged without affecting the coherence of a text, provided the challenge is motivated and the reader is prepared for it" (Baker 1992: 249). Unfortunately, the mixed reception that met my translation of Tarchetti's *Passion* indicates that such a challenge, even though rationalized explicitly, can indeed meet with uncooperative readers: Barbara Grizzuti Harrison refused to depart from her realist expectations and therefore found the translation incoherent. Yet *Passion* showed that minoritizing translation can still move between cultural constituencies precisely because its heterogeneous discourse is able to support diverse notions of coherence that circulate among different constituencies. Current linguistics-oriented approaches lack not only the theoretical assumptions to conceptualize and execute such literary translation projects, but the methodological tools to analyze them.

Pragmatic or technical translation would seem to be better suited to theorization according to Grice's maxims. In fact, translators of scientific, commercial, legal, and diplomatic documents will be bound, by their contracts or by the conditions of their employment in agencies, to honor those maxims because the texts they translate give priority to communication in institutional terms. The translation of technical documents (e.g. scientific research, product warranties, birth certificates, peace treaties) usually occurs in such narrowly defined situations, with specialized readerships and standardized terminologies devised precisely to escape the continual variation in natural languages. Any implicature in these documents tends to be purely conventional, hardly brought into existence by the flouting that occurs in conversation. The ethics I formulated for translating literary texts, then, must be revised to accommodate the different conditions of technical translation: here good translating adheres to the conventions of the field or discipline or the practical purpose that the document is designed to serve. This is a purely functional standard, which will eventually force the evaluation of the translated text to take into account its social effects, possibly the economic and political interests it serves (e.g. Does the translator wish to translate – an instruction manual, an advertisement, a labor contract – for a transnational corporation that engages in questionable labor practices?).

Yet even with technical translation certain situations and projects may arise to warrant a violation of a Gricean maxim. In translating advertisements, a translator may find it useful to frustrate domestic expectations of a foreign culture, perhaps departing from reigning ethnic stereotypes so as to invest a product with a distinctively domestic charisma. This departure will obviously be intended to increase the effectiveness of the advertising copy in a different culture. But insofar as it occurs in a translation, the possible responses will proliferate according to different segments of the domestic audience.

During 1988, for example, British and Italian television ran advertisments for an Italian car (the Fiat Tipo) which were identical in deploying an ethnic stereotype, "the coldness and self-control of the English gentleman," and then climactically inverting it (Giaccardi 1995: 188). Filmed in English with subtitles added for the Italian audience, the advertisements featured an "imperturbable" gentleman who is silently reading a newspaper in the backseat of a taxi but who, after glimpsing an attractive woman driving a Fiat Tipo, urges his driver to follow her, heedless of traffic rules (ibid.: 165, 174). The Italian version made the stereotype more explicit and then exaggerated the deviation from it, the gentleman's abrupt emotional excitement. The English title, "Taxi Driver," was replaced by a specific English location, "Londra, Settembre 1988," and the gentleman's relatively restrained response, "Lovely," was translated into more emphatic Italian: "Splendida!" (ibid.: 189).

The advertisements worked by departing from a stereotype widely held among viewers in both countries. Yet only the English version can be satisfactorily explained as a successful irony, a Gricean implicature, and therefore a form of cooperative conversation: it left the stereotype intact partly by giving the gentleman an "Oxbridge" accent, highlighting a class code that is immediately intelligible to the English audience. "The transgression itself," in other words, "unfolds according to conventional schemes" (ibid. 190). The Italian version seems less cooperative, its effect less predictable, especially with educated Italian viewers who know English: it threatened to call attention to the conventionality of the stereotype because the translation was so exaggerated, so out of synch with the English soundtrack, with the tone of "Lovely."

Diplomatic and legal interpreting can easily involve violations of the Gricean maxim of truthfulness. In interpreting for geopolitical negotiations, a translator may wish to remove satirical innuendo, a kind of implicature that would obstruct communication by creating antagonism between the negotiators. And in court interpreting, a translator may correct grammatical errors, avoid reproducing hesitations and verbal slips, and delete culture-specific formulas, all to increase domestic intelligibility, interest, and even sympathy (Morris 1995). In these cases, the translator not only violates some conversational maxim, but raises the question of whether the translation practice can accurately be called mere communication as opposed to mysti-fication, naturalization, or palliation. And clearly the translators' violations will carry ethical and political implications, not only in their usefulness to the field that the translating is designed to serve, but also in their concern with the larger issues of peaceful international relations and the fair admin-istration of justice.

The scientific model

The most worrisome tendency in linguistics-oriented approaches is their promotion of scientific models. Because language is defined as a set of system-atic rules autonomous from cultural and social variation, translation is studied as a set of systematic operations autonomous from the cultural and social formations in which they are executed. Translation theory then becomes the synchronic description of two ideal objects: the linguistic practices that the translator performs to render the foreign text, like calque or "compen-sation" (see Harvey 1995), and the "typical situations in which certain kinds of translation are preferred" (Neubert and Shreve 1992: 34, 84–88). Yet insofar as such approaches exclude the theory of the remainder, they purify translation practices and situations of their social and historical variables, leaving literary and technical translators alike unequipped to reflect on the cultural meanings, effects, and values produced by those practices.

Keith Harvey's synthesis of the research on compensation, for example, the most comprehensive and nuanced to date, is designed to develop a set of concepts that can describe a translation practice, mainly in pedagogy (Harvey 1995: 66, 77). In Harvey's account, translators may compensate for the loss of a feature in the foreign text by adding the same or a similar feature at the same or another point in the domestic text. Thus, in trans-lating Tarchetti's *Fosca*, when I rendered "il tempo vola quando si è felici" ("time flies when one is happy") as "time flies when you're having fun," I was performing what Harvey calls a "generalized" compensation, "where the target text includes stylistic features that help to naturalize the text for the target reader and that aim to achieve a comparable number and quality of effects, without these being tied to any specific instances of source text loss" (ibid.: 84). In resorting to a colloquial catchphrase, I was compensating generally for the characters' habitual use of conventionalized language, cultural clichés. Yet the colloquialism I used released a domestic remainder that created multiple effects, not all of which were predictable, although their impact definitely depended on the reader's motivations: the colloquialism was capable of increasing the consistency of the characters, but also of breaking the realist illusion and calling attention to the translated status of my text. My rationale for producing these effects, at once ethical and political, was peculiarly domestic, designed for contemporary American culture, and therefore it included but surpassed the intention to compensate for a stylistic effect in a nineteenth-century Italian text.

In one of Harvey's own examples, the compensation similarly introduces a domestic remainder that actually alters the significance of the foreign text. An English version of the French cartoon strip *Asterix* omits a Spanish maid's "misuse of the French language," but apparently compensates for the omission by assigning the maid's employer and his friend pastiches of wine connoisseur-ship and Samuel Johnson's enlightenment humanism (ibid.: 69–71). Here the compensation spares the Spanish working-class immigrant from satire while shifting it to the French bourgeoisie through features that are directed to a more elite domestic readership (insofar as identifying the cultural allusions requires an educated reader). The remainder released in the English version can be seen as reflecting an ethnic or national rivalry between the British and the French.

Harvey seems to recognize that any compensation does much more than supply an equivalent feature in the translation. "Effect," he observes in discussing Gutt (1991), "turns out to be a function of the reader's own motivation for reading a text, and even of the various conventions that determine response in different cultures, rather than the inherent property of a particular text" (Harvey 1995: 73). But Harvey believes that "it is important to retain the term [compensation] for essentially stylistic, text-specific features and effects," since "the larger issues of the mismatch between social and cultural practices go well beyond it and threaten to make the concept too general to be of any pedagogical use or theoretical value" (ibid.: 71, 69). Without a theory of the remainder, however, a descriptive frame-work can't explain how text-specific features produce different effects according to different reader motivations and cultural conventions. And to explain how my compensatory renderings in *Passion* divided domestic reader-ships, a social theory of cultural value (e.g. Bourdieu) is necessary.

The important point is that translators should be able to provide such expla-nations as a rationale for choosing between different textual practices, different forms of compensation, and even different projects, i.e., whether to contract for them in the first place. Otherwise descriptive frameworks for textual practices are likely to encourage mechanical, unreflective translating that is not concerned with its value – or only with its utilitarian and economic as opposed to cultural and political values. "The scientific model taking language as an object of study," remark Deleuze and Guattari, "is one with the political model by which language is homogenized, centralized, standardized, becom-ing a language of power, a major or dominant language" (Deleuze and Guattari 1987: 101). Yet by repressing the heterogeneity of language, the scientific model prevents translators from understanding and evaluating what their practices admit and exclude, and what social relations those practices make possible.

A similar kind of repression has long occurred in translation research that aims to address larger cultural issues, but insists on a strictly empirical approach to them. Initially developed in the 1970s and subsequently refined in numerous papers and case studies, Gideon Toury's orientation is avowedly scientific, avoiding prescriptive accounts of translation to examine actual translation practices (cf. Shreve 1996). He sets out from the assertion that "translations are facts of target cultures" (Toury 1995: 29), the domestic situations where foreign texts are chosen for translation and discursive strategies are devised to translate them. And within that situation he emphasizes the "norms" that constrain the translator's activity (ibid.: 53), the diverse values that shape translation decisions, and that are themselves shaped by translations, or, more generally, by patterns of importing foreign forms and themes. Toury is less interested in the "adequacy" of a translation to the foreign text because he knows that "shifts" always occur between them, and in any case, a measurement of adequacy, even the identification of a "source" text, involves the usually implicit application of a domestic norm (ibid.: 56–57, 74, 84). His project is rather to describe and explain the domestic "acceptability" of a translation, the ways in which various shifts constitute a type of "equivalence" which conforms to domestic values at a certain historical moment (ibid.: 61, 86).

There can be no doubt about the historical importance of Toury's work. With such other like-minded theorists as Itamar Even-Zohar, André Lefevere, and José Lambert, Toury helped to establish translation studies as a distinct discipline by defining the object of study, the target text circulating in a "polysystem" of cultural norms and resources (for a survey of this group, see Gentzler 1993: chap. 5). Today Toury's target emphasis is shared by any scholar or translator who would address translation in its own terms. His concepts and methods have in effect become basic guidelines (even when they aren't explicitly attributed to him) because they make translation intelligible in linguistic and cultural terms. When studying translation you can't avoid comparing the foreign and translated texts, looking for shifts, inferring norms, even when you know that all these operations are no more than interpretations constrained by the domestic culture. Although Toury does not refer to Lecercle's concept of the remainder, translation shifts might be construed as encompassing it: shifts involve the inscription of domestic values in the foreign text.

Nonetheless, some two decades later, the limitations of Toury's project emerge more clearly. The claim of science has come to seem theoretically naive or perhaps disingenuous. Toury feels that he must base translation research on a scientific model to establish translation studies as a legitimate discipline. "No empirical science can make a claim for completeness and (relative) autonomy unless it has a proper *descriptive branch*," he writes, and no translation scholars can be called "descriptive" unless "they refrain from value judgments in selecting subject matter or in presenting findings, and/or refuse to draw any conclusions in the form of recommendations for 'proper' behaviour" (Toury 1995: 1, 2; his emphasis). Yet Toury is here repressing his own disciplinary interests. His project is motivated fundamentally by the effort to install translation studies in academic institutions. The target emphasis isn't merely necessary to conduct translation research; it is also implicated in academic empire-building insofar as Toury imagines his audience to be scholars, not translators, and expects his theory to prevail over others that are not scientific.

What's missing is a recognition that judgments can't be avoided in this or any other cultural theory. Even at the level of devising and executing a research project, a scholarly interpretation will be laden with the values of its cultural situation. Toury seems aware of this point, as when he suddenly encourages skepticism about descriptions of norms:

> One thing to bear in mind, when setting out to study norm-governed behaviour, is that there is no necessary identity between the norms themselves and any formulation of them in language. Verbal formulations of course reflect *awareness* of the existence of norms as well as of their respective significance. However, they also imply other interests, particularly a desire to *control* behaviour – i.e., to dictate norms rather than merely account for them. Normative formulations tend to be slanted, then, and should always be taken with a grain of salt.
>
> (Toury 1995: 55; his emphases)

The context of this passage suggests that Toury has in mind the accounts of translation norms given by the translators who followed (or violated) them. But there is no reason why that last sentence couldn't apply as well to a translation scholar formulating the norms that govern a body of translations (or Toury's desire to conceptualize translation studies and thereby control the behaviour of translation scholars). The formulations are always interpretations, and they are made in relation to (and possibly against) previous formulations in the field, but also in relation to the hierarchy of values that define the culture at large.

The very ability to perceive a value shaping a translation suggests a degree of critical detachment from it, not necessarily sympathetic identification. Toury, for instance, describes a Hebrew revision of Shakespeare's sonnets to the young man where the gender of the addressee is changed to female. And he explains this revision by noting that the translations were written in the early twentieth century for an audience of religious Jews for whom "love between two men [. . .] was simply out of bounds" (Toury 1995:

118). Yet Toury's account, even if he doesn't brand the translation homophobic, is nonetheless distanced from homophobia and perhaps favorable in its description of same-sex relationships ("love between two men"). Moreover, since he refers to the translator's decision as a "compromise" that involved "voluntary *censorship*" (ibid.; his emphasis), it seems clear that his formulation of the norm is slanted toward liberalism. If he shared the translator's conservatism, Toury might have called the translation a voluntary expression of moral propriety.

The insistence on value-free translation studies prevents the discipline from being self-critical, from acknowledging and examining its dependence on other, related disciplines, from considering the wider cultural impact that translation research might have. Toury's method for descriptive research, setting out from comparative analyses of the foreign and translated texts to elucidate shifts and identify the target norms that motivate them – this method must still turn to cultural theory in order to assess the significance of the data, to analyze the norms. Norms may be in the first instance linguistic or literary, but they will also include a diverse range of domestic values, beliefs, and social representations which carry ideological force in serving the interests of specific groups. And they are always housed in the social institutions where translations are produced and enlisted in cultural and political agendas.

Over the past two decades, the claim of science has effectively isolated translation studies from precisely the theoretical discourses that would enable scholars to draw incisive conclusions from their data while recognizing the constraints of their own cultural situation. Proponents of empirical description like Evan-Zohar and Toury, whose work is rooted in Russian Formalism and structuralist linguistics, have ignored the radical changes that various theoretical developments caused in literary and cultural studies – namely, varieties of psychoanalysis, feminism, Marxism, and poststructuralism. These are all discourses that insist on the difficulty of separating fact from value in humanistic interpretation. Without them the translation theorist cannot begin to think about an ethics of translation, or the role played by translation in political movements, issues that seem more crucial today than sketching narrow disciplinary boundaries. The scientific model would perpetuate the marginality of translation studies by discouraging an engagement with the trends and debates that have fueled the most consequential thinking about culture.

My recommendation is that empirical approaches, whether based on linguistics or on polysystem theory, be qualified and supplemented by the concept of the remainder and the social and historical thinking that it demands of translators and translation scholars. There can be no question of choosing between adhering to the constants that linguistics extracts from language or placing them in continuous variation because language is a continuum of dialects, registers, styles, and discourses positioned in a hierarchical arrangement and developing at different speeds and in different ways. Translation, like any language use, is a selection accompanied by exclusions, an intervention into the contending languages that constitute any historical conjuncture, and translators will undertake diverse projects, some that require adherence to the major language, others that require minoritizing subversion. Text linguistics, pragmatics, and polysystem theory can be useful in training translators and analyzing translations, provided that the descriptive frameworks devised by these approaches are joined to a theory of the heterogeneity of language and its implication in cultural and political values. Thus, May relies on Gricean conversation to analyze an English translation of a Russian novel, revealing how the translator did not compensate for an implicature in the foreign text and wound up omitting a self-reflexive register in the narrative (May 1994: 151–152). Yet she explains this omission by situating it in the Anglo-American translation tradition, where the dominance of fluent strategies results in "clashing cultural attitudes toward narrative and style in the original and target languages," as well as a "struggle between translator and narrator for control of the text's language" (ibid.: 59).

In searching for a common ground between the empirical approaches and what I shall call the cultural materialist orientation made possible by the remainder, it seems important to question the notion that translation theory and practice can be understood and advanced simply by studying empirical data like textual evidence. To yield any insights, textual features must still be processed on the basis of particular theoretical assumptions – without this processing they can't be called "evidence" of anything – and these assumptions should be submitted to on-going scrutiny and revision. Neubert and Shreve's call for an empirical approach to translation studies, despite their insistence to the contrary, will not produce inferences verified by observing actual translation practices, but deductions from the idealized concepts of text linguistics and pragmatics that constitute their guiding principles – the application of Beaugrande and Dressler (1981) and Grice to translation. By the same token, Toury's view that translation studies should coolly infer "regularities of behaviour" and predictable "laws" mystifies the values implicit in his descriptions and may well discourage the study and practice of translation experimentalism. As a result, the inferences made by these approaches ultimately serve to confirm assumptions about language and textuality that appear reductive and conservative, especially from the standpoint of an American literary translator.

Studying the remainder in translation does not entail abandoning the empirical description of recurrent textual practices and typical situations. It rather offers a way to articulate and clarify – in terms that are at once textual and social – the ethical and political dilemmas that translators face when working in any situation. Our aim should be research and training that produces readers of translations and translators who are critically aware, not predisposed toward norms that exclude the heterogeneity of language.

2

AUTHORSHIP

Perhaps the most important factor in the current marginality of translation is its offense against the prevailing concept of authorship. Whereas authorship is generally defined as originality, self-expression in a unique text, translation is derivative, neither self-expression nor unique: it imitates another text. Given the reigning concept of authorship, translation provokes the fear of inauthenticity, distortion, contamination. Yet insofar as the translator must focus on the linguistic and cultural constituents of the foreign text, translation may also provoke the fear that the foreign author is not original, but derivative, fundamentally dependent on pre-existing materials. It is partly to quell these fears that translation practices in English cultures (among many others) have routinely aimed for their own concealment, at least since the seventeenth century, since John Dryden (Venuti 1995a; Berman 1985). In practice the fact of translation is erased by suppressing the linguistic and cultural differences of the foreign text, assimilating it to dominant values in the target-language culture, making it recognizable and therefore seemingly untranslated. With this domestication the translated text passes for the original, an expression of the foreign author's intention.

Translation is also an offense against a still prevailing concept of scholarship that rests on the assumption of original authorship. Whereas this scholarship seeks to ascertain the authorial intention that constitutes originality, translation not only deviates from that intention, but substitutes others: it aims to address a different audience by answering to the constraints of a different language and culture. Instead of enabling a true and disinterested understanding of the foreign text, translation provokes the fear of error, amateurism, opportunism – an abusive exploitation of originality. And insofar as the translator focusses on the linguistic and cultural constituents of the foreign text, translation provokes the fear that authorial intention cannot possibly control their meaning and social functioning. Under the burden of these fears, translation has long been neglected in the study of literature, even in our current situation, where the influx of poststructuralist thinking has decisively questioned author-oriented literary theory and criticism.

Whether humanist or poststructuralist, contemporary scholarship tends to assume that translation does not offer a true understanding of the foreign text or a valuable contribution to the knowledge of literature, domestic or foreign.

The effects of this assumption are evident in the hiring, tenure, and promotion practices of academic institutions, as well as in academic publishing. Translation is rarely considered a form of literary scholarship, it does not currently constitute a qualification for an academic appointment in a particular field or area of literary study, and, compared to original compositions, translated texts are infrequently made the object of literary research. The fact of translation tends to be ignored even by the most sophisticated scholars who must rely on translated texts in their research and teaching.

And when translation isn't simply ignored, it is likely to suffer a wholesale reduction to linguistic correctness, especially by foreign-language academics who repress the domestic remainder that any translation releases and so refuse to regard it as a conveyor of literary values in the target culture. Hence, translations that were much celebrated in previous periods, that were powerful in creating domestic audiences for a foreign author or text, are typically dismissed as unacceptable if they contain lexical and syntactical errors. The American translator Helen Lowe-Porter, whose versions of Thomas Mann's fiction were praised as "very competent" at mid-century, established his reputation as a major German writer among contemporary English-language readers (*Times Literary Supplement* 1951). Yet she was subsequently attacked for her "linguistic incompetence" by British specialists in German literature who found her work "seriously flawed" (Luke 1970; Buck 1995). Her errors and "imprecision – in which the translator flagrantly reinterprets the author's words" – have come to be regarded as a scandalous debasement of the German texts (Buck 1995; Luke 1995).

Behind this seemingly common-sense view, however, lies a greater scandal, a veneration of foreign languages and literatures that is irrational in its extremity since it is unlikely to find any translation acceptable. Yes, translation errors should be corrected, but errors do not diminish a translation's readability, its power to communicate and to give pleasure. Foreign-language academics fear translation because it appears to threaten fairly rote foreign-language study (which is all that is needed to detect translation errors). In more paranoid cases, with shrinking enrollments, the fear may be that translation might decrease and ultimately stop such study. And yet without instruction in foreign languages translators aren't formed, and translation can't occur or be studied.

The academic veneration of foreign languages and literatures is disingenuous as well. Fueled by a sense of self-preservation, it doesn't value the text itself so much as the text inscribed with whatever interpretation currently prevails among academic specialists. It is this interpretation that specialists expect every translation to communicate in their insistence on linguistic correctness and precision. In John Woods's recent version of Mann's novel *Buddenbrooks* a syntactical error was decried, not simply for being a "plain incomprehension," but for destroying an "antithesis (backed by a long Romantic tradition) between the 'hot day' of life and the 'cool night' of death" (see the exchange between Luke 1995 and Venuti 1995b).

When texts from the academic canon of foreign literatures are translated by non-specialists, foreign-language academics close ranks and assume a don't-tread-on-my-patch attitude. They correct errors and imprecisions in conformity with scholarly standards and interpretations, excluding other possible readings of the foreign text and other possible audiences: for example, belletristic translations that may slight accuracy for literary effect so as to reach a general readership with different values. Lowe-Porter's version of Mann's novella *Death in Venice*, criticized for giving a "false perception" of the "interaction" between the ageing writer Aschenbach and the enchanting youth Tadzio, could just as well be described as recasting their homoerotic dynamic to suit the greater moral strictness of an American audience during the 1930s (Buck 1995). In a key passage, for instance, Mann's German is noncommittal, referring to Aschenbach's "intoxication" (*der Rausch*) with the boy – "der Rausch ihm zu teuer war" – whereas Lowe-Porter's English inscribes a censure by substituting "illusion": "his illusion was far too dear to him" (Mann 1960: 494; Mann 1936: 414).

The refusal to consider the cultural values conveyed by translation uncovers the elitism at the core of academic institutions, which are designed to function, after all, by selectively bestowing the qualification to take part in scholarly debate. If these revelations are damaging, it is primarily because they issue into paradox: translation exposes a deep unwillingness among foreign-language specialists to think about the differences introduced by moving between languages and cultures, a kind of thinking that foreign-language study makes possible in the first place and should aim to promote. By depreciating translation, these specialists express a chauvinistic investment in a foreign language that ignores the cultural conditions under which that language must be taught.

To explore these continuing scandals, I want to consider the literary form known as "pseudotranslation," an original composition that its author has chosen to present as a translated text. The reception of a pseudotranslation can illuminate the status and manifold effects of actual translations because it "constitutes a convenient way of introducing novelties into a culture," marking the limits of dominant values by precipitating changes in them (Toury 1995: 41). The novelties are most likely to be literary forms and themes that are new to or currently marginal in the domestic culture, so that the pseudotranslator typically exploits accepted translation practices to work with cultural materials that might otherwise be excluded or censored. Yet the novelties may also include new conceptions of authorship and scholarship, especially when the foreign language and literature that figure in the fiction of the pseudotranslation have achieved canonical status in the domestic culture. Pseudotranslation, since it involves a concealment of authorship, inevitably provokes a reconsideration of how an author is defined in any period, leading either to a reactionary imposition of the dominant conception or to an unsettling revision that sparks new literary trends.

The derivations of authorship

The literary hoax perpetrated by the French writer Pierre Louÿs, the book-length collection of prose poems he entitled *Les Chansons de Bilitis* (1895), must certainly be classed among the most intriguing of pseudotranslations. Louÿs presented his text as a French translation from the Greek poetry of Bilitis, a woman who was said to be Sappho's contemporary. Yet most of his readers knew that none of Bilitis's poetry survived, and that in fact she seems never to have existed, whether in the sixth century B.C. or in some other period of antiquity. Louÿs described his project in a letter to a French scholar in 1898: "Les Chansons de Bilitis sont toutes apocryphes, à l'exception de sept ou huit, imitées de divers auteurs" ("The songs of Bilitis are all apocryphal, with the exception of seven or eight, imitated from various authors") (Louÿs 1990: 318). This hoax is remarkable for its demystification of dominant cultural values, not only the academic reception of classical Greek literature and of Sappho's poetry in particular, but also concepts of authorship and historical scholarship that still prevail today. On the one hand, *Les Chansons de Bilitis* exposed the multiple conditions of authorship, questioning the claim of originality; on the other hand, it exposed the many values that inform scholarship, questioning the claim of historical truth. Louÿs's hoax is transgressive on several levels, some of which escape his control – such as the use to which I am putting it in this chapter. And, most importantly for my purposes, his hoax derives its transgressive power mainly from simulating (and occasionally being) a translation.

By deliberately presenting himself as a translator instead of an author, Louÿs directed his reader's attention to the cultural materials from which he produced his text. This was of course done to give Bilitis an air of authenticity, but it also implied that Louÿs was not an authentic author. The first favorable reviewers, most of whom either knew or sensed that Bilitis was a fiction, tended to regard Louÿs's writing as derivative, a "délicieux pastiche," wrote the *Echo de Paris* (Clive 1978: 111). And even when reviewers explicitly recognized his authorship, they defined it not as self-expression, but as scholarship, although cast in the emotionally evocative language of poetry. "L'érudition, le détail technique de reconstitution ne blessent jamais ici" ("The learning, the technical detail of reconstruction never offend here"), wrote the *Mercure de France*, because "M. Pierre Louÿs est tout à fait un poète: sa forme savante qui gênait l'émotion a soudain pu l'enserrer" ("Mr. Pierre Louÿs is entirely a poet: his scholarly form, which restrains emotion, can suddenly encompass it") (Mauclair 1895: 105). Louÿs's hoax blurred the distinctions between translation, authorship, and scholarship. As soon as the reader realized that Bilitis was invented, and that Louÿs's text derived from numerous literary and scholarly sources, authorship was redefined as historical research that takes the form of a literary imitation which incorporates translation.

Louÿs initially planned to publish his text with detailed scholarly notes that identified his sources. He chose to withhold these notes, but they survive and reveal quite clearly his intention to play havoc with the question of authorship. One annotation states that "Une mauvaise variante de cette idylle est attribuée à Hedylus dans l'*Anthologie Palatine* (V.199)" ("A bad variant of this idyll is attributed to Hedylus in the *Greek Anthology*") (Louÿs 1990: 218). The French text described thus is actually Louÿs's imitation of Hedylus's poem, not his translation of an "idylle" by Bilitis that happened to be badly imitated by Hedylus. The note supports the hoax by aiming, in one stroke, to establish Bilitis's existence in literary history and to assign her poetry to the academic canon of classical literature. She is implicitly characterized as a major poet considered worthy of imitation by later and lesser poets such as Hedylus (who was active in the third century B.C.). Louÿs makes the same gesture in his biographical essay on Bilitis, where he observes that another Greek poet, Philodemus, "l'a pillée deux fois" ("pilfered her [poetry] twice") (ibid.: 35). For any reader aware of the fiction, such comments resonate with dizzingly complex ironies: they indicate that Louÿs's authorship hinges on his production of a derivative text, an adaptation or partial translation, while slyly suggesting that he is the author of classical poems imitated by later classical poets, or in other words that he is himself a classical poet. The pseudo-attributions allow Louÿs to displace Hedylus and Philodemus as the author of poems preserved in the *Greek Anthology*. Here authorship involves a competition with a canonical poet, a game of poetic one-upmanship, in which a text by that poet is imitated through adaptation or translation (or plagiarized: "pillée").

This construction of authorship is, moreover, masculinist. Louÿs exemplifies the connection that exists in male-dominated societies between homosocial desire and the structures that maintain and transmit patriarchal power (see Sedgwick 1985: chap. 1). He is the author of his text by virtue of his competition with other male poets, his emulative rivalry with them, and the arena in which they compete is the representation of female sexuality. Louÿs's fiction dwells almost exclusively on Bilitis's sexual experience. In the biography that he constructs explicitly in the preface and more indirectly in the poems, her life is divided into three moments, each linked to a specific locale and a specific form of sexual activity. First, she passes a precocious girlhood in Pamphylia, where she takes a masturbatory pleasure in straddling tree limbs, is raped by a goatherd, and bears a daughter whom she abandons. She then travels to Mytilene, where she is seduced by Sappho and subsequently engages in various lesbian affairs, including a decade-long relationship with a young girl who abandons her. Finally, she travels to Cyprus, where she becomes a courtesan consecrated to Aphrodite until age compels her to forego prostitution.

In the individual texts that support this biographical narrative, Louÿs competes against classical poets in representing the female as an object of male sexuality. The poem "Conversation," included in Bilitis's "Epigrammes dans l'Île de Chypre" ("Epigrams on the Island of Cyprus"), incorporates his partial translations of two Greek poems – one by Philodemus, one anonymous – in which a man negotiates with a prostitute for her services (*Greek Anthology*, V.46 and 101). Louÿs also chose to adapt the poem by Hedylus in which a virgin is raped in her sleep:

> Oinos kai proposeis katekoimisan Aglaoniken
> ai doliai. kai eros edus o Nikagoreo.
> Es para Kypridi tauta murois eti panta mudonta
> keintai. parthenion ugra laphura pathon.
> sandala. kai malakai. maston endumata. mitrai.
> upnou kai skulmon ton tote marturia.
> (transcribed from Paton 1956)

> Wine and toasts sent Aglaonice to sleep,
> both crafty, plus the sweet love of Nicagoras.
> She laid before Kypris this scent still dripping all over,
> the moist spoils of virgin desire.
> Her sandals and the soft band that wrapped her breasts
> are proof of her sleep and his violence then.

Louÿs's version, entitled "Le Sommeil interrompu" ("Interrupted Sleep"), records that crucial moment in Bilitis's life when she was raped by the goatherd:

> Toute seule je m'étais endormie, comme une perdrix dans la bruyère. Le vent léger, le bruit des eaux, la douceur de la nuit m'avaient retenue là.

> Je me suis endormie, imprudente, et je me suis réveillée en criant, et j'ai lutté, et j'ai pleuré; mais déjà il était trop tard. Et que peuvent les mains d'une enfant?

> Il ne me quitta pas. Au contraire, plus tendrement dans ses bras, il me serra contre lui et je ne vis plus au monde ni la terre ni les arbres mais seulement la lueur de ses yeux.

> À toi, Kypris victorieuse, je consacre ces offrandes encore mouillées de rosée, vestiges des douleurs de la vierge, témoin de mon sommeil et de ma résistance.
> (Louÿs 1990: 74)

All alone I was falling asleep, like a partridge in the heather. The light wind, the sound of the waters, the sweetness of the night were holding me there.

I fell asleep, imprudent, and awoke with a cry, and struggled, and wept; but already it was too late. Besides, what can a child's hands do?

He did not leave me. On the contrary, his arms clasped me more tenderly against himself and I saw nothing in the world, neither earth nor trees, but only the gleam in his eyes.

To you, victorious Kypris, I consecrate these offerings still wet with dew, vestiges of the virgin's sorrows, witness to my sleep and my resistance.

Louÿs's literary competition with Hedylus results in deviations that exaggerate the image of the female as sexually desirable and submissive to the male. Perhaps the most significant change is Louÿs's shift from a third- to a first-person persona. Hedylus's poem questions Nicagoras's motives by indicating that his "wine and toasts" are deceptive, intended to put Aglaonice to sleep and thus make her vulnerable to his "violence." Louÿs's poem, in contrast, shows the victim blaming herself: Bilitis suggests that, like a game bird ("perdrix"), she will naturally be pursued by men, so it is "imprudent" of her to sleep alone and in the open air. Bilitis subscribes to a patriarchal representation of herself as a sexual object, aware of her desirability, but also of her helplessness before male aggression. Louÿs underscores her acquiescence by omitting the explicit mention of male "violence" in Hedylus and focussing instead on female "resistance" finally overcome. Bilitis depicts herself as possessing a child-like weakness ("les mains d'une enfant"), clasped in the goatherd's arms, enchanted by the gaze he has fixed on her ("la lueur de ses yeux"). Louÿs's authorship, both derivative and masculinist, is established by an adaptation that revises Hedylus's image of male sexual violence, not merely by substituting a mystification, but by assigning it to a female poet who in effect confirms it. The fiction of translation again calls attention to the conditions of Louÿs's authorship, although with an outcome that he may not have anticipated: to create the appearance that he had translated an authentic classical poet, he was led to add annotations that simultaneously identify his sources and reveal his authorial identity to be a masculinist construction.

We can extend this reading further by observing that Louÿs imagined his audience as primarily male, literary, and bohemian, an exclusive group who rejected bourgeois values in art and morality. In a letter written to his brother Georges in 1895, Louÿs confided that "Je voudrais beaucoup avoir un public féminin" ("I would like to have a female readership"), but this seemed unlikely to him because "les femmes n'ont que la pudeur des mots" ("women experience only the shame of words"), so concerned with respectability as to be hypocritical: "Je crois bien que si la préface de Bilitis la représentait comme un monstre de perversité, pas une des dames que je connais n'avouerait avoir lu le volume" ("I truly believe that if the preface to Bilitis represented her as a monster of perversity, none of the women I know would admit to reading the volume") (Louÿs 1990: 314). The literary competition that established Louÿs's authorship was conducted before other male writers, acquaintances such as André Gide and Stéphane Mallarmé who knew of the hoax and praised his writing. And the competition included canonized French poets like Baudelaire. *Les Fleurs du mal* (1856) linked Sappho with lesbianism in poems that provoked the government censor, most notably "Lesbos" and the two entitled "Femmes damnées" (see DeJean 1989: 271–273), while *Le Spleen de Paris* (1869) developed a poetic prose that could incorporate various genres, narrative, lyric, and dramatic. Louÿs, however, refined the polymorphous Baudelairean prose poem by reducing it to a four-strophe text, and his depictions of sexual activity exceeded Baudelaire's, not merely because they avoided any moral judgment, but because they were graphic, constituting a form of pornography that titillated male readers. Henri de Régnier, who published an appreciative article on Louÿs's text in the *Mercure de France*, wrote to him that "La lecture de Bilitis m'a jeté dans des transports érotiques que je vais satisfaire aux dépens de l'honneur de mon mari ordinaire [*sic*]" ("Reading Bilitis has thrown me into erotic raptures which I satisfy at the cost of my honor as an ordinary husband") (Louÿs 1990: 329).

What *Les Chansons de Bilitis* expressed was Louÿs's own sexuality, as well as that of his male readers; and the form of his expression shows that his sexuality was equally derivative, that his desire was not self-originating but culturally constructed. This is borne out by the autobiographical dimension of the text. Louÿs wrote most of it during 1894, when he made a short visit to Algeria and had a liaison with Meryem bent Ali, a sixteen-year-old girl who was cited by her initials in the dedication to the first edition. Meryem belonged to the Oulad Naïl tribe, in which young girls traditionally resorted to prostitution to earn their dowry (see Clive 1978: 102–106 and Louÿs 1992). They were introduced by Gide, to whom Louÿs sent a revealing description of her: "elle est Indienne d'Amérique, et par moments Vierge Marie, et encore courtisane tyrienne, sous ses bijoux qui sont les mêmes que ceux des tombeaux antiques" ("she is an American Indian, and at moments the Virgin Mary, and again a Tyrian prostitute, beneath her jewels which are the same as those from ancient tombs") (Clive 1978: 106).

Louÿs's desire for Meryem was determined by various cultural codes: it was a romantic fascination with the alien that was simultaneously bohemian, antiquarian, and Orientalist. His letter to Gide rests on a stereotype of North

African women that is both racist and masculinist. As Edward Said has observed, "in the writing of travellers and novelists" like Flaubert and Louÿs, "[eastern] women are usually the creatures of a male power-fantasy. They express unlimited sensuality, they are more or less stupid, and above all they are willing" (Said 1978: 207–208). Louÿs's experience with Meryem can be detected in several poems, but it also resulted in the Orientalist themes that recur throughout his scholarly apparatus. His fictive biography of Bilitis assigns her a Greek father and a Phoenician mother, and he annotates the poem entitled "Les Bijoux" ("The Jewels") with a glance at the present: "Il est remarquable qu'à l'époque actuelle, ce système de bijoux a été conservé sans aucun changement par les Oulad Naïl" ("It is remarkable that in the present era this ensemble of jewels has been preserved without any change by the Oulad Naïl") (Louÿs 1990: 223). What Louÿs expressed in *Les Chansons de Bilitis* was partly his desire for Meryem, if not his heterosexual promiscuity in general, yet that desire was already a translation of his readings in classical Greek literature. In 1894 he wrote to brother Georges that "j'ai écrit vingt pièces nouvelles, en grande partie inspirées par des souvenirs d'Algérie où j'ai pu vivre toute l'Anthologie pendant un mois" ("I have written twenty new pieces, inspired for the most part by memories of Algeria where I was able to live out the entire Greek Anthology in a month") (ibid.: 311).

The prejudices of scholarship

By blurring the distinction between translation and authorship, Louÿs's hoax inevitably questioned scholarship that defined historical truth as a verification of authorial originality. *Les Chansons de Bilitis* is an elaborate parody of a scholarly translation, in which he invented not merely a classical text by a Greek poet, but a modern edition by a German professor whose name, "G. Heim," puns on the German word for "secret" or "mysterious," *geheim*. In the poems themselves, Louÿs paid a scholarly attention to detail. For instance, he used an archaic spelling for Sappho in the Dorian dialect, "Psappha," as well as various Greek words that relate specifically to classical culture, like "Héraïos," the month in the Greek calendar consecrated to Hera, and "métôpion," a perfume that originated in Egypt (Louÿs 1990: 33, 88, 133, 145). And the biography of Bilitis, as Joan DeJean has pointed out, "is situated in the interstices of Sappho scholarship. Louÿs weaves Bilitis into Psappha's life as her rival for one of the beloved girls actually mentioned by Sappho, Mnasidika" (DeJean 1989: 277).

In his correspondence Louÿs admitted that his intention was to debunk the prevailing concept of scholarship. He sent a copy of his text to a classical scholar precisely to deceive him. When the scholar responded that Bilitis's poems "ne sont pas pour moi des inconnus" ("are not unknown to me"), Louÿs attributed this delusion to the assumption that historical research affords unmediated access to the truth or even enables a total identification with past cultures (Louÿs 1990: 320). He framed the scholar's reasoning as an impossible syllogism: "Comme archéologue et comme *athénien*, je dois connaître tout ce qui est grec. Or Bilitis est un auteur grec. Donc je dois connaître Bilitis" ("As an archaeologist and *Athenian*, I must know everything that is Greek. Now Bilitis is a Greek author. Therefore I must know Bilitis") (ibid.; Louÿs's emphasis). Louÿs thus suggested that, like his counterfeit translation, scholarship is engaged in historical invention, which, however, can pass for truth because it shares the cultural authority enjoyed by academic institutions ("archéologue").

At the same time, Louÿs demonstrated that translation can be a form of historical scholarship, that it can constitute a scholarly invention of the classical text for the modern reader, but that unlike most scholarship it does not conceal its status as an invention or its historical difference from the classical text. This is how Louÿs described his project to his brother: "tout en évitant les anachronismes trop grossiers, je ne perdrai pas de temps à ménager une impossible vraisemblance" ("while avoiding anachronisms that are too gross, I shall not waste any time in contriving an impossible verisimilitude") (Louÿs 1990: 311). Louÿs expected his readers to recognize that he was not presenting ancient poems, but modern derivations. And his readers complied: the reviewer for *Gil Blas* observed, with some uncertainty, that "Si c'est une traduction véritable, ce doit être une traduction assez libre, car, tant que s'évoque l'esprit grec, ces poèmes paraissent imprégnés aussi quelque peu d'esprit moderne" ("If this is a real translation, it must be a rather free translation, since, insofar as the Greek spirit is evoked, these poems also seem imbued a little with a modern spirit") (Clive 1978: 111). Louÿs's hoax makes clear that both scholarship and translation are necessarily anachronistic: however much grounded in research, their representations of the past are likely to possess "une impossible vraisemblance" because they are motivated by present cultural values.

This point was dramatically made by an unexpected development. In 1896 the influential classical scholar, Ulrich von Wilamowitz-Moellendorf, published an extremely negative review of *Les Chansons de Bilitis*. Wilamowitz saw through the hoax. He noted that Louÿs's effort to create the appearance of authenticity was learned ("In gewissem Sinne ist auch P.L. ein Classicist" ("In a certain sense, even P.L. is a classicist") (Wilamowitz 1913: 69), and he found some of the texts persuasive imitations of classical literature ("Fast das ganze letzte Buch der Bilitis würde sich in hellenistische Epigramme übersetzen lassen" ("Almost the entire last book of Bilitis could be translated into Hellenistic epigrams") (ibid.: 68)). But he faulted Louÿs for factual errors and anachronisms:

> wenn er so viel tut, um im Detail antik zu scheinen, so fordert er die Kritik des Sachkenners heraus, der ihm dann doch sagen muß, daß es im Altertum in Asien keine Kamele gab, daß Hasen keine

Opfertiere sind, daß "Lippen rot wie Kupfer, Nase blauschwarz wie Eisen, Augen schwarz wie Silber", drei ganz unantike Vergleiche sind.

(ibid.: 64)

by striving so hard to appear ancient in each detail, he challenges the critique of the expert who feels compelled to tell him that ancient Asia knew no camels, that rabbits are no sacrificial animals, that "lips red as copper, the nose blue-black as iron, eyes black as silver" are entirely unancient comparisons.

For Wilamowitz, only scholarship was capable of discovering historical truth, and it did so through an imaginative identification with the authorial "individuality" that was uniquely expressed in the text:

So wird emsige Beobachtung mancherlei ermitteln; aber in der Lyrik vollends ist die Individualität die Hauptsache, und sie läßt sich auf diesem Wege nimmermehr zurückgewinnen. In solchen Fällen kann das beste nur durch nachschaffende poetische Intuition geleistet werden: Welckers Macht beruht darauf, daß er die Gottesgabe dieser Phantasie besaß.

(Wilamowitz 1913: 70)

industrious observation will unearth a lot; but in poetry individuality is what ultimately matters, and it can never be retrieved by [Louÿs's] method. In such cases the best accomplishments can only be achieved through imitative poetic intuition: Welcker's power rests on his divine gift of this imagination.

In this revealing passage, Wilamowitz indicated the necessity of careful research ("industrious observation"), but confessed that scholarship goes beyond the historical record by relying on the scholar's "poetic intuition." What keeps this intuition from being merely a modern invention is apparently a "divine" omniscience, the scholar's ability to transcend his historical moment in the retrieval of the ancient author's intention. Louÿs's texts lacked this transcendence because they contained too many details that were recognizably modern, addressed to a modern readership. Wilamowitz called them "leere Bruchstücke [. . .], mehr oder minder schief übersetzt und damit dem Publicum imponiren will" ("vapid fragments [. . .], more or less unevenly translated, in order to impress the public") (ibid.: 69).

Yet Louÿs's hoax was so powerfully transgressive that it forced Wilamowitz to reveal the modern values informing his scholarship. This is evident, first, in the mention of Friedrich Gottlieb Welcker, the early nineteenth-century philologist. Wilamowitz's critique of Louÿs rested on an acceptance of the German tradition of Sappho scholarship, specifically Welcker's view that

Sappho was not homosexual. Wilamowitz asserted that "mit voller Zuversicht bekenne ich mich zu dem Glauben, daß Welcker Sappho von einem herrschenden Vorurteil befreit hat" ("in full confidence I confess to the belief that Welcker has liberated Sappho from the dominant prejudice"); she was "eine vornehme Frau, Gattin und Mutter" ("a noble woman, wife, and mother") (Wilamowitz 1913: 71, 73). Welcker's reading of Sappho, however, was hardly an intuition that escaped the contingencies of his moment: as DeJean has argued, "at the time of the French Restoration and in a period of rising German nationalism, Welcker posited an essential bond between male physical beauty, militarism, and patriotism on the one hand and Sappho's chastity on the other" (DeJean 1989: 205). Welcker's Sappho was a distinctively German invention: she functioned in a "nationalistic program for civic virtue" as a teacher who prepared virgins for marriage and the production of "new citizens" (ibid.: 218, 219).

In Wilamowitz's review, some eighty years later, the nationalism survived not only in his strenuous denial of Sappho's homosexuality – most of his review is devoted to this question – but also in some rather explicit statements of his prejudices. His homophobia was linked to a belief in German cultural superiority: "In Deutschland brüsten sich die Kreise, die mit der Tendenz der Bilitis sympathisiren, meist mit ihrer Bildungslosigkeit" ("In Germany, those circles who sympathize with Bilitis's tendencies usually boast of their lack of cultivation") (Wilamowitz 1913: 68). And Louÿs's Orientalism provoked an anti-Semitic reaction in a footnote where Wilamowitz commented on the name "Bilitis":

> Offenbar ist das der syrische Name der Aphrodite, den ich meist Beltis geschrieben finde. Vor den Semiten hat der Verfasser jenen unberechtigten Respect, der wissenschaftlich längst überwunden immer noch hie und da grassiert. Er läßt sie in Pamphylien sich mit den Hellenen mischen, fabelt von *rhythmes difficiles de la tradition sémitique* und versichert, daß die Sprache seiner Bilitis eine Masse phoenikischer Vocabeln enthalte. Lauter Undinge. Aber Mr. Louys hat auch die aphroditegleiche Schönheit seines Romanes aus Galilaea stammen lassen und zu ihren Ehren erotische Stücke des Alten Testamentes herangezogen. Er wird wohl für die Semiten eine angeborene Vorliebe haben.
>
> (Wilamowitz 1913: 64)

Apparently this is the Syrian name of Aphrodite, which for the most part I have found written as Beltis. The author shows the Semites that inappropriate respect which, although it has scientifically been overcome for a long time, still flourishes here and there. He has them mix themselves with the Hellenes in Pamphylia, tells fables about the *rhythmes difficiles de la tradition sémitique*, and assures us that the language of his Bilitis contains numerous Phoenician words. All nonsense. But Mr. Louys also has the Aphrodite-like beauty of his novel [*Aphrodite*, published in 1896] originate in Galilee and in her honor has referred to erotic pieces of the Old Testament. He must have an innate preference for the Semites.

Louÿs's hoax posed a serious threat to classical scholarship because his representation of ancient Greek culture challenged the nationalist and racist values that figured in the German reception of Sappho's poetry. Wilamowitz felt compelled to review *Les Chansons de Bilitis* in order to reaffirm Welcker's image of the chaste Sappho against the degradations of the distrustful French (see Calder 1985: 86–87). He lamented that "er außerhalb Deutschlands nicht so vollkommen triumphirt, wie bei uns" ("outside of Germany [Welcker] has not triumphed as perfectly as among us") (Wilamowitz 1913: 71). Ever ready to taunt the dour academic, Louÿs responded to the review by involving Wilamowitz in the hoax: the fictive bibliography appended to the 1898 edition of the text attributed a German edition to "le professeur von Willamovitz-Moellendorff. – *Goettingische Gelehrte*. – Goettinge, 1896," the place and the year in which the German philologist had published his attack (Louÿs 1990: 194).

Redefining translation

Louÿs's hoax prompts a reconsideration of the distinctions that are currently drawn between translation, authorship, and scholarship. Translation can be considered a form of authorship, but an authorship now redefined as derivative, not self-originating. Authorship is not *sui generis*; writing depends on pre-existing cultural materials, selected by the author, arranged in an order of priority, and rewritten (or elaborated) according to specific values. Louÿs made this clear in a letter to his brother on the eve of the second edition of *Les Chansons de Bilitis*:

> Je crois justement que l'originalité du livre vient de ce que la question pudeur n'est jamais posée. En particulier, je crois que la *seconde* partie semblera très nouvelle. Jusqu'ici, les lesbiennes étaient toujours représentées comme des femmes fatales (Balzac, Musset, Baudelaire, Rops) ou vicieuses (Zola, Mendès, et auprès d'eux cent autres moindres). Même Mlle de Maupin, qui n'a rien de satanique, n'est pourtant pas une femme ordinaire. C'est la première fois [. . .] qu'on écrit une idylle sur ce sujet-là.
>
> (Louÿs 1990: 317)

I believe that the originality of the book derives precisely from the fact that the modesty question is never posed. In particular, I believe that the *second* part will appear very new. Until now, lesbians have always been represented as femmes fatales (Balzac, Musset, Baudelaire, Rops) or vicious (Zola, Mendès, and another hundred lesser writers). Even Mlle. de Maupin, who is not at all satanic, is nonetheless not an ordinary woman. This is the first time [. . .] that an idyll has been written on this topic.

Louÿs felt that his derivative text made him an original author, but only in the sense that it transformed previous representations of female homosexuality and cast them in a different genre ("une idylle"). From this point of view, what distinguishes translation from original composition is mainly the closeness of the mimetic relation to the other text: translation is governed by the goal of imitation, whereas composition is free, relatively speaking, to cultivate a more variable relation to the cultural materials it assimilates.

Translation can also be considered a form of scholarship. Both translation and scholarship rely on historical research in their representations of an archaic or foreign text, but neither can produce a representation that is completely adequate to the author's intention. On the contrary, both translation and scholarship answer to contemporary, domestic values that necessarily supplement that intention: in effect, they reinvent the text for a specific cultural constituency that differs from the one for which it was initially intended. Thus, Mallarmé wrote to Louÿs that

Un charme si exquis de ce livre, à la lecture, est de se rendre compte que le grec idéal, qu'on croit entendre derrière, est précisément le texte lu en votre langue.

(Louÿs 1990: 331)

One of the exquisite charms of reading this book is to realize that the Greek ideal, which one seems to hear behind it, is precisely the text read in your language.

Mallarmé, who was aware of the fiction, nonetheless took pleasure in reading Louÿs's poems as a translation ("entendre derrière"), yet a translation that was so successful as to displace the Greek texts. From this point of view, what distinguishes translation from scholarship is mainly the necessity of a performative relation to the other text: translation must perform or enact its representation in its very language, whereas scholarship enjoys the freedom, relatively speaking, to lay out its representation in commentary.

Louÿs's pseudotranslation undoubtedly introduced novelties into French literary culture, not only the frank portrayal of female sexuality, but more self-conscious concepts of translation, authorship, and scholarship. And these novelties produced unexpected consequences. Although *Les Chansons de Bilitis* can be seen as expressing the masculinist and heterosexual desires of its author and his male readers, Louÿs's graphic depiction of Bilitis's homosexuality also inspired the lesbian writings of Natalie Clifford Barney and Renée Vivien, including Vivien's French translation of Sappho's poetry. The construction of the lesbian author that emerges here depends on a deeply sympathetic identification with Louÿs's texts which, just as with his male readers, involved titillation. "Bilitis," Barney wrote to Louÿs in 1901, "m'a donné des extases plus éperdues et des tendresses plus tendres que n'importe qu'elle [sic] autre maîtresse" ("has given me more distracted ecstasies and more tender endearments than any other mistress") (Louÿs 1990: 333). Barney's first evocation of lesbianism, the 1902 volume *Cinq petits dialogues grecs* (*Five Little Greek Dialogues*), proclaimed the derivative nature of her authorship: it was "presented almost as a companion piece to *Bilitis*," dedicated to Louÿs by "une jeune fille de la societé future" ("a young girl from the future society") he had mentioned in the dedication to his own text (DeJean 1989: 280). Barney's authorship hinged on an emulative rivalry with Louÿs, and the arena in which this rivalry occurred was the representation of female sexuality. She simultaneously shared and revaluated the sexual identity he fashioned for Bilitis, replacing the masculinist voyeurism of his circle with a lesbian utopianism.

Vivien's 1903 version of Sappho similarly reflects the redefinition of translation initiated by Louÿs's hoax. She, like Barney, saw her own sexuality mirrored in *Les Chansons de Bilitis*, including it among the "livres inséparables de ma pensée, et de mon existence" ("books that are inseparable from my thinking, and my existence") (Louÿs 1990: 333). She also followed Louÿs in representing Sappho as homosexual and thus rejecting the German philological tradition that insisted on the Greek poet's chastity (DeJean 1989: 249–250). Vivien's carefully planned edition shows that she took an authorial approach to translation which indicated the derivative nature of her authorship, its reliance on domestic cultural materials, while making clear that her historical scholarship was serving certain sexual values in the present. She provided not only the Greek texts, but close prose versions followed by freer renderings in verse that often expanded fragments into complete poems. The juxtaposition of the elliptical prose to the polished poetry in traditional stanzaic forms highlights Vivien's deliberate reliance on the French representation of Sappho's homosexuality:

> Tu nous brûles.
> Mes lèvres ont soif de ton baiser amer,
> Et la sombre ardeur qu'en vain tu dissimules
> Déchire mon âme et ravage ma chair:
> Eros, tu nous brûles . . .
> (Vivien 1986: 161)

> You burn us.
> My lips are thirsty for your bitter kisses,

And the dark ardor that you hide in vain
Tears my soul and ravages my flesh:
    Eros, you burn us . . .

Vivien's translation is authorial, not by virtue of her identification with Sappho, but through her emulative rivalry with her French predecessors: she both drew on and revaluated the French tradition of Sappho speculation that goes back to a canonical figure like Baudelaire, "a misogynist with no concern for the reality of female homosexuality" (DeJean 1989: 285). In resorting to the sort of pastiche that Louÿs developed in *Les Chansons de Bilitis*, a mixture of translation and imitation, Vivien made Sappho's poetry available to a lesbian readership, yet without concealing the fact that her French version answered to the sexual values of this constituency.

Because the effects of translation are unpredictable and potentially contradictory, determined by many different cultural and social factors, it can be disruptive of scholarly canons and is likely to face repression. Yet this very unpredictability makes translated texts deserving of the scholar's attention as much as the foreign texts they translate. The study of translations is truly a form of historical scholarship because it forces the scholar to confront the issue of historical difference in the changing reception of a foreign text. Translation, with its double allegiance to the foreign text and the domestic culture, is a reminder that no act of interpretation can be definitive for every cultural constituency, that interpretation is always local and contingent, even when housed in social institutions with the apparent rigidity of the academy. In such settings, translation is scandalous because it crosses institutional boundaries: not only does translation require scholarly research to move between languages, cultures, and disciplines, but it compels the scholar to consider constituencies beyond the academy – for example, the overwhelming majority of English-language readers who need translations because foreign-language study has declined as English has achieved global dominance. At the present time, translation studies comprise an area of research that uncomfortably exposes the limitations of English-language scholarship – and of English.

3

COPYRIGHT

Copyright, the legal codes and conventions that govern the ownership of intellectual works, describes a narrow space for translation. The history of copyright since the eighteenth century reveals a movement toward reserving for the author the right to copy and circulate his or her work, including the right to license translations of it into foreign languages (Kaplan 1967; Rose 1993). In current copyright law, with international treaties that extend the rights of nationals to foreigners, authors worldwide enjoy an exclusive right in any translation of their works for a term of the author's life plus fifty years – unless the translation was made in the service of an employer or on a work-for-hire basis, in which case the employer enjoys an exclusive right in the translation (for the UK and the US, see Copyright, Designs and Patents Act 1988 (c. 48), sections 2(1), 11(1) and (2), 16(1)(e), 21(3)(a)(i), and 17 US Code, sections 101, 106(2), 201(a) and (b) (1976); Bently 1993 offers a comprehensive account). Although the provisions of actual publishing contracts can vary widely, in principle copyright law places strict limitations on the translator's control of the translated text.

From the viewpoint of translators and translation, these limitations carry some troubling consequences, both economic and cultural. By subordinating the translator's rights to the author's, the law permits the author to shrink the translator's share in the profits of the translation. A 1990 survey conducted by the PEN American Center indicates that most translations in the United States are done on a work-for-hire basis, whereby the translator receives a flat fee with no percentage of the royalties or subsidiary rights sales (e.g. a periodical publication, a license for a paperback edition, or an option by a film production company); in the relatively few instances where contracts give translators a portion of this income, the percentages range from 5 to 1 percent of the royalties for a hardback edition and from 50 to 10 percent of subsidiary rights sales (Keeley 1990). Translators in the United Kingdom face similar contractual terms (Glenny 1983), although the unequal distribution of profits is also indicated by the allotment of loan payments under the Public Lending Right, with the author receiving 70 and the translator 30 percent.

Because copyright law decisively contributes to this unfavorable economic situation, it diminishes the incentive *for translators* to invest in translation projects. The many literary magazines published in English today confirm that translators are in fact willing to make such an investment: they regularly contribute translations of foreign poetry, fiction, and nonfiction to these magazines without the promise of a book contract, usually for little or no payment, mainly on the strength of a deep engagement with the foreign text and culture. Yet the exclusive translation right given to authors means that it is customarily they (or publishers as their assignees) who initiate translations in an effort to sell licenses and create foreign-language markets for their works, and so they directly approach foreign publishers, who then commission translators. The law prevents translators from acquiring sufficient bargaining power to change this situation, unless of course the translator is one of the very few who manage to gain public recognition because publishers repeatedly commission them. But even in these cases actual publishing practices reveal the subordination of translators. William Weaver, the leading English-language translator of Italian fiction since the 1950s, has published over sixty book-length translations, all of which originated with publishers' commissions (telephone interview: 24 September 1994). Current copyright law, then, ensures that translation projects will be driven by publishers, not by translators.

As a result, publishers shape cultural developments at home and abroad. Seeking the maximum returns for their investments, they are more likely to publish domestic works that are also publishable in foreign countries, yet are not so culturally specific as to resist or complicate translation. And their publishing decisions may target specific foreign markets for the sale of translation licenses. Goldstein sketches a hypothetical case: "knowing that the French and German language markets belong exclusively to it, a publisher of English language works may decide to invest in works that, once translated, will appeal to these audiences as well" (Goldstein 1983: 227). By the same token, publishers who purchase translation rights are more likely to focus on foreign works that are easily assimilable to domestic cultural values, to prevailing trends and tastes, targeting specific markets so as to avoid the potential loss involved in creating new ones. When a translation becomes a bestseller, for example, it motivates the translation of similar kinds of foreign works. Immediately after the enormous success of Umberto Eco's *The Name of the Rose* (1983) in Weaver's translation, American publishers eagerly pursued the translation rights for any historical novel that resembled Eco's (McDowell 1983). An increasing trend since the 1980s, similarly, has been to invest in the translation of foreign works involved in tie-ins because film or dramatic adaptations promise wider reader recognition and greater sales. Publishers can thus determine not merely patterns of exchange with foreign cultures, but the range of translation practices devised by translators in the domestic culture.

Translation discredits the legal institutions that maintain this situation by exposing a basic contradiction in their aims and operations. In diminishing the translator's incentive for investment, copyright law deviates from its "traditional goals" of encouraging and rewarding creative efforts (Bently 1993: 495). The law now curtails creativity in translation, the invention of translation projects and methods, as well as the creativity in literature that is inspired by the availability of foreign works in inventive translations. This problem is particularly exacerbated in the United States and the United Kingdom, where the volume of translation has remained relatively low throughout the post-World War II period.

The history of copyright shows that earlier translators did not suffer the same legal limitations as their successors today. On the contrary, translation was advantaged by the centuries-long, sometimes contradictory development of authorial rights in copyright law. There have been decisions in which the translator's copyright in the translated text was not only recognized, but given priority over that of an author or employer. And, ironically enough, cases that proved decisive in reserving copyright for the author contained alternative definitions of translation that were much more favorable to translators.

These alternatives from the past can be useful in challenging the present legal status of translation. They make clear that the historical development of an exclusive authorial copyright coincides with, and indeed depends on, the emergence of a Romantic concept of original authorship that negates the translator's work. But they also enable the formulation of a different concept of authorship, one in which the translator is seen as a species of author, and originality is revised to embrace diverse writing practices. What I shall present here is a genealogy of copyright that contests the cultural assumptions of the law and aims to foster legislative reform designed to further both the interests of translators and the practice of translation.

The current situation

Current copyright law defines translation inconsistently. On the one hand, the author is distinguished from, and privileged over, the translator. Copyright is reserved for the author, the producer who originates the form of the underlying work, and it covers only that form, the medium of expression as opposed to the idea or information expressed. The author's copyright encompasses not only reproductions, printed copies of the work, but also derivative works or adaptations, a category that explicitly includes translations, as well as such other derivative forms as dramatizations, film versions, abridgements, and musical arrangements. On the other hand, however, copyright in a derivative work can be reserved for its producer, although without excluding the right of the author who produced the underlying work (CDPA 1988, sections 1(1)(a), 16(1)(e), 21(3)(a)(i); 17 US Code, sections 102(a) and (b), 103(a), 106(2) (1976)). Here the translator is recognized as an author: according to contemporary commentary, a translator can be said to author a translation because translating originates a new medium of expression, a form for the foreign text in a different language and literature (see Skone James *et al.* 1991: 3–34 and Chisum and Jacobs 1992: 4C(1)(c)). Yet this difference in the linguistic and literary medium is evidently not so substantive as to constitute a truly authorial originality for the translator, since it does not in any way limit the right of the foreign author in the translation. When copyright law treats derivative works, it contradicts its key principle: that authorship consists of original expression, and hence that legal protection is given only to forms, not ideas (this contradiction appears in other jurisdictions too: for Canada, see Braithwaite 1982: 204; for France, see Derrida 1985: 196–199). In current law, the producer of a derivative work is and is not an author.

This contradiction indicates that copyright law must be protecting something else to the detriment of derivative works like translations. And that something else, I want to suggest, includes the individualistic concept of authorship that remains an important assumption in literary scholarship. According to this fundamentally Romantic concept, the author freely expresses personal thoughts and feelings in the work, which is thus viewed as an original and transparent self-representation, unmediated by transindividual determinants (linguistic, cultural, social) that might complicate authorial identity and originality (for a literary history of this concept, see Abrams 1953; for histories of its economic and legal conditions, see Woodmansee 1984, Saunders 1992, and Rose 1993). A translation, then, can never be more than a second-order representation: only the foreign text can be original, authentic, true to the author's psychology or intention, whereas the translation is forever imitative, not genuine, or simply false. Copyright law reserves an exclusive right in derivative works for the author because it assumes that literary form expresses a distinct authorial personality – despite the decisive formal change wrought by works like translations.

This is evident in an American case concerning a literary translation, *Grove Press, Inc. v. Greenleaf Publishing Co.* (247 F. Supp. 518; EDNY 1965), in which the decision waffled on the definition of originality as the criterion of authorship. Grove Press was seeking an injunction against Greenleaf, who published without authorization *The Thief's Journal*, Bernard Frechtman's 1954 English version of Jean Genet's *Journal du Voleur*. The court found that Greenleaf's publication infringed Genet's copyright in the French text:

> It is obvious that Greenleaf copied not only the words of Frechtman, the translator, but also the content and meaning of those words as created in Jean Genet's original biographical story. This creation included the entire plot, scenes, characters and dialogue of the novel, i.e., the format and pattern. Greenleaf copied two things, (1) the words and (2) the story.
>
> (524–525)

Although this decision linked Genet's authorship to the specific formal orga-nization of the French text ("the format and pattern"), the sense of form was inconsistent and confused. Elements of literary form were cited ("plot, scenes, characters and dialogue"), but copyright was vested in "the content and meaning of those words as created in Jean Genet's original biographical story." The medium of expression vanished before the ideas expressed. The "words" in this instance were English, not French, and they were "created" or chosen by Frechtman, not by Genet. Yet they communicated a "story" that was "original" because it originated with the French author, with his life. The judge was uncertain about the precise genre of Genet's work, describing it as both an autobiography and a "novel," because the criterion of authorship was ultimately not formal, but thematic or semantic. The judge's certainty was that Frechtman's translation reproduced the meaning of the French text and therefore the author's intention.

The Romantic concept of authorship thus elides any distinction between reproducing a work and preparing a derivative work based on it, even though copyright law lists these two actions as distinct rights reserved for the author. An unauthorized translation infringes the author's copyright because the translator produces an exact copy of the form and content of the under-lying work. A translation is not regarded as an independent text, interposing linguistic and literary differences which are specific to the translating culture, which are added to the foreign text to make it intelligible in that culture, and which the foreign author did not anticipate or choose. The foreign author's originality is assumed to transcend any such differences, so that the translation can be viewed as effectively identical to the foreign text. What copyright law protects is a concept of authorship that is really not inscribed in a material form, but rather is immaterial, a god-like essence of individuality that lacks cultural specificity and permeates various forms and media.

The most explicit legal version of this concept is *droit moral* or rights of per-sonality, which developed in French, German, and Scandinavian jurisdictions during the nineteenth century and achieved international currency with the Rome Revision (1928) of the Berne Convention for the Protection of Literary and Artistic Works (see Saunders 1992: chap. 3). Under the *droit moral*, the identity between author and work is phrased in moralistic terms, with the work considered an embodiment of the author's person. A 1934 commentary on the Rome Revision described the legal thinking behind this concept:

> Above and beyond the pecuniary and patrimonial right, we under-stand that the author exercises a lofty sovereignty over his work, such that when it is damaged he is injured. Publication is envisaged as a phenomenon that extends the personality of the author and thus exposes him to further injuries because the surface of his vulner-ability has been enlarged.
>
> (Saunders 1992: 31)

The *droit moral* gives the author various personal rights, including the right to be identified as author, the right to control the first publication, and the right to object to a distorted treatment of the work which may damage the author's reputation. Derivative works like translations could conceivably provoke a legal action under this last right, which has been included in the *droit moral* section of the Berne Convention since the Brussels Revision (1948). In principle, legal protection against distortions endows authors with enormous power over every aspect of the translating process, permitting them to develop their own idea of what constitutes the integrity of their work in a foreign language.

Interestingly, British law, although it recognizes the author's "moral rights," is alone in specifically excluding translations from the right to object to a distorted treatment (CDPA 1988, section 80(2)(a)(i)). Is translation excluded in this case because it is assumed to communicate the foreign author's personality without distortion? Or is the assumption that another authorial personality has intervened, the translator's, which is communicated in the translation and therefore requires protection in dealings with the domestic publisher and the foreign author? Bently suggests that "the legislature effected a broad exclusion of translations in order to recognise the difficulty and subjectiveness of determinations of the quality of translations" (Bently 1993: 514).

Whatever rationale may be offered for this exclusion, it seems clear that *droit moral* further restricts the translator's rights, yet without in any way resolving the inconsistencies in current legal definitions of translation. Copyright law admits that translation sufficiently alters the form of the foreign text to be copyrightable by the translator. Yet to allow the foreign author to assert a moral right of integrity over the translation would be to deny this basis of the translator's authorship. The economic disadvantage to the translator (and the publisher of the translation) is clear: as Bently puts it, "to require the author's approval [. . .] would be to give him a second opportunity to bargain in a situation where the derivative user has made considerable investment" (Bently 1993: 513).

The inconsistencies arise, moreover, not just between copyright codes at different levels of jurisdiction, national and international, but within the very international treaties that were designed to foster greater uniformity in the protection of intellectual works. The Berne Convention did not recognize the translator's copyright in the translated text until the Paris Revision (1971), yet this new awareness of translation produced no change in the author's exclusive right to license derivative works. The pertinent article reads: "Translations, adaptations, arrangements of music and other alterations of a literary or artistic work shall be protected as original works without prejudice to the copyright in the original work" (2(3)). The repetition of "original" here calls attention to the shifting concept of authorship in international copyright law. The autonomy of translation as original work is enhanced by separating author from translator. But the originality that entitles translators to legal protection is obviously not the same as that of foreign authors, who still enjoy "the exclusive right of making and authorising the translation of their works" (article 8). The UNESCO recommendation to improve the status of translators, adopted by the General Conference at Nairobi (22 November 1976), actually repeats the wording of the Berne Convention and thereby continues the subordination of translators to the authors of the underlying works (article II.3).

The contradictory development of original authorship

The ambiguous legal status of translation stretches back before the legislation that reserved copyright for the author. In Tudor and Stuart England, copyright was a right to publish held, not by an author, but by a printer or bookseller who belonged to the Stationers' Company, a guild established by the royal government to regulate the publishing industry and to censor books that were suspect on religious or political grounds (Patterson 1968: chap. 4). Stationers held an exclusive copyright in perpetuity. Nonetheless, they did recognize an authorial property right: authors were paid for the permission to print their copy and permitted to revise it. At least one entry in the Stationers' Register (dated "9no Decembris 1611") suggests that stationers might also recognize the author's translation right:

> Samuell Macham. Entred for his Copy vnder th'handes of Master warden Lownes, A booke called *Polemices sacræ pars prior, Roma Irreconsiliabilis, Authore* Josepho Hall Theologiae Doctore.

> *Item* Entred for his Copy the same booke to be printed in Englishe yf ye Author please to haue it translated.
> (Arber 1875–94: 473)

But, despite such rare instances, the line between translation and authorship was not always clearly drawn in the literary and publishing practices of this period. Authorship was seen as encompassing the creative use of other texts, foreign as well as domestic (see Greene 1982), and both translators and authors yielded their copyright to the stationer. Sir Thomas Wyatt's sonnets, to take one famous example, imitated and in several instances translated specific Italian poems by Petrarch and others, but when Wyatt's poetry was first published in *Tottel's Miscellany* (1557), he was identified as the author, not the translator.

The Romantic concept of original authorship emerged relatively late in the history of copyright. Although the first English formulations of this concept occurred in literary treatises like Edward Young's *Conjectures on Original Composition* (1759), it did not prevail in copyright law until the middle of the nineteenth century (see Ginsburg 1990: 1873–88). In an 1854 case before the House of Lords, *Jeffreys v. Boosey* (4 HLC 815, 869; 10 Eng. Rep. 681), a justice answered the claim that copyright "is a mental abstraction too evanescent and fleeting to be property" by invoking the distinction between the medium of expression and the idea expressed – only to collapse it. "The claim is not to ideas," he argued at first, "but to the order of the words, and [. . .] this order has a marked identity and a permanent endurance." Yet it quickly became clear that the "identity" the justice had in mind was in fact a mental abstraction, since the work was analogous to the author's physiognomy:

> Not only are the words chosen by a superior mind peculiar to itself, but in ordinary life no two descriptions of the same fact will be in the same words, and no two answers to your Lordships' questions will be the same. The order of each man's words is as singular as his countenance.
>
> (ibid.)

Although copyright was vested in the medium of expression, the medium was characterized as a transparent representation of the author's personality, a "mind" of a "superior" and "peculiar" kind. The importance assigned to an abstraction like personality inevitably evaporated form, with the result that the scope of the author's copyright was expanded to include any alteration in "the order of the words," no matter how substantial. Accordingly, the period that saw the authorial personality prevail in the courts also saw the institution of statutes that gave the author the right to prepare derivative works like translations. Although the Statute of Anne, the first act to protect authorial rights, was instituted in 1710, British law did not give the author an exclusive translation right until 1852 (Copyright Act, 15 & 16 Vict., c.12), American law not until 1870 (Act of 8 July, ch. 230, s. 86, 16 Stat. 198).

The law was slow to recognize this right partly because another, conflicting concept of authorship had prevailed before the mid-nineteenth century. According to this concept, copyright was reserved for the author, not because the work represented a personality, but because it was a product of labor, not because it expressed thoughts and feelings, but because it resulted from an investment of time and effort, both mental and physical. As one justice asserted in the 1769 case *Millar v. Taylor* (4 Burr. 2303; 98 Eng. Rep. 201; KB), a landmark in the establishment of authorial rights, "it is just, that an author should reap the pecuniary profit of his own ingenuity and labour." Copyright was found to exist in the common law: the author enjoyed a perpetual right in the work. The decision assumed that this right was natural, following John Locke's theory of private property. In his *Second Treatise of Civil Government* (1690), Locke argued that every Man has a *Property* in his own *Person*. This no Body has any Right to but himself. The *Labour* of his Body, and the *Work* of his Hands, we may say, are properly his. Whatsoever then he removes out of the State that Nature hath provided, and left it in, he hath mixed his *Labour* with, and joyned to it something that is his own, and thereby makes it his *Property*.

(Locke 1960: 305–306)

As this passage suggests, the concept of authorship as labor investment is just as individualistic as the Romantic insistence on personality: an author is completely autonomous from nature and from other persons; authoring is a free appropriation of natural materials. And the defining characteristic of authorship, labor, turns out to be just as immaterial as personality: the author's labor grants a natural right over a work that is itself natural, with both right and work transcending any specific cultural determinations or social constraints. Of course the very fact that the author's copyright requires legal protection, developed in various cases and enacted by various statutes, indicates that the relation between an individual and the product of that individual's labor is not natural, but legally constructed in response to changing cultural and social conditions. In *Millar v. Taylor*, these conditions included Locke's liberal theory of private property, as well as a book industry that functioned as a market for copyrights and so devised a concept of authorship by which authors were entitled to transfer their rights to booksellers. "The right of authors was merely a thread amid the complex relations between state interest, common-law rights to intellectual property, and commercial competition emerging throughout the eighteenth century" (Stewart 1991: 15; for the social conditions of the Statue of Anne, see Rose 1993: chap. 3 and Saunders 1992: chap. 2). The material conditions of authors' rights are denied as much by Lockean possessive individualism as by the Romantic theory of personal expression.

The concept of authorship as labor is interesting, not for its liberal assumptions, but for its enlargement of the scope of copyright law to address what today are classified as derivative works. The cases that defined authorial rights in the wake of the Statute of Anne acknowledged a translation to be an independent work which did not infringe the copyright of the author who produced the underlying work. A key case is *Burnett v. Chetwood* (2 Mer. 441; 35 Eng. Rep. 1008 (1720)). The executor of Thomas Burnett's estate was seeking to enjoin the defendant from publishing an unauthorized English translation of Burnett's Latin work, *Archaeologia Philosophica* (1692), a theological treatise which included a dialogue between Eve and the serpent that embarrassed the author when translated (for an account of the circumstances, see Rose 1993: 49–51). The court granted the plantiff's suit, although the decision was neither an application of the statute to protect Burnett's copyright nor an implicit recognition of his moral right to protect his reputation.

The justice was less interested in interpreting copyright law than in making a paternalistic gesture of censorship:

> *Lord Chancellor* said, that though a translation might not be the same with the reprinting the original, on account that the translator has bestowed his care and pains upon it, and so not within the prohibition of the act, yet this being a book which to his knowledge (having read it in his study), contained strange notions, intended by the author to be concealed from the vulgar in the Latin language, in which language it could not do much hurt, the learned being better able to judge of it, he thought it proper to grant an injunction to the printing and publishing it in English; that he lookt upon it, that this Court had a superintendency over all books, and might in a summary way restrain the printing or publishing any that contained reflections on religion or morality.

The decision wound up supporting what was "intended by the author," but it actually involved a legal definition of translation that put it outside of the author's copyright. Agreeing with the defendant's counsel that authorship consisted of labor invested in the production of a work, the Lord Chancellor distinguished between "reprinting the original" and translating it and hence assumed that the translator was an author, not a copyist. In *Millar v. Taylor*, the justices drew this distinction even more sharply. Although they found that the author held a perpetual copyright, one believed that "certainly bona fide imitations, translations, and abridgements are different; and in respect of the property, may be considered as new works," whereas another asserted that a purchaser of a book "may improve upon it, imitate it, translate it; oppose its sentiments: but he buys no right to publish the identical work" (98 Eng. Rep. 203, 205). In the early history of copyright law, the author was given only the right to reproduce the work, not to prepare a derivative work based on it. In fact, a translation was seen, not as derivative, but as original, or "new," because it resulted from the translator's labor. *Wyatt v. Barnard* (1814) found that "Translations, if original, [. . .] could not be distinguished from other Works," and so a copyright could be held in a translation by the translator or by the translator's employer, unless that translation copied another translated text – i.e., unless it was not *original* (3 Ves. & B. 77; 35 Eng. Rep. 408; Ch.). Originality was assumed to be a precise selection and arrangement of words, regardless of whether those words were intended to imitate another work.

The concept of authorship as labor investment thus led to an emphasis on form as the basis of copyright, and this emphasis supported the translator's right in the translation. In *Burnett v. Chetwood*, the defendant's counsel observed that the Statute of Anne, insofar as it was intended to promote creativity and the dissemination of knowledge, protected only the form of the author's work, not the content ("the sense"), and therefore the translator's creation of a different form for that content excluded the translation from the author's copyright. Translation, counsel concluded, "should rather seem to be within the encouragement than the prohibition of the act" (1009). The assumption here was twofold: on the one hand, the ideas in the underlying work were regarded as public knowledge upon publication, so that an author could own no more than their initial medium of expression; on the other hand, the translator's form-creating labor — the "skill in language" that resulted in the production of "his own style and expressions" — made him the owner of the translation that disseminated those ideas (ibid.). A similar assumption underlay the decision in *Donaldson v. Beckett* (1774). This crucial case upheld the Statute of Anne, but repealed the perpetual right given to the author in *Millar v. Taylor* precisely because, in Lord Camden's words, "science and learning are in their Nature *publici Juris*, and they ought to be as free and general as Air or Water" (Parks 1975: 53). For Camden, any perpetual right, whether grounded in the author's ideas or form, would hinder their circulation in derivative works. If copyright were vested "in the Sentiments, or Language," he pointed out, "no one can translate or abridge them," an effect that was contrary to the aims of the statute (ibid.: 52).

This line of thinking received its most extreme articulation in an American case, *Stowe v. Thomas* (23 Fed. Cas. 201 (No. 13514) (CCEDPa 1853)). The court found that an unauthorized German translation of Harriet Beecher Stowe's novel, *Uncle Tom's Cabin* (1852), did not infringe her copyright in the English text. Citing such earlier cases as *Burnett v. Chetwood* and *Millar v. Taylor*, the judge recognized the decisive intervention of the translator's labor: "The same conceptions clothed in another language cannot constitute the same composition," since "to make a good translation of a work often requires more learning, talent and judgment than was required to write the original" (208). The judge limited Stowe's right to the actual language of her novel because granting her control over translations would interfere with the circulation of her ideas, thereby contradicting the constitutional view of authorial copyright as a legal means "to promote the Progress of Science and useful Arts" (US Constitution, article I, section 8, clause 8 (1790)). The decision sought to foster the cultural creativity reflected in derivative works — however uneven in quality they might be — while strictly defining copyright infringement as unauthorized reproduction:

> By the publication of Mrs. Stowe's book, the creations of the genius and imagination of the author have become as much public property as those of Homer or Cervantes. All her conceptions and inventions may be used and abused by imitators, play-rights and poetasters. All that now remains is the copyright of her book; the exclusive right to print, reprint and vend it, and those only can be called infringers of her rights, or pirates of her property, who are guilty of printing,

publishing, importing or vending without her license, "copies of
her book." A translation may, in loose phraseology, be called a transcript or copy of her thoughts or conceptions, but in no correct
sense can it be called a copy of her book.

(208)

Stowe v. Thomas in effect gave translators an exclusive copyright in their
translations, distinct from the copyright in the underlying work held by its
author. And this meant, in principle, that translators could control every
step in the translation process, from choosing a foreign text to translate, to
developing a translation method, to authorizing the publication of the translated text.

Yet *Stowe v. Thomas* never achieved the authority of a precedent; in the
history of copyright, the case has proved to be eccentric. For precisely during
the period when it recognized translators as authors by virtue of their form-
creating labor, the Romantic concept of authorship came to dominate
the law, dooming translation to the ambiguous legal status that it currently
occupies. This development can be glimpsed in *Byrne v. Statist Co.* (1 KB
622 (1914)), a British case that is sometimes cited for its recognition of the
translator's rights, but that actually circumscribes them within narrow bounds.

The court decided that a newspaper had infringed a translator's copyright
by publishing his translation without his permission. The judge agreed with
the plaintiff's counsel that the translator owned the copyright in the translation according to the recently instituted act:

> This translation was an "original literary work" within s. 1, sub-s.
> 1, of the Copyright Act, 1911. It is "original" because it is not a
> mere copy of the work of another person. Originality of idea is
> not necessary; it is sufficient if the work is in substance a new thing
> involving fresh skill and labour. This translation is "original" work
> in that sense, and it is "literary" work [. . .] The plaintiff is the
> "author" of the work, and is therefore the owner of the copyright
> therein.

Although the concepts favorable to the translator seem to be in place
here – authorship as labor investment, originality as form – they were radically
qualified by the Copyright Act of 1911. This same act defined translation
as a "mere copy" by reserving for the author the exclusive right "to produce,
reproduce, perform, or publish any translation of the work" (1 & 2 Geo.
5, c. 46, 1(2)(b)). In *Byrne v. Statist Co.*, both the translator and the infringing
newspaper had in fact purchased a translation right from the foreign author;
the newspaper, however, neglected to approach the translator as well for
permission to reprint his translation. This case certainly recognized the translator as an author, but not one whose copyright in the translation superseded

or in any way limited the foreign author's. The act, therefore, was implicitly defining authorship as something less tangible than labor, something that transcended formal changes, an abstraction that negated the translator's work: the foreign author's ideas, intention, or personality.

The formal basis of the translator's authorship

The history of copyright may indeed contain alternative definitions of translation that favor translators. But the neglect into which these definitions have fallen, their sheer lack of legal authority today, indicates that they require substantial rethinking to challenge the dominance of the Romantic concept of authorship and to prove useful in legislative reform. This rethinking must encompass the basic concepts of copyright law, beginning with the understanding of form that defines authorship.

The early cases conceive of linguistic and literary form as transparent communication. Meaning is assumed to be an unchanging essence embedded in language, not an effect of relations between words that is unstable, varying with different contexts. Hence the clothing metaphors that recur in the cases: an author is said to clothe meaning in language; a translator then communicates the meaning of the foreign text by changing its linguistic clothes. In copyright law, this concept of form first appeared in *Burnett v. Chetwood*, where, however, it was simultaneously put into question. The defendant's counsel argued that a translation "may be called a different book" because

> the translator dresses it up and clothes the sense in his own style and expressions, and at least puts it into a different form from the original, and *forma dat esse rei*.
>
> (1009)

The Latin axiom was drawn from the Aristotelian metaphysics that prevailed in medieval scholastic philosophy: in a fairly close rendering, "form brings things into existence." The counsel apparently cited this metaphysical principle to establish the relative autonomy of the translation from the foreign text: translating is seen as form-creating, and therefore the translation can be said to exist as an object independent of the underlying work on which it is based. Yet the axiom also suggests that the translation effectively *creates* the foreign text in another language, that the different form created by the translator brings into existence another text with a different meaning. If *forma dat esse rei*, form cannot easily be detached from content, nor can formal changes preserve the same content unchanged. Hence, the translator's new "style and expressions" must produce a new "sense."

The decision itself supports this understanding of form, because it documents the fact that the meaning of Burnett's Latin treatise changed when translated into English. The plaintiff's counsel found the translation a mixture of error and parody, "the sense and words of the author mistaken, and represented in an absurd and ridiculous manner" (1009). The Lord Chancellor saw the change wrought by the translation in social terms: the "strange notions" of the *Archaeologia Philosophica*, he noted, were "learned" and innocuous in Latin, but "vulgar" and potentially harmful in English. The meanings of the two texts, then, were determined by the writers' creation of different forms that addressed different audiences. The reference to these audiences demonstrates that authorship is not individualistic, but collective: the form of the work does not originate simply with the author as "his own style and expressions," but is in effect a collaboration with a specific social group, wherein the author takes into account the cultural values characteristic of that group.

This collective concept of authorship applies to both the translation and the underlying work. The texts at issue in *Byrne v. Statist Co.* were a Portuguese speech delivered by a Brazilian governor to the state legislature and plaintiff's English translation published as an "advertisement" in an influential London-based newspaper, the *Financial Times* (624). The different social situations for which the texts were written ensured that they would take different forms and carry different meanings for their readers. The governor's speech was political, serving as "a message to the General Assembly of that State dealing with its finances," whereas Byrne's translation was commercial, designed to provide information for potential investors (623). The social function of each text was inscribed in its form, most obviously in each author's use of a specific language for a specific audience, but also in the different literary and rhetorical structures chosen by each author to signify in a different social context. The collective nature of authorship becomes clear in the judge's statement of the facts, which reports Byrne's detailed description of his own translation:

> He cut down the speech by about one third. He edited it by omitting the less material parts. He divided it into suitable paragraphs, and supplied head-lines appropriate to those paragraphs. He told me too that the *Financial Times* sets a high standard of literary style and that his translation conformed to that high standard.
>
> (624)

The commercial function that Byrne's translation was intended to perform required not only that it communicate the same financial information as the governor's speech, but that this information be assimilated to domestic cultural values, rewritten according to a new stylistic "standard" in English, edited according to a new, distinctively journalistic format ("paragraphs" and "head-lines"), and reinterpreted according to an English investor's sense of pertinence (the omission of "less material parts").

Byrne v. Statist Co. indicates that the form of a work is not only collaborative, constituted by a relation with an audience, but derivative, not originating in the author's personality or productive labor on raw nature, but drawn from pre-existing cultural materials. The Brazilian governor's speech was written in the style of a political address, Byrne's translation in the style of business journalism. The styles preceded the composition of the texts and determined their meanings, however much those styles were elaborated and fitted to a specific purpose and occasion. The copyrightable form in a work, then, is not self-originating, but uniquely derived: the precise selection, arrangement, and elaboration of materials that already exist in a culture, not merely the lexicon, syntax, and phonology that define a particular language, but the structures and themes that have accumulated in the various cultural discourses of that language – literary, rhetorical, political, commercial, and so forth. It is from these materials, never raw or natural, always culturally coded by previous uses, that an author produces a form determined by an address to a particular cultural constituency.

Still, the collective authorship of a translation differs in an important way from that of the underlying work. Even though every work appropriates other works to some extent, a translation is engaged in two, simultaneous appropriations, one of the foreign text, the other of domestic cultural materials. The relation between translation and foreign text is mimetic and interpretive, governed by canons of accuracy and methods of interpretation that vary culturally and historically, whereas the relation between translation and domestic culture is mimetic and communicative, governed by an imitation of cultural materials to address audiences that are culturally and historically specific. In translating, the interpretation of the foreign text and the address to an audience are mutually determining, although in any given translation one of these determinants may outweigh the other: the projected audience may decisively shape the translator's interpretation, or the translator's interpretation may decisively define the audience.

Contemporary translations, unlike such other derivative forms as dramatic or film adaptations, are bound to a much closer relation to the underlying work, partly because of the Romantic concept of authorship. The dominance of this concept instills in translators and their publishers a deference to the foreign text that discourages the development of innovative translation methods which might seem distorting or false in their interpretations. Today, a dramatic or film adaptation of a novel may deviate widely from the plot, characterizations, and dialogue in that novel, but a translation is expected to imitate these formal elements without revision or deletion.

Nonetheless, the closeness of the relation between translation and foreign text should not be taken as implying that the two works are identical, or that the translation is not an independent work of authorship. If authorship is collective, if a work both collaborates with and derives from a cultural context, then the translation and the foreign text are distinct projects because they involve different intentions and contexts. The significance of a foreign novel in the foreign literature where it was produced will never be exactly the same as the significance of that novel in a translation designed for circulation in another language and literature. This goes some way toward explaining why bestsellers don't always repeat their success in a foreign country when translated.

The variation in significance, moreover, cannot be limited or preempted by the appearance of the same author's name on the foreign text and the translation. For readers of the foreign text, that name will project a different identity, tied to the foreign language and the cultural traditions of the foreign country, than the somewhat domesticated identity projected by the translation. To take an extreme yet illuminating example, ever since Islamic fundamentalists called for the death of the British writer Salman Rushdie because they judged his novel *The Satanic Verses* (1988) to be blasphemous of the Koran, the name "Salman Rushdie" has differed in meaning, depending not only on the cultural values that a reader brings to any book attributed to this writer, but also on the language in which it circulates. The identity linked to Rushdie's name is likely to vary according to whether a book of his is published in English or in an Arabic translation.

Copyright law has failed to acknowledge the manifold relations that determine any translation because it has been dominated by individualistic concepts of authorship, whether Lockean or Romantic, whether grounded in labor or in personality. These concepts have diminished the legal status of derivative forms, while concealing the degree to which the underlying work is itself derivative. A collective concept of authorship offers a precise definition of form to distinguish between a translation and the foreign text it translates: the collaborative and derivative dimensions of form result in linguistic and cultural differences that can serve as the basis for the translator's claim to copyright, but also for an argument in favor of restricting the foreign author's right in the translation.

Remedies

Current copyright law, however, lacks the conceptual tools to formulate such a restriction. British and American codes (among others) provide for a "joint work," for instance, yet the concept of authorship assumed here is not in fact collective, but individualistic, resting on the notion of organic unity that has long dominated literary criticism (see Venuti 1985–86). Thus, a joint work is regarded as seamlessly unified: the "contributions" of "each author" are "not distinct" or are "merged into inseparable or interdependent parts of a unitary whole" (CDPA 1988, section 10(1); 17 US Code, sections 101, 201(a)). In the case of a derivative form like translation, the contributions of the translator and the foreign author can be distinguished: the translation imitates the linguistic and literary values of a foreign text, but the imitation is cast in a different language with relations to a different cultural tradition. As a result, the translator contributes a form that partly replaces and in general qualifies the form contributed by the foreign author. A foreign novelist may be said to contribute the characters in a novel to the translation, but the nature of those characters as evidenced in dialogue or description will inevitably be altered by the values of the translating language and culture, by the release of a domestic remainder during the translation process. The notion of indistinct contributions still rests on the individualistic assumption that linguistic and literary form enables transparent communication by a single person, as opposed to communication determined collectively by cultural materials and social contexts.

The definition of a joint work is particularly inhospitable to derivative forms like translation because it stipulates an "intention" to collaborate shared by the authors "at the time the writing is done" (HR Rep. No. 1476, 94th Cong., 2nd Sess. 103, 120; cf. Jaszi 1994: 40, 50–55 on "serial collaborations"). The assumption is that the work is produced by two individuals in concert and over a well-defined period of time. Yet this does not take into account the reality of translation projects today. According to current practices, several years are likely to elapse between the publication of a foreign text and its translation, unless the foreign text was written by an author of previous international bestsellers and is therefore of immediate interest to publishers worldwide. The development of a translation project requires numerous tasks that vary in complexity, but all of which are time-consuming: these tasks begin with the domestic publisher's selection of a foreign text to translate and include the negotiation of translation rights with the foreign author or publisher, the commissioning of a translator, and the editing of the translation. The publication of a translation can thus be considered a collective project, involving the collaboration of many agents at different stages. The foreign author's participation is of course indispensable, but it may finally be limited to the writing of the foreign text that is the basis of the project. What argues against viewing a translation as a joint work is not merely the different times at which foreign author and translator make their contributions, but the absence of a shared intention. Foreign authors generally address a linguistic and cultural constituency that does not include the readers of their works in translation. Translators address a domestic constituency whose demand for intelligibility in the terms of the translating language and culture exceeds the foreign author's intention as realized in the foreign text.

Recent cases and commentary suggest that a translation may be considered a "fair use" of a foreign text which is exempt from the foreign author's exclusive copyright in derivative works. A use of a copyrighted work is defined as fair when it serves "purposes such as criticism, comment, news reporting, teaching (including multiple copies for classroom use), scholarship, or research" (17 US Code, section 107; for the comparable British concept of "fair dealing," see CDPA 1988, sections 29(1), 30(1) and (2)). Many kinds of translations, both literary and technical, serve such purposes, and in the case of literary works a translation can always be seen as an interpretation of the foreign text, a criticism or commentary that determines its meaning for a domestic audience.

A fair-use argument for translation can be developed further on the basis of *Campbell v. Acuff Rose Music, Inc.* (1994), in which the United States Supreme Court held that a rap song, 2 Live Crew's "Pretty Woman," may constitute a fair use of the rock ballad which it parodied, Roy Orbison's "Oh, Pretty Woman" (114 S.Ct. 1164; the decision is discussed in Greenhouse 1994). The court stated that "like less ostensibly humorous forms of criticism," parody "can provide social benefit by shedding light on an earlier work, and, in the process, creating a new one" (1171). Parody, like translation, involves an imitative rewriting of an underlying work, while the mimetic relation between translation and foreign text may sometimes be parodic. The English translation in *Burnett v. Chetwood*, for example, was described as an "absurd and ridiculous" version of Burnett's Latin treatise. A translation can be viewed, more generally, as one of those "less ostensibly humorous forms of criticism" to which the justice referred, a commentary on the foreign text that is subtly enacted through imitation.

Yet a fair-use argument for translation may falter on the additional factors that must be considered for any such exemption from the foreign author's exclusive copyright. Recent cases make clear that the most important of these factors are "the purpose and character of the use, including whether such use is of a commercial nature," "the amount and substantiality of the portion used in relation to the copyrighted work as a whole," and "the effect of the use upon the potential market for or value of the copyrighted work" (17 US Code, section 107(1), (3), and (4)).

A translation, insofar as it is written in a different language for a different culture, does not limit the potential market for the foreign text in its own language and culture. In fact, the translation of a work into many languages could increase its literary and commercial value at home by demonstrating its value abroad. Nor does a translator use too much of the foreign text to sustain a fair-use defense. Today, a translation is expected to render the foreign text in its entirety; if a translation alters or omits substantial portions of that text, it would no longer be considered a translation, but another kind of derivative form, such as an adaptation or abridgement. More importantly, the peculiar kind of writing involved in any translation forces a distinction between copying and imitating the foreign text. A translation does not copy in the sense of repeating that text verbatim; rather, the translation enters into a mimetic relation that inevitably deviates from the foreign language by relying on target-language approximations. Even though a contemporary translation is required to imitate the entire foreign text, their linguistic and cultural features are sufficiently distinct to permit them to be considered autonomous works.

The factor that might finally mark an unauthorized translation as an infringement under the fair-use provision is the purpose and character of the use to which the translator puts the copyrighted work. Certainly, translators select and translate foreign texts for purposes that can be described as cultural or even "educational." Translations do not just increase knowledge in diverse humanistic and technical fields; they can also exert a decisive influence on the development of disciplines and professions. And translations can be enlisted in the service of political agendas that hinder or promote cultural and social change (for examples of such agendas, see Cronin 1996 and Simon 1996). At the same time, however, translators are also motivated by a significant commercial interest, since they aim to profit from their translations. It is this very interest that copyright law was designed to protect so as to encourage the creation of cultural and educational works. But the fair-use provision frustrates this design by assuming, quite contradictorily, that authors of derivative works like translations should not share the commercial motives of other authors.

Perhaps the most effective way to calibrate the competing interests in a translation project is the one that takes into account the actual dealings of translators, publishers, and authors, as well as the inevitability of cultural change. By far the most important consideration here is time. If an author or publisher does not sell the translation rights for a work soon after its first publication, any project to translate it will most likely originate in the translating culture and require several years to develop. During this period, a work that initially lacked value in the translating culture comes to be valuable through the efforts of a translator or publisher, notably through translating and publishing strategies that address domestic cultural constituencies and locate or establish markets for the translation. A translation, in turn, is produced at a particular moment in the history of a culture. It loses cultural and commercial value when new domestic trends and constituencies emerge to diminish its market, leading the publisher to stop reprinting, if not to invest in another translation of the same foreign work.

These considerations suggest the need for limitations of both the foreign author's and the translator's copyrights. Limiting the foreign author's right in the translation to a definite period — say, five years — will encourage translators and domestic publishers by increasing the incentive for investment in translations. If the foreign text is not translated within the five-year period, the first translator or publisher to publish a translation of it thereafter should not only be permitted to copyright the translation, as current law provides, but should also enjoy an exclusive translation right in the foreign text. Yet given the fact that translations date and lose their readerships, the translator's exclusive right should last, not for the full term of the copyright, but only for the length of time that the translation is kept in print by the publisher. Such limitations will motivate publishers to develop and issue more translations without the added burden of paying foreign authors for rights. Translators will be motivated to apply and enhance their expertise in foreign languages and cultures by inventing translation projects that answer to their own sense of domestic cultural values – without fear of legal reprisals from foreign authors or of uninformed, cost-conscious rejections from domestic publishers. The out-of-print provision will stimulate innovation in translating and publishing because it requires a more careful reflection on the domestic readerships that already exist or might be created for foreign works. (This proposal resembles, but goes far beyond, the three-year limitation of the foreign author's translation right provided by the British Copyright Act of 1852, a limitation that was in any case removed in 1911; see Bently 1993: 501–505 for a discussion of the legislative changes.)

Current copyright law does not define a space for the translator's authorship that is equal to, or in any way restricts, the foreign author's exclusive right. Yet it acknowledges that there is a material basis to warrant some such restriction. The collective concept of authorship outlined here puts the translator on an equal legal footing with the author of the underlying work. According to this concept, copyright would be grounded on precise formal features which show that similar procedures are involved in creating the foreign text and the translation, and these procedures occur with sufficient autonomy, in different linguistic and cultural contexts, to allow the works to be viewed as independent. Without a greater recognition of the collective nature of authorship, translators will continue to be squeezed by unfavorable, if not simply exploitative, contracts. Individualistic notions of intellectual property will continue to seem pious fictions used by authors and publishers to add a patina of legitimacy to their money grabs. And publishers around the world will continue to support the unequal patterns of cross-cultural exchange that have accompanied economic and political developments in the post-World War II period. It is the sheer global reach of translation, its strategic and irreplaceable value in negotiating cultural differences, that lends urgency to the need for a clarification and improvement of its legal status.

4

THE FORMATION OF
CULTURAL IDENTITIES

Translation is often regarded with suspicion because it inevitably domesticates foreign texts, inscribing them with linguistic and cultural values that are intelligible to specific domestic constituencies. This process of inscription operates at every stage in the production, circulation, and reception of the translation. It is initiated by the very choice of a foreign text to translate, always an exclusion of other foreign texts and literatures, which answers to particular domestic interests. It continues most forcefully in the development of a translation strategy that rewrites the foreign text in domestic dialects and discourses, always a choice of certain domestic values to the exclusion of others. And it is further complicated by the diverse forms in which the translation is published, reviewed, read, and taught, producing cultural and political effects that vary with different institutional contexts and social positions.

By far the most consequential of these effects – and hence the greatest potential source of scandal – is the formation of cultural identities. Translation wields enormous power in constructing representations of foreign cultures. The selection of foreign texts and the development of translation strategies can establish peculiarly domestic canons for foreign literatures, canons that conform to domestic aesthetic values and therefore reveal exclusions and admissions, centers and peripheries that deviate from those current in the foreign language. Foreign literatures tend to be dehistoricized by the selection of texts for translation, removed from the foreign literary traditions where they draw their significance. And foreign texts are often rewritten to conform to styles and themes that *currently* prevail in domestic literatures, much to the disadvantage of more historicizing translation discourses that recover styles and themes from earlier moments in domestic traditions.

Translation patterns that come to be fairly established fix stereotypes for foreign cultures, excluding values, debates, and conflicts that don't appear to serve domestic agendas. In creating stereotypes, translation may attach esteem or stigma to specific ethnic, racial, and national groupings, signifying respect for cultural difference or hatred based on ethnocentrism, racism, or patriotism. In the long run, translation figures in geopolitical relations by establishing the cultural grounds of diplomacy, reinforcing alliances, antagonisms, and hegemonies between nations.

Yet since translations are usually designed for specific cultural constituencies, they set going a process of identity formation that is double-edged. As translation constructs a domestic representation for a foreign text and culture, it simultaneously constructs a domestic subject, a position of intelligibility that is also an ideological position, informed by the codes and canons, interests and agendas of certain domestic social groups. Circulating in the church, the state, and the school, a translation can be powerful in maintaining or revising the hierarchy of values in the translating language. A calculated choice of foreign text and translation strategy can change or consolidate literary canons, conceptual paradigms, research methodologies, clinical techniques, and commercial practices in the domestic culture. Whether the effects of a translation prove to be conservative or transgressive depends fundamentally on the discursive strategies developed by the translator, but also on the various factors in their reception, including the page design and cover art of the printed book, the advertising copy, the opinions of reviewers, and the uses made of the translation in cultural and social institutions, how it is read and taught. Such factors mediate the impact of any translation by assisting in the positioning of domestic subjects, equipping them with specific reading practices, affiliating them with specific cultural values and constituencies, reinforcing or crossing institutional limits.

I want to develop these observations by examining several translation projects from different periods, past and present. Each project exhibits in an especially clear way the process of identity formation at work in translation, as well as its various effects. The aim is to consider how translation forms particular cultural identities and maintains them with a relative degree of coherence and homogeneity, but also how it creates possibilities for cultural resistance, innovation, and change at any historical moment. For notwithstanding the fact that translation is summoned to address the linguistic and cultural difference of a foreign text, it can just as effectively foster or suppress heterogeneity in the domestic culture.

The identity-forming power of translation always threatens to embarrass cultural and political institutions because it reveals the shaky foundations of their social authority. The truth of their representations and the subjective integrity of their agents are founded not on the inherent value of authoritative texts and institutional practices, but on the contingencies that arise in the translation, publication, and reception of those texts. The authority of any institution that relies on translations is susceptible to scandal because their somewhat unpredictable effects exceed the institutional controls that normally regulate textual interpretation, such as judgments of canonicity (see Kermode 1983). Translations extend the possible uses of foreign texts among diverse audiences, institutionally based or not, producing results that may be both disruptive and serendipitous.

The representation of foreign cultures

In 1962 the classical scholar John Jones published a study that challenged the dominant interpretation of Greek tragedy, which, he argued, was not only articulated in academic literary criticism, but inscribed in scholarly editions and translations of Aristotle's *Poetics*. In Jones's view, "the *Poetics* which we have appropriated to ourselves derives jointly from modern classical scholarship, and from Romanticism" (Jones 1962: 12). Guided by a Romantic concept of individualism, in which human agency is seen as self-determining, modern scholars have given a psychological cast to Aristotle's concept of tragedy, shifting the emphasis from the action to the hero and the audience's emotional response. This individualistic interpretation, Jones felt, obscures the fact that "the centre of gravity of Aristotle's terms is situational and not personal," that ancient Greek culture conceived of human subjectivity as socially determinate, "realised in action and recognised – intelligibly differentiated – through its truth to type" and "status" (ibid.: 16, 55). Jones's study was favorably reviewed on publication, despite some complaints about his unfamiliar "jargon" and "a certain opacity of language," and over the next two decades it gained enormous authority in classical scholarship (Gellie 1963: 354; Burnett 1963: 177). By 1977 it had established a "new orthodoxy" on the question of characterization in Aristotle's *Poetics* and Greek tragedy, overcoming the long dominance of the hero-centered approach and receiving both assent and further development in the work of leading scholars (Taplin 1977: 312; Goldhill 1986: 170–171).

Jones's study proved so effective in causing a disciplinary revision partly because he critiqued the standard translations of Aristotle's treatise. He shrewdly demonstrated that scholarly translators imposed the individualistic interpretation on the Greek text through various lexical choices. From Ingram Bywater's 1909 version he quoted the passage in which Aristotle discusses *hamartia*, the error of judgment made by characters in tragedies. Jones read the English translation symptomatically, locating "discrepancies" or deviations from the Greek that reveal the work of the translator's ideology, Romantic individualism:

> There are three discrepancies to be noted between Bywater's translation and the Greek original. Where he has "a good man" the Greek has "good men"; where he has "a bad man" the Greek has "bad men"; and where he renders "the change in the hero's fortunes" the Greek has "the change of fortune." The first and second of his alterations are not quite as trivial as they seem, for they contrive jointly to suggest that Aristotle has in mind a single dominant figure throughout, when in fact his discourse shifts from plural to singular. These two alterations help pave the way for the third, which is, in the whole range of its implications, momentous. [. . .] Aristotle's

69

demand that the change of fortune shall be brought about by the *hamartia* of "the intermediate kind of personage" does not entitle us to style that personage the Tragic Hero; for to call him the hero can only mean that we put him at the centre of our ideal play – as commentator after commentator has alleged that Aristotle does, thrusting the hero on his treatise.

(Jones 1962: 19–20)

Jones was careful to stress that the discrepancies in Bywater's translation are not errors, but calculated choices designed "to make Aristotle's indisputable meaning plainer than it would otherwise have been" (Jones 1962: 20). Nonetheless, to make the meaning plain was to make it anachronistic by assimilating the Greek text to a modern cultural concept, "the now settled habit in which we see action issuing from a solitary focus of consciousness – secret, inward, interesting" (ibid.: 1962: 33). The same Romantic inscription is evident in scholarly renderings of the Greek word *mellein*. Jones pointed out that this verb can have several meanings, including "to be about to do," "to be on the point of doing," and "to intend doing." Both Bywater and Gerald Else (1957) made choices that psychologize Aristotle's concept of tragic action by introducing intentionality and introspection: "intending to kill," "intending to betray," "meditating some deadly injury" (Jones 1962: 49).

The case of Jones shows that, despite strict canons of accuracy, even academic translations construct distinctly domestic representations of foreign texts and cultures. And these representations, assigned varying degrees of institutional authority, may reproduce or revise dominant conceptual paradigms in academic disciplines. Translations can precipitate a disciplinary revision because the representations they construct are never seamless or perfectly consistent, but often contradictory, assembled from heterogeneous cultural materials, domestic and foreign, past and present. Thus, Jones was able to detect what he called "discrepancies" in Bywater's translation, discontinuities with the Greek text that signaled the intervention of a modern individualistic ideology.

Yet disciplines also change because competing representations emerge to challenge those in dominance. Although Jones undoubtedly illuminated neglected and distorted aspects of Aristotle's *Poetics* and Greek tragedy, he was himself translating and therefore constructing a domestic representation that was also anachronistic to some extent, even though more compelling than the current academic orthodoxy. As reviewers suggested, Jones's concept of determinate subjectivity reveals an "existentialist manner of thinking" that enabled him both to question the individualism of classical scholarship and to develop an interdisciplinary method of reading, not psychological but "sociological" and "anthropological" (Bacon 1963: 56; Burnett 1963: 176–177; Lucas 1963: 272). At points, Jones's critique of the orthodox reading clearly resembled the thinking of philosophers like Nietzsche who were important for the emergence of existentialism. Just as *On the Genealogy of Morals* treated the concept of an autonomous subject as "the misleading influence of language," whereby "'the doer' is merely a fiction added to the deed," so Jones pointed to the grammatical category underlying the hero-centered approach to Greek tragedy: "the status of action must always be adjectival: action qualifies; it tells us things we want to know about the individual promoting it [. . .] the state of affairs 'inside' him who acts" (Nietzsche 1967: 45; Jones 1962: 33). Jones's study was able to establish a new orthodoxy in classical scholarship because it met scholarly standards for textual evidence and critical argument, but also because it reflected the rise of existentialism as a powerful current in post-World War II culture. His critique of the authoritative English translations, along with his own versions of the Greek text, brought about a disciplinary revision by importing cultural values, domestic and foreign, from outside the boundaries of the discipline – notably a concept of determinate subjectivity that was elaborated in German and French philosophers like Heidegger and Sartre and given international currency through translations.

Thus, when an academic translation constructs a domestic representation of a foreign text and culture, this representation can alter the institution where it is housed because disciplinary boundaries are permeable. Although defined by precise qualifications and practices and by a hierarchical arrangement of themes and methodologies, an academic discipline does not reproduce them in an untroubled fashion because it is prone to conceptual infiltrations from other fields and disciplines, both in and out of the academy. And since these boundaries can be crossed, the traffic in cultural values can take diverse forms, not only circulating among academic disciplines, as in the case of Jones, but also moving from one cultural institution to another, as when the academy influences the nature and volume of translations issued by the publishing industry. Here a specific cultural constituency controls the representation of foreign literatures for other constituencies in the domestic culture, privileging certain domestic values to the exclusion of others and establishing a canon of foreign texts that is necessarily partial because it serves certain domestic interests.

A case in point is the translation of modern Japanese fiction into English. As Edward Fowler (1992) indicated, American publishers like Grove Press, Alfred Knopf, and New Directions, noted for their concern with literary as well as commercial values, issued many translations of Japanese novels and story collections during the 1950s and 1960s. Yet their choices were very selective, focussing on relatively few writers, mainly Tanizaki Jun'ichiro, Kawabata Yasunari, and Mishima Yukio. By the late 1980s a reviewer who is also a poet and translator could say that "for the average Western reader, [Kawabata's novel] Snow Country is perhaps what we think of as typically 'Japanese': elusive, misty, inconclusive" (Kizer 1988: 80). The same cultural image was assumed by another, more self-conscious reviewer, who, when confronted with an English version of a comic Japanese novel, wondered skeptically: "Could it be that the novel of delicacy, taciturnity, elusiveness, and languishing melancholy – traits we have come to think of as characteristically Japanese – is less

71

characteristic than we thought?" (Leithauser 1989: 105). American publishers, Fowler argued, established a canon of Japanese fiction in English that was not only unrepresentative, but based on a well-defined stereotype that has determined reader expectations for roughly forty years. Moreover, the cultural stereotyping performed by this canon extended beyond English, since English translations of Japanese fiction were routinely translated into other European languages during the same period. In effect, "the tastes of English-speaking readers have by and large dictated the tastes of the entire Western world with regard to Japanese fiction" (Fowler 1992: 15–16).

Among the many remarkable things about this canon formation is the fact that the English-speaking tastes in question belonged to a limited group of readers, primarily academic specialists in Japanese literature associated with trade publishers. The translations of Tanizaki, Kawabata, and Mishima were produced by university professors such as Howard Hibbett, Donald Keene, Ivan Morris, and Edward Seidensticker who advised editors on which Japanese texts to publish in English (Fowler 1992: 12 n. 25). It has been suggested that their translating was homogenizing, avoiding any language that "might not have been said or written by a modern American university professor of modest literacy, and concomitantly modest literary gifts" (Miller 1986: 219). The various interests of these academic translators and their editors – literary, ethnographic, economic – were decisively shaped by an encounter with Japan around World War II, and the canon they established constituted a nostalgic image of a lost past. Not only did the translated fiction often refer to traditional Japanese culture, but some novels lamented the disruptive social changes wrought by military conflict and Western influence; Japan was represented as "an exoticized, aestheticized, and quintessentially *foreign* land quite antithetical to its prewar image of a bellicose and imminently threatening power" (Fowler 1992: 3; his emphasis).

The nostalgia expressed by the canon was distinctly American, not necessarily shared by Japanese readers. Keene, for example, a critic and translator of considerable authority in English-language culture, disagreed on both literary and political grounds with the lukewarm Japanese reception of Tanizaki's novels. "Tanizaki seems to have been incapable of writing a boring line," Keene felt, while expressing particular admiration for *The Makioka Sisters*, a novel that was banned by the militaristic government in the early 1940s: "the leisurely pace of its account of prewar Japan seems to have exasperated those who insisted on a positive, exhortatory literature suited to the heroic temper of the times" (Keene 1984: I, 721, 774). Thus, the nostalgic image projected by the canon could carry larger, geopolitical implications: "the aestheticized realms [in the novels selected for translation] provided exactly the right image of Japan at a time when that country was being transformed, almost overnight in historical terms, from a mortal enemy during the Pacific War to an indispensable ally during the Cold War era" (Fowler 1992: 6). The English-language canon of Japanese fiction functioned as a domestic cultural support for American diplomatic relations with Japan, which were also designed to contain Soviet expansionism in the East.

This case shows that even when translation projects reflect the interests of a specific cultural constituency – here an elite group of academic specialists and literary publishers – the resulting image of the foreign culture may still achieve national dominance, accepted by many readers in the domestic culture whatever their social position may be. An affiliation between the academy and the publishing industry can be especially effective in molding a broad consensus, since both possess cultural authority of sufficient power to marginalize noncanonical texts in the domestic culture. The Japanese novels that were not consistent with the postwar academic canon because they were comic, for example, or represented a more contemporary, westernized Japan – these novels were not translated into English or, if translated, were positioned on the fringes of English-language literature, published by smaller, more specialized publishers (Kodansha International, Charles E. Tuttle) with limited distribution (Fowler 1992: 14–17).

Moreover, the canon did not undergo any significant change during the 1970s and 1980s. The volume of English-language translations suffered a general decline, weakening any effort to widen the range of Japanese novels available in English versions; in the hierarchy of languages translated into English, Japanese ranked sixth after French, German, Russian, Spanish, and Italian (Venuti 1995a: 13; Grannis 1993: 502). Perhaps more importantly, the institutional programs developed to improve cross-cultural exchange between the United States and Japan continued to be dominated by "a professional group of university professors and corporate executives (the latter mostly publishers and booksellers) – men whose formative experiences have been shaped by World War II" (Fowler 1992: 25). As a result, the lists of Japanese texts proposed for English translation simply reinforced the established criteria for canonicity, including a special emphasis on the war era and reflecting a "concern with 'high culture' and with the experiences of Japan's intellectual and social elite" (ibid.: 27).

What this suggests is that translation projects can effect a change in a domestic representation of a foreign culture, not simply when they revise the canons of the most influential cultural constituency, but when another constituency in a different social situation produces and responds to the translations. By the end of the 1980s the academic canon of Japanese literature was being questioned by a new generation of English-language writers and readers. Born after the Pacific War and under the global reach of American hegemony, they were skeptical of "the down-dragging melancholy of so much Japanese fiction" and more receptive to different forms and themes, including comic narratives that display the deep entrenchment of Western cultural influences in Japan (Leithauser 1989: 110).

Anthologies seem to have played a role in this canon reformation, since, as Lefevere has shown, "once a certain degree of early canonization has been attained" by a foreign literature in translation, "new anthologies can accept that emerging canon, try to subvert it, or try to enlarge it" (Lefevere 1992a: 126–127). In 1991, for example, Alfred Birnbaum, an American journalist who was born in 1957 and has lived in Japan since childhood, edited an anthology entitled *Monkey Brain Sushi*. As the sensational title suggests, Birnbaum sought to challenge the academic canon and reach a wider English-language audience with the most recent Japanese fiction. His introduction makes clear that he deliberately avoided the "staples of the older diet," like Tanizaki, Kawabata, and Mishima, in favor of writers who "were all born and raised in an Americanized postwar Japan" and whose books are "what most people really read" (Birnbaum 1991: 1; for a similar translation project, see Mitsios 1991). Unlike the older anthologies that established the academic canon – e.g. Keene's Grove Press collection (1956) – Birnbaum's was published by the small American branch of a Tokyo-based press, Kodansha, and neither the editor nor his three collaborators were affiliated with academic institutions. The early indications are that anthologies like *Monkey Brain Sushi* and Helen Mitsios's *New Japanese Voices* have indeed reformed the canon of Japanese fiction for a popular readership: not only have these books been reprinted in paperback editions, but in their wake several novels by young Japanese writers have been published in English with critical and commercial success.

Perhaps the clearest sign of the change is Banana Yoshimoto's *Kitchen* (1993), which was excerpted in Mitsios's anthology. Yoshimoto was published by one of the presses important for creating the academic canon, Grove, but not on the advice of academic specialists: the editor learned of it through an Italian translation – a change from the period when English was the language through which Japanese fiction was disseminated in European cultures (Harker 1994: 4). The two pieces in *Kitchen*, a novella and a short story, represent Japanese characters who are youthful and extremely Westernized, traits that were repeatedly cited as sources of fascination in the reviews. Interestingly, some reviewers assimilated the title piece to aspects of Japanese fiction highlighted by the academic canon. "Ms. Yoshimoto's story," wrote Kakutani in the *New York Times*, "turns out not to be a whimsical comedy of manners but an oddly lyrical tale about loss and grief and familial love" (Kakutani 1993: C15). In a study of the various factors determining the production and reception of *Kitchen*, Harker attributed its success to the creation of a "middle-brow" audience for Japanese fiction, an audience that is rather different from the elite academic specialists who formerly selected the texts for translation, even if it still betrays the residual influence of their decades-long dominance. In Harker's view, the appeal of the translation was due to

> a writer who explodes the image of Japanese literature as inscrutable and uninteresting with subject matter which is upbeat, vaguely titillating,

and accessibly philosophical; offhand references to American popular culture which create a sense of familiarity for English readers; an accessible yet still "oriental" translation; and skillful packaging and marketing. The success of *Kitchen*, ultimately, comes from both its effective utilization, and deformation, of common cultural tropes of "Japanese-ness."

(Harker 1994: 1–2)

If the new wave of translated Japanese fiction brings about an enduring canon reformation, it too may harden into a cultural stereotype of Japan – especially if Japanese remains low in the hierarchy of languages translated into English and a narrow range of Japanese texts is made available. Obviously, this stereotype will differ from its predecessor in being neither exoticized nor aestheticized, and it will carry rather different geopolitical implications from those that obtained in the post-World War II period. Since the new fiction projects the image of a highly Americanized Japanese culture, at once youthful and energetic, it can implicitly answer to current American anxieties about Japan's competitive strength in the global economy, offering an explanation that is reassuringly familiar and not a little self-congratulatory: the image permits Japanese economic power to be seen as an effect of American cultural domination on a later, postwar generation. Thus, Birnbaum's introduction to his canon-revising anthology informed American readers that, "trade imbalance notwithstanding, the Japanese have been enthusiastic importers of Western language" (Birnbaum 1991: 2). The Japanese title of Yoshimoto's novella is in fact a Japanized English word, transliterated as *Kitchin* (Hanson 1993: 18). The image of contemporary Japanese culture projected by the new fiction may also be traced with a nostalgia for a lost past, although a past that is American, not Japanese: the period from the mid-1940s to the late 1960s, when American hegemony had yet to be decisively challenged at home or abroad.

The creation of domestic subjects

In the foregoing cases, not only do translation projects construct uniquely domestic representations of foreign cultures, but since these projects address specific cultural constituencies, they are simultaneously engaged in the formation of domestic identities. When Jones's existentialist-informed translations of Aristotle displaced the dominant academic reading, they acquired such institutional authority as to become a professional qualification for classical scholars. Specialists in Aristotle and Greek tragedy are expected to demonstrate familiarity with Jones's study in teaching and research publications. Accordingly, Jones rates a mention in introductory surveys of criticism, whether they are devoted to the tragic genre or to specific tragedians (e.g. Buxton 1984). He has also influenced research in such other areas of classical literature as Homeric poetry (Redfield 1975: 24–26). Similarly, the postwar canon of Japanese fiction in English translation shaped the preferences of both the publishers who invested in elite foreign literature and the readers interested in it. Familiarity with Tanizaki, Kawabata, and Mishima became the mark of a literary taste that was both discriminating and knowledgeable, backed by scholarly credentials.

Of course, the cultural agents who carried out these translation projects did not plan or perhaps even anticipate such domestic effects as the establishment of a professional qualification and the creation of literary taste. They were scholars, translators, and publishers who were more immediately concerned with questions specific to their respective disciplines and practices, questions of academic knowledge, aesthetic value, and commercial success. The history of translation reveals other projects that were designed precisely to form domestic cultural identities by appropriating foreign texts. In these cases, the translations have tended to be highly literary, designed to foster a new literary movement, constructing an authorial subject through an affiliation with a particular literary discourse.

Ezra Pound, for instance, saw translation as a means of cultivating modernist poetic values like linguistic precision. In 1918 he published a "brief recapitulation and retrospect" of the "new fashion in poetry" in which he offered the aspiring modernist poet a recipe for self-fashioning (Pound 1954: 3). "Translation," he wrote, is "good training, if you find that your original matter 'wobbles' when you try to rewrite it. The meaning of the poem to be translated can not 'wobble'" (ibid.: 7). Modernist poets like Pound translated foreign texts that supported modernist poetic language: "In the art of Daniel and Cavalcanti," he remarked, "I have seen that precision which I miss in the Victorians" (ibid.: 11). Pound fashioned himself as a modernist poet-translator partly by competing against Victorian translators of the poems he valued, imitating yet exceeding them in specific translation choices. He introduced his translation of Guido Cavalcanti's poetry by admitting that "in the matter of these translations and of my knowledge of Tuscan poetry, Rossetti is my father and mother, but no one man can see everything at once" (Anderson 1983: 14).

The case of Pound suggests not merely that translation can be instrumental in the construction of an authorial identity, but also that this construction is at once discursive and psychological, worked out in writing practices open to psychoanalytic interpretation. Pound's translations staged an oedipal rivalry in which he challenged Rossetti's canonical status by translating poetry the Victorian poet had translated, Cavalcanti's idealized representations of women (Venuti 1995a: 197). In the process Pound defined himself both as modernist and as male. He felt that his translations supplied what had "escaped" Rossetti, namely "a robustezza, a masculinity" (Anderson 1933: 243). Which is to say that, in his own view, Pound bettered his poetic father in capturing the female image presented by a foreign poetry.

Because translation can contribute to the invention of domestic literary discourses, it has inevitably been enlisted in ambitious cultural projects, notably the development of a domestic language and literature. And such projects have always resulted in the formation of cultural identities aligned with specific social groups, with classes and nations. During the eighteenth and nineteenth centuries German translation was theorized and practiced as a means of developing a German-language literature. In 1813 the philosopher Friedrich Schleiermacher pointed out to his scholarly German audience that "much of what is beautiful and powerful in our language has in part either developed by way of translation or been drawn out by translation" (Lefevere 1992b: 165). Schleiermacher put translation in the service of a bourgeois cultural elite, a largely professional readership which preferred a highly refined German literature grounded in classical texts. Yet he and contemporaries like Goethe and the Schlegel brothers viewed these minority values as defining a national German culture to the exclusion of various popular genres and texts – mainly the sentimental realism, Gothic tales, chivalric romances, and didactic biographies preferred by the largest segment of German-language readers (Venuti 1995a: 105–110).

In 1827 Goethe noted that "flagging national literatures are revived by the foreign," and he then proceeded to describe the specular mechanism by which a domestic subject is formed in translation:

> In the end every literature grows bored if it is not refreshed by foreign participation. What scholar does not delight in the wonders wrought by mirroring and reflection? And what mirroring means in the moral sphere has been experienced by everyone, perhaps unconsciously; and, if one stops to consider, one will realize how much of his own formation throughout life he owes to it.
>
> (Berman 1992: 65)

Translation forms domestic subjects by enabling a process of "mirroring" or self-recognition: the foreign text becomes intelligible when the reader recognizes himself or herself in the translation by identifying the domestic values that motivated the selection of that particular foreign text, and that are inscribed in it through a particular discursive strategy. The self-recognition is a recognition of the domestic cultural norms and resources that constitute the self, that define it as a domestic subject. The process is basically narcissistic: the reader identifies with an ideal projected by the translation, usually values that have achieved authority in the domestic culture and dominate those of other cultural constituencies. Sometimes, however, the values may be currently marginal yet ascendant, mobilized in a challenge to the dominant. At Goethe's moment, when the Napoleonic wars threatened to extend French domination into Prussia, a compelling ideal was a nationalist concept of a distinctively German literary culture, underwritten by the translation of canonical foreign texts but still to be realized. As Berman remarked of Goethe's thinking, "foreign literatures become the mediators in the internal conflicts of national literatures and offer them an image of themselves they could not otherwise have," but which, we may add, they nonetheless desire (Berman 1992: 65). Hence, the reader's self-recognition is also a misrecognition: a domestic inscription is taken for the foreign text, dominant domestic values for the reader's own, and the values of one constituency for those of all others in the domestic culture. Goethe's mention of "scholar" is a reminder that the subject constructed by this nationalist agenda for translation entails an affiliation with a specific social group, here a minority with sufficient cultural authority to set itself up as the arbiter of a national literature.

Translations thus position readers in domestic intelligibilities that are also ideological positions, ensembles of values, beliefs, and representations that further the interests of certain social groups over others. In cases where translations are housed in institutions like the church, the state, or the school, the identity-forming process enacted by a translated text potentially affects social reproduction by providing a sense of what is true, good, and possible (this thinking relies on Althusser 1971; Therborn 1980; Laclau and Mouffe 1985). Translations may maintain existing social relations by investing domestic subjects with the ideological qualification to assume a role or perform a function in an institution. Technical translations – legal or scientific texbooks, for example – enable agents to achieve and maintain levels of expertise. But they may also bring about social change by revising such qualifications and thereby modifying institutional roles or functions.

Consider the controversies surrounding the translation of the Bible in the early Christian Church. The Septuagint, the Greek version of the Old Testament prepared by Hellenistic Jews in the third century B.C., still commanded enormous authority some six centuries later: it was the ground of all theological and exegetical speculation, and it displaced the Hebrew text as the source of the Latin translations that were widely used by Christian congregations in the late Roman Empire. Augustine, bishop of Hippo, feared Jerome's project of translating the Old Testament directly from the Hebrew because it threatened the ideological consistency and institutional stability of the Church. In a letter to Jerome written in 403, Augustine explained that "many problems would arise if your translation began to be read regularly in many churches, because the Latin churches would be out of step with the Greek ones" (White 1990: 92). Augustine then described an incident which demonstrated that early Christian identity was deeply rooted in the Septuagint and in the Latin translations made from it; to introduce Jerome's translation from the Hebrew would throw this identity into crisis and ultimately play havoc with Church organization by alienating believers:

> when one of our fellow bishops arranged for your translation to be read
> in a church in his diocese, they came across a word in your version of
> the prophet Jonah which you had rendered very differently from the
> translation with which they were familiar and which, having been read

by so many generations, was ingrained in their memories. A great uproar ensued in the congregation, especially among the Greeks who criticised the text and passionately denounced it as wrong, and the bishop (the incident took place in the city of Oea) was compelled to ask the Jews to give evidence. Whether out of ignorance or spite, they replied that this word did occur in the Hebrew manuscripts in exactly the same form as in the Greek and Latin versions. In short, the man was forced to correct the passage in your version as if it were inaccurate since he did not want this crisis to leave him without a congregation. This makes us suspect that you, too, can be mistaken occasionally.

(ibid.: 92–93)

The Septuagint-based Latin translation used at Oea formed Christian identities by sustaining a self-recognition that defined orthodox belief: members of the congregation recognized themselves as Christians on the basis of an institutionally validated translation that was "familiar" and "ingrained in their memories." The furor caused by Jerome's version from the Hebrew shows that the continued existence of the institution requires a relatively stable process of identity formation enacted not simply by a particular translation, but by the repeated use of it – "read by so many generations." It is also clear that the institution ensures the stability of the identity-forming process by erecting a criterion for translation accuracy: members of the congregation, especially Greeks, judged a Latin version of the Old Testament "correct" when they found its renderings consistent with the authoritative Greek version, the Septuagint.

Yet a cultural practice like translation can also precipitate social change because neither subjects nor institutions can ever be completely coherent or sealed off from the diverse ideologies that circulate in the domestic culture. Identity is never irrevocably fixed but rather relational, the nodal point for a multiplicity of practices and institutions whose sheer heterogeneity creates the possibility for change (Laclau and Mouffe 1985: 105–114). Jerome insisted on a return to the Hebrew text partly because his cultural identity was Latin as well as Christian and distinguished by a highly refined literary taste. Educated in Rome, "he was part of a culture in which sensitivity to a foreign language was an integral element," so that "he was capable of appreciating the aesthetic merits of works in a language not his own," like the Hebrew Bible (Kamesar 1993: 43, 48–49). The polylingualism of Latin literary culture combined with Christian belief to motivate Jerome's study of Hebrew, eventually enabling his discovery that the authoritative Greek translations and editions were deficient: his Latin versions of them, as he explained to Augustine, contained typographical indicators for passages where "the Septuagint expands on the Hebrew text" or "something has been added by Origen from the edition of Theodotion" (White 1990: 133). Jerome's complicated cultural make-up led him to question the Septuagint. Whereas its authority among the Church

Fathers rested on a belief in its divine inspiration as well as the Apostles' approval of its use, Jerome's concern for textual integrity and doctrinal authenticity judged it inadequate, flawed by omissions and expansions that reflected the values of its pagan patron and corrupted by variants that accumulated in successive editions (Kamesar 1993: 59–69).

Jerome's translation did finally displace the Septuagint, becoming the standard Latin version of the Bible throughout the medieval period and beyond while exerting "an incalculable influence not only on the piety but on the languages and literatures of Western Europe" (Kelly 1975: 162). This success was due in large part to Jerome's discursive strategies and to the prefaces and letters in which he defended his version. His translation discourse reveals his cultural diversity. On the one hand, he Latinized characteristic features of the Hebrew text by revising simple paratactic constructions into complex suspended periods and by replacing the formulaic repetition of words and phrases with elegant variations (Sparks 1970: 524–526). On the other hand, he Christianized Judaic themes by rewriting "a large number of passages in such a way as to give them a much more pointedly Messianic or otherwise Christian implication than the Hebrew permitted" (Kelly 1975: 162). In adopting such discursive strategies, Jerome's translation appealed to Christians who, like him, were schooled in Latin literary culture.

In defending his translation, furthermore, he anticipated the objections of such Church officials as Augustine, who feared that a return to the Hebrew text would weaken institutional stability. Although extremely critical of the Septuagint, Jerome shrewdly represented his Latin version not as a replacement, but as a supplement, which, like other Latin versions, would aid in the interpretation of the authoritative Greek translation and "protect Christians from Jewish ridicule and accusations that they were ignorant of the true Scriptures" (Kamesar 1993: 59). Jerome's version was thus presented as an institutional support, assisting in theological and exegetical speculation and in debates with the members of a rival religious institution – the synagogue – who cast doubt on the cultural authority of Christianity.

The controversies in the early Christian Church make clear that translations can alter the functioning of any social institution because translating, by definition, involves the domestic assimilation of a foreign text. This means that the work of translation must inescapably rely on cultural norms and resources that differ fundamentally from those circulating in the domestic culture (cf. Robyns 1994: 407). Thus, as Augustine's letter reported, the bishop at Oea was forced to resort to Jewish informants to assess the correctness of Jerome's version from the Hebrew text, even though the criterion of accuracy (namely fidelity to the Septuagint) was formulated and applied within the Christian Church. By the same token, Jerome's departures from the Septuagint occasionally followed other, more literal Greek versions of the Old Testament made by Jews and used in synagogues (White 1990: 137). Since the task of translation is to make a foreign text intelligible in domestic terms, the institutions that use translations are open to infiltrations from different and even incompatible cultural materials that may controvert authoritative texts and revise prevailing criteria for translation accuracy. Perhaps the domestic identities formed by translation can avoid the dislocations of the foreign only when institutions regulate translation practices so restrictively as to efface and hence defuse the linguistic and cultural differences of foreign texts.

The ethics of translation

If translation has such far-reaching social effects, if in forming cultural identities it contributes to social reproduction and change, it seems important to evaluate these effects, to ask whether they are good or bad, or whether the resulting identities are ethical. It will be useful to start, once again, with Antoine Berman, whose thinking underwent an interesting turn just before his untimely death.

Berman based his concept of a translation ethics on the relationship between the domestic and foreign cultures that is embodied in the translated text (for a possible taxonomy of such relationships, see Robyns 1994). Bad translation shapes toward the foreign culture a domestic attitude that is ethnocentric: "generally under the guise of transmissibility, [it] carries out a systematic negation of the strangeness of the foreign work" (Berman 1992: 5). Good translation aims to limit this ethnocentric negation: it stages "an opening, a dialogue, a cross-breeding, a decentering" and thereby forces the domestic language and culture to register the foreignness of the foreign text (ibid.: 4). Berman's ethical judgments hinge on the discursive strategies applied in the translation process. The question is whether they are thoroughly domesticating or incorporate foreignizing tendencies, whether they resort to "trumpery" by concealing their "manipulations" of the foreign text or show "respect" for it by "offering" a "correspondence" that "enlarges, amplifies, and enriches the translating language" (Berman 1995: 92–94).

It is worth emphasizing that, apart from discursive strategies, the very choice of a foreign text for translation can also signify its foreignness by challenging domestic canons for foreign literatures and domestic stereotypes for foreign cultures. And, as Berman came to recognize, even the most domesticating translator (his example is the influential seventeeth-century translator of classical texts, Perrot d'Ablancourt) can't simply be dismissed as unethical if he "doesn't dissimulate his cuts, his additions, his embellishments, but exposes them in prefaces and notes, frankly" (ibid.: 94). On the contrary, we must admire the sheer achievement of boldly domesticating translations, the fact that the translators produced a "textual work" with its own aims and strategies "in more or less close correspondence to the textuality of the original" (ibid.: 92).

A translation ethics, clearly, can't be restricted to a notion of fidelity. Not only does a translation constitute an interpretation of the foreign text, varying

81

with different cultural situations at different historical moments, but canons of accuracy 'are articulated and applied in the domestic culture and therefore are basically ethnocentric, no matter how seemingly faithful, no matter how linguistically correct. The ethical values implicit in such canons are generally professional or institutional, established by agencies and officials, academic specialists, publishers, and reviewers and subsequently assimilated by translators, who adopt varying attitudes towards them, from acceptance to ambivalence to interrogation and revision. Any evaluation of a translation project must include a consideration of discursive strategies, their institutional settings, and their social functions and effects.

Institutions, whether academic or religious, commercial or political, show a preference for a translation ethics of sameness, translating that enables and ratifies existing discourses and canons, interpretations and pedagogies, advertising campaigns and liturgies – if only to ensure the continued and unruffled reproduction of the institution. Yet translation is scandalous because it can create different values and practices, whatever the domestic setting. This is not to say that translation can ever rid itself of its fundamental domestication, its basic task of rewriting the foreign text in domestic cultural terms. The point is rather that a translator can choose to redirect the ethnocentric movement of translation so as to decenter the domestic terms that a translation project must inescapably utilize. This is an ethics of difference that can change the domestic culture.

In the projects we have examined, the identity-forming process was repeatedly grounded in domestic ideologies and institutions. This suggests that they were all engaged in an ethnocentric reduction of possibilities, excluding not only other possible representations of foreign cultures, but also other possible constructions of domestic subjects. Yet distinctions can be drawn among the projects. The English-language canon of Japanese fiction, for example, was maintained for some three decades by a network of translators and institutions. Although it did indeed represent the Japanese texts as foreign and create a wide English-language audience for them, the privileged concept of foreignness was distinctively American and academic, reflecting a domestic nostalgia for an exotic prewar Japan and marginalizing texts that couldn't be assimilated to the stereotype. A translation project following an ethics of difference will make available both the exotic and the Americanized (among other excluded forms and themes), inevitably domesticating the texts to some extent, but at the same time representing the diversity of the Japanese narrative tradition by restoring those segments of it that were formerly neglected. The restoration may indeed be a domestic reconstruction with its own partialities, but it nonetheless seeks to compensate for a previous exclusion, however partially defined. The recent translations of Japanese fiction, particularly the Americanized novels of Banana Yoshimoto, constitute such a restoration.

To limit the ethnocentric movement inherent in translation, a project must take into account the interests of more than just those of a cultural constituency that occupies a dominant position in the domestic culture. A translation project must consider the culture where the foreign text originated and address various domestic constituencies. Jones's translations of Aristotle truly decentered the reigning academic versions because his project was open to foreign cultural values that were not located in the English-language academy: the features of the archaic Greek text that were repressed by the modern Anglo-American ideology of individualism became visible from the vantage point of the modern Continental philosophy of existentialism, disseminated in philosophical treatises and literary texts. A translation project motivated by an ethics of difference thus alters the reproduction of dominant domestic ideologies and institutions that provide a partial representation of foreign cultures and marginalize other domestic constituencies. The translator of such a project, contrary to the notion of "loyalty" developed by translation theorists like Nord (1991), is prepared to be disloyal to the domestic cultural norms that govern the identity-forming process of translation by calling attention to what they enable and limit, admit and exclude, in the encounter with foreign texts.

Yet a translation project that seeks to limit its ethnocentric movement can eventually establish a new orthodoxy. It too may become exclusionary and therefore vulnerable to displacement by a later project designed to rediscover a foreign text for a different constituency. William Tyndale's 1525 English version of the New Testament challenged the authority that Jerome's Latin version had acquired in the Catholic Church, and the challenge was essential to the formation of a different religious identity, the English Protestant. Thomas More was quick to perceive the ideological decentering effected by Tyndale's own return to the Greek text: Tyndale, in More's view, "changed the word church [*ecclesia* in the Greek] into this word congregation, because he would bring it in question which were the church and set forth Luther's heresy that the church which we should believe and obey, is not the common known body of all Christian realms remaining in the faith of Christ" (Lefevere 1992b: 71).

A translation ethics of difference reforms cultural identities that occupy dominant positions in the domestic culture, yet in many cases this reformation subsequently issues into another dominance and another ethnocentrism. In 1539 the translator Richard Taverner, "in place in the official Protestant propaganda machinery at the start of official Protestantism in England," introduced subtle revisions to Tyndale's version of the Bible that reveal a different ideological slant, more populist and less institutional: Taverner chose the most familiar and accessible language, using the simple "cursed" instead of Tyndale's ritualistic "excommunicate," and the homely "moche people were slayne" instead of Tyndale's ecclesiastical "there was a plague in the congregation of the lord" (Westbrooke 1997: 195). Such revisions, although significant enough to mark perhaps a theological difference with Tyndale, were hardly intended by Taverner, a Clerk of the Signet under Henry VIII, to provoke institutional change. Nor did a change occur, even if a revision like "cursed" did make its way into the King James Bible (1611).

A translation practice that rigorously redirects its ethnocentrism is likely to be subversive of domestic ideologies and institutions. It too would form a cultural identity, but one that is simultaneously critical and contingent, constantly assessing the relations between a domestic culture and its foreign others and developing translation projects solely on the basis of changing assessments. This identity will be truly intercultural, not merely in the sense of straddling two cultures, domestic and foreign, but crossing the cultural borders among domestic audiences (cf. Pym 1993). And it will be historical, distinguished by an awareness of domestic as well as foreign cultural traditions, including traditions of translation. "A translator without a historical conscious-ness [*conscience*]," wrote Berman, remains a "prisoner to his representation of translating and to those representations that convey the 'social discourses' of the moment" (Berman 1995: 61).

Yet is it feasible for a translator to pursue an ethics of difference consci-entiously? To what extent does such an ethics risk unintelligibility, by decentering domestic ideologies, and cultural marginality, by destabilizing the workings of domestic institutions? Can a translator maintain a critical distance from domestic norms without dooming a translation to be dismissed as unreadable?

Banana Yoshimoto's *Kitchen* can help to address these questions – at least for literary translation. The English version was successful in reaching a diverse readership and altering the English-language canon of modern Japanese fiction. Yet Yoshimoto's novels have been attacked for failing to interrogate American cultural values. Miyoshi has judged them to be naively written celebrations of an Americanized Japan, unlike the work of some other Japanese women novelists who are "critically alert and historically intelligent" (Miyoshi 1991: 212, 236). Tanizaki's novels offer a compelling contrast: Miyoshi wrote of *The Makioka Sisters* that "if the work's apparent lack of interest in the war is a mark of the author's resistance" against Japanese mili-tarism, "its indifference to the postwar years may also point to a criticism of the Occupation-imposed reforms" (ibid.: 114). From this point of view, then, the ethical move would be to translate Tanizaki instead of Yoshimoto, in contrast to what I – following Fowler's critical account of American trans-lation patterns – have argued.

This case indicates the need for a more nuanced concept of the trans-lator's deviation from domestic cultural norms. What distinguishes Miyoshi's position from Fowler's is that Miyoshi sought out texts that are critical of American global hegemony in economic and political affairs, whereas Fowler discriminated between specific values *within* American culture. While both lines of thinking are important today for any ethical translation, Fowler's realized that domestic canons for foreign literatures are always already in place when a translation project is developed, and that therefore an ethics of difference must take these canons into account. Put another way, any agenda of cultural resistance for translation must take specifically cultural forms, must choose foreign texts and translation methods that deviate from those that are currently canonical or dominant. This deviation can definitely be found in a writer like Yoshimoto – especially in Megan Backus's English version of *Kitchen*.

This version is highly readable, but it is also foreignizing in its translation strategy. Instead of cultivating a seamless fluency that invisibly inscribes American values in the text, Backus developed an extremely heterogeneous language that communicates the Americanization of Japan, but simultaneously foregrounds the differences between American and Japanese culture for an English-language reader. The translation generally adheres to the standard dialect of current English usage, but this is mixed with other dialects and discourses. There is a rich strain of colloquialism, mostly American, both in the lexicon and the syntax: "cut the crap," "home-ec" (for "Home Economics"), "I'm kind of in a hurry," "I perked up," "I would sort of tortuously make my way," "night owl," "okay," "slipped through the cracks," "smart ass," "three sheets to the wind," "woozy" (Yoshimoto 1993: 4, 6, 19, 29, 42, 47, 63, 70, 92, 103). There is also a recurrent, slightly archaic formality used in passages that express the fey romanticism to which the narrator Mikage is inclined. "I'm dead worn out, in a reverie," she says at the opening, combining the poetical archaism "reverie" with the colloquial "dead worn out" (ibid.: 4). Similarly, when she first meets Yuichi, beginning the relationship that drives the narrative, he sends her language shifting through registers and references, from high-tech slang to Hollywood love talk to mystical theology:

> His smile was so bright as he stood in my doorway that I zoomed in for a closeup on his pupils. I couldn't take my eyes off him. I think I heard a spirit call my name.
>
> (ibid.: 6)

There are, moreover, many italicized Japanese words scattered throughout the text, mostly for food – "katsudon," "ramen," "soba," "udon," "wasabi" – but including other aspects of Japanese culture, like clothing ("obi") and furnishings ("tatami mat") (ibid.: 40, 61, 78, 83, 89, 98, 100).

The heterogeneity of Backus's translation discourse undoubtedly indicates that Yoshimoto's characters are Americanized Japanese. The very language of the translation thus makes the same point that is made in the Japanese text by the many allusions to American popular culture, to comic strips (Linus from *Peanuts*), television programs (*Bewitched*), amusement parks (Disneyland), and restaurant chains (Denny's) (ibid.: 5, 31, 90, 96). But since the discourse contains so many deviations from standard English, the translation offers an estranging experience to an English-language reader, who is constantly made aware that the text is a translation because the discursive effects work only in English, releasing a distinctively American remainder. The first ethical move with *Kitchen* was the decision to translate a Japanese novel that runs counter to the post-World War II canon of this genre in English. But the second was to develop a translation discourse that is foreignizing in its deviation from dominant linguistic norms, that brings the awareness that the translation is only a translation, imprinted with domestic intelligibilities and interests, and therefore not to be confused with the foreign text.

Miyoshi did not consider these effects because his approach to Yoshimoto's fiction focussed entirely on the Japanese text and its Japanese reception. The Americanized Japan represented in this fiction can only have a different cultural and political significance for American readers who experience Backus's foreignizing translation. The limitations of neglecting the issue of translation become most apparent in the passages Miyoshi quoted to demonstrate that "there is no style, no poise, no imagery" in Yoshimoto's writing (Miyoshi 1991: 236). He needed to *translate* the Japanese text of *Kitchen* to make his point for the English-language reader, but the difference created by the shift to English did not in fact exist for him. When his translation of a passage is juxtaposed to Backus's, the foreignizing tendencies in her writing emerge quite clearly:

> I placed the bedding in a quiet well-lit kitchen, drawing silently soft sleepiness that comes with saturated sadness not relieved by tears. I fell asleep wrapped in a blanket like Linus.
>
> (Miyoshi 1991: 236)

> Steeped in a sadness so great I could barely cry, shuffling softly in gentle drowsiness, I pulled my futon into the deathly silent, gleaming kitchen. Wrapped in a blanket, like Linus, I slept.
>
> (Yoshimoto 1993: 4–5)

Backus's version is clearly the more evocative of the two. It typically opens with the sort of romantic poeticism that characterizes Mikage (the subtly metaphorical "steeped in a sadness"), communicated through a suspended syntactical construction that is fluent but formal, even faintly archaic, in its complexity. The lexicon begins to change noticeably with the translator's retention of the Japanese word, "futon," and then again with the American cultural reference ("Linus"). The pop familiarity of this reference is somewhat defamiliarized by its placement in a construction that resembles the more formal syntax used in the first sentence. Compared to the heterogeneity of Backus's version, Miyoshi's is more strongly domesticating, assimilating the Japanese text to the standard dialect of English, so familiar as to be transparent or seemingly untranslated – even in his eyes. The features of Yoshimoto's Japanese that provoked his criticism are transformed in

English, but it is only Backus's English that invites the critical reflection that Miyoshi valued. The linguistic and cultural differences introduced by any translation can permit a foreign text that seems aesthetically inferior and politically reactionary at home to carry opposite valences abroad.

Location and audience are of crucial importance. Translations of Yoshimoto's fiction are different or deviant from reigning canons, because these translations were not developed by or designed for the American cultural elite who established those canons. On the contrary, her success in translation is a result of her appeal to a wider, middle-brow readership, youthful and educated, although not necessarily academic. Miyoshi was certainly right to question the Americanized themes in Yoshimoto's fiction, to view them as evidence of the cultural imperialism that the United States has conducted since World War II. But he seems to have sought a highly literary form of narrative that in English-language culture appeals to a relatively narrow audience. In suggesting that Yoshimoto doesn't deserve to be translated, Miyoshi would prevent a larger American constituency from evaluating the impact of American culture abroad. My conclusion, then, is that translating Yoshimoto at the present moment is a worthwhile move for an English-language translator to make, an ethical act that can introduce a significant difference into American culture.

The case of Yoshimoto shows, finally, that translation concerned with limiting its ethnocentrism does not necessarily risk unintelligibility and cultural marginality. A translation project can deviate from domestic norms to signal the foreignness of the foreign text and create a readership that is more open to linguistic and cultural differences – yet without resorting to stylistic experiments that are so estranging as to be self-defeating. The key factor is the translator's ambivalence toward domestic norms and the institutional practices in which they are implemented, a reluctance to identify completely with them coupled with a determination to address diverse cultural constituencies, elite and popular. In attempting to straddle the foreign and domestic cultures as well as domestic readerships, a translation practice cannot fail to produce a text that is a potential source of cultural change.

5

THE PEDAGOGY OF
LITERATURE

The reflections that follow derive fundamentally from the current predicament of English-language translation in the global cultural economy. Since World War II, English has remained the most translated language worldwide, but one of the least translated into. The translations issued by British and American publishers currently comprise about 2 to 4 percent of their total output each year, approximately 1,200 to 1,600 books, whereas in many foreign countries, large and small, West and East, the percentage tends to be significantly higher: 6 percent in Japan (approximately 2,500 books), 10 in France (4,000), 14 in Hungary (1,200), 15 in Germany (8,000) (Grannis 1993). In 1995, Italian publishers issued 40,429 volumes, 25 percent of which were translations (10,145); English towered over other source languages at 6,031 translations (Peresson 1997). In 1995, American publishers issued 62,039 volumes, 2.65 percent of which were translations from 17 languages (1,639); neither of the most frequently translated languages, French and German, accounts for more than 500 translations (Ink 1997). This asymmetry in translation patterns ensures that the United States and the United Kingdom enjoy a hegemony over foreign countries that is not simply political and economic, as the particular case may be, but cultural as well.

The international sway of English coincides with the marginality of translation in contemporary Anglo-American culture. Although British and American literature circulates in many foreign languages, commanding the capital of many foreign publishers, the translating of foreign literatures into English attracts relatively small investment and little notice. Translation is underpaid, critically unrecognized, and largely invisible to English-language readers. The power of Anglo-American culture abroad has limited the circulation of foreign cultures at home, decreasing the domestic opportunities for thinking about the nature of linguistic and cultural difference. Of course, no language can entirely exclude the possibility of different dialects and discourses, different cultural codes and constituencies. And this fact is borne out by the current variety of Englishes, not just the differences between British and American usage, but the diverse linguistic and cultural forms that exist within English-speaking nations. Nonetheless, the risk posed by the marginal position of translation is a cultural narcissism and complacency, an unconcern with the foreign that can only impoverish British and American culture and foster values and policies grounded in inequality and exploitation.

The marginality of translation reaches even to educational institutions, where it is manifested in a scandalous contradiction: on the one hand, an utter dependence on translated texts in curricula and research; on the other hand, a general tendency, in both teaching and publications, to elide the status of translated texts as translated, to treat them as texts originally written in the translating language. Although since the 1970s translation has emerged more decisively as a field of academic study and as an area of investment in academic publishing, institutionalized as the creative writing workshop, the certificate program, the curriculum in translation theory and criticism, and the book series dedicated to literary translations or translation studies – despite this increasing recognition, the fact of translation continues to be repressed in the teaching of translated literature. My aim is to explore two questions raised by this repression. What are its cultural and political costs, i.e., what knowledges and practices does it make possible or eliminate? And what pedagogy can be developed to address the issue of translation, especially the remainder of domestic values inscribed in the foreign text during the translating process?

Translation in the classroom

Given the unavoidable use of translations in colleges and universities, the repression is remarkably widespread. But it is perhaps most acute in the United States, where undergraduates are required to take "humanities" or "Great Books" courses devoted to the canonical texts of Western culture. The readings consist overwhelmingly of English translations from archaic and modern languages. Beyond such first- and second-year courses, translations are indispensable to undergraduate and graduate curricula in numerous disciplines, including comparative literature, philosophy, history, political science, anthropology, and sociology. Some foreign-language departments have responded to fluctuating enrollments during the post-World War II period by instituting courses in which specific foreign literatures are read solely in English translation. But whether the issue of translation is addressed in these courses remains doubtful – given the cool reception that foreign-language faculties have given to translation as a method of foreign-language instruction.

Over the past twenty years translation also made possible the developments in cultural theory that have radically transformed Anglo-American literary criticism, introducing new methodologies of greater sophistication and explanatory power, linking culture to social and political issues, and spawning such interdisciplinary tendencies as cultural studies. These concepts, debates, and curriculum revisions are in many cases concerned with the question of linguistic and cultural difference that lies at the heart of translation: for example, the issue of ethnic and racial ideologies in cultural representations; the elaboration of postcolonial theory to study colonialism and colonized cultures throughout world history; and the emergence of multiculturalism to challenge European cultural canons, especially as embodied in Great Books courses. Yet teaching and research have tended not to address their dependence on translation. Little attention is given to the fact that the interpretations taught and published in academic institutions are often at some remove from the foreign-language text, mediated by the translation discourse of the English-language translator.

The extent of this repression can be gauged from *Approaches to Teaching World Literature*, a series published by the Modern Language Association of America (MLA). Begun in 1980 and now totaling more than fifty volumes, the series assembles bibliographical data and pedagogical techniques for canonical literary texts, archaic and modern, including ones written in foreign languages. It also constitutes a broad sampling of current teaching practices in the United States and Canada. As the series editor points out in a general preface, "the preparation of each volume begins with a wide-ranging survey of instructors, thus enabling us to include in the volume the philosophies and approaches, thoughts and methods of scores of experienced teachers." Among the foreign-language texts selected for treatment are Dante's *Divine Comedy* (1982), Cervantes's *Don Quixote* (1984), Camus's *The Plague* (1985), Ibsen's *A Doll's House* (1984), the *Iliad* and *Odyssey* (1987), Goethe's *Faust* (1987), Voltaire's *Candide* (1987), the Hebrew Bible (1989), García Márquez's *One Hundred Years of Solitude* (1990), and Montaigne's *Essays* (1994). In the volumes devoted to foreign-language texts, the bibliographical section, entitled "Materials," routinely contains a discussion of translations which evaluates them mainly according to utilitarian criteria: accuracy, accessibility to contemporary students, market availability, popularity among the survey respondents. Yet in the pedagogical section, entitled "Approaches," translation is rarely made a topic of discussion, even though many of the essays refer explicitly to the use of English-language versions in the classroom.

An essay in the volume on Dante, for instance, "Teaching Dante's *Divine Comedy* in Translation," describes an undergraduate course on medieval Italian literature offered at the University of Toronto. Despite the title, only one paragraph in this seven-page essay is reserved for comments on translation. After indicating that the main "problem" confronting late twentieth-century readers of Dante is cultural "distance," the instructor adds:

> There is another barrier between the students and Dante in this course: language. We read the *Divine Comedy* in translation, and no matter how good the translation is, it can never be Dante. No translator can hope to capture the flow and rhythm of Dante's verse, simply because of the intrinsic differences between English and Italian. There is another hazard in translation. In the original text

there are always ambiguities that the translator cannot reproduce. Before a difficult passage, he or she is obliged to adopt a critical stance. Thus, any translation of the *Divine Comedy* is heavily colored by the translator's interpretation of it. Interpretive options that exist in Dante's Italian are eliminated, and ambiguities, perhaps unknown to the original, are created. Not even prose translations can escape this kind of distortion: in their effort to secure the letter, they completely destroy the spirit. That is why I prefer a verse translation. In my opinion, it is worth sacrificing a little accuracy for a sense of Dante's poetry. Although it is not without shortcomings, I use Dorothy Sayers' translation of the *Divine Comedy*.

(Iannucci 1982: 155)

Here the paragraph ends. It shows the instructor's fairly sophisticated understanding of how translation both loses linguistic and cultural features of the foreign text and adds others specific to the target-language culture. But the elliptical reference to Dorothy Sayers's version makes clear that this understanding is not brought into the classroom in any systematic or otherwise illuminating way. The instructor asserts that "the objective of this course is twofold: first, to help the students comprehend Dante's poetic world in the context of medieval culture and, second, to make them aware of the critical process itself" (ibid.). Yet what seems to be missing is any consequential awareness that at least *two* different critical processes are at work: the translator's, the "interpretation" represented by Sayers's version, and the instructor's, his reconstruction of "Dante's poetic world" in the form of "ten introductory lectures designed to bridge the historical and cultural gaps between us and Dante and to establish a critical framework within which to interpret the poem" (ibid.).

The problem is that neither translation nor lecture can "bridge" these "gaps" entirely. Thus, although the instructor aims to remove every "barrier" between the student and the Italian text, he believes, somewhat contradictorily, that "the *Divine Comedy* needs mediation, now more than ever, if we are to avoid a simplistic, anachronistic reading" (ibid.). This mediation inevitably erects another barrier: it reflects contemporary scholarship on Dante's poem and medieval Italian culture, "the latest literature on the subject," "modern critical opinion, at least in North America" (ibid.: 156). The reading in this course can't avoid anachronism and the "distortion" of "ambiguities, perhaps unknown to the original," because it is based on a British translation published in the 1940s in a mass-market paperback series, the Penguin Classics, and taught in a Canadian university in the late 1970s.

In failing to teach the translated status of the text, the instructor bears out Jacques Derrida's suggestive remark that translation is a "political-institutional problem of the University: it, like all teaching in its traditional form, and perhaps all teaching whatever, has as its ideal, with exhaustive translatability, the effacement of language" (Derrida 1979: 93–94). Current pedagogy implicitly conceives of translation as communication unaffected by the language that makes it possible, or in Derrida's (translator's) words, "governed by the classical model of transportable vocality or of formalizable polysemia" (ibid.: 93). To think of translation as "dissemination," however, as the release of different meanings owing to the substitution of a different language, raises a political problem: it questions the distribution of power in the classroom by exposing the linguistic and cultural conditions that complicate the instructor's interpretation. Studying the meanings that Sayers's English version inscribes in Dante's Italian text would weaken the interpretive authority of the instructor who teaches that his reading is true or adequate to the Italian, despite his assimilation of modern scholarship and the students' use of the translation. Although the instructor's essay reveals his awareness that translation involves an unpredictable dissemination of meaning, that a ratio of loss and gain occurs between source- and target-language texts, his teaching assumes that this ratio has been overcome, that his interpretation is a transparent English-language translation.

What is preserved here is the authority not merely of the instructor's interpretation, but of the language in which it is communicated – English. For, as Derrida observes, the ideal of translatability that currently informs the university also "neutralizes [a] national language" (1979: 94), i.e., the fact that the language of instruction is not impartial in its representation of foreign texts, but *national*, specific to English-speaking countries. The repression of translation in the classroom conceals the inevitable inscription of British and American cultural values in the foreign text, yet simultaneously treats English as the transparent vehicle of universal truth, thus encouraging a linguistic chauvinism, even a cultural nationalism.

This is more likely to occur in humanities courses, where a translation of a canonical foreign text may be enlisted in domestic agendas. The reactionary defense of the Great Books that emerged in the 1980s, for example, has often assumed a continuity between them and a national British or American culture while ignoring important cultural and historical differences, including those introduced by translation. William Bennett's controversial report on humanities education in the United States is typical. Speaking as the director of the National Endowment for the Humanities, the appointee of a conservative presidential administration, Bennett argued that the canonical texts of European literature and philosophy must be "the core of the American college curriculum" because "we are a part and a product of Western civilization" – even though the students in "core" courses cannot read the Western languages in which most of those texts were written (Bennett 1984: 21). As Guillory has pointed out, "the translation of the 'classics' into one's own vernacular is a powerful institutional buttress of imaginary cultural continuities; it confirms the nationalist agenda by permitting the easy appropriation of texts in foreign languages" (Guillory 1993: 43). When the issue of translation is repressed in the teaching of translated texts, the translating language and culture are valorized, seen as expressing the truth of the foreign, whereas in fact they are constructing an image bent to the intelligibilities and interests of certain domestic groups – in Bennett's case, an elite projecting an image of an American national culture.

A pedagogy of translated literature can help students learn to be both self-critical and critical of exclusionary cultural ideologies by drawing attention to the situatedness of texts and interpretations. Translations are always intelligible to, if not intentionally made for, specific cultural constituencies at specific historical moments. The repression of translation makes ideas and forms appear to be free-floating, unmoored from history, transcending the linguistic and cultural differences that required not merely their translation in the first place, but also their interpretation in a classroom. The effort to reconstruct the period in which the foreign text was produced, to create a historical context for interpretation, does not so much compensate for the loss of historicity as complicate and exacerbate it: students are encouraged to regard their historical interpretations as immanent in the texts, not determined by translation discourses and critical methodologies that answer to the cultural values of different, later moments. As a result, students develop a concept of interpretive truth as a simple adequacy to the text, ignoring the fact that they are actively constituting it by selecting and synthesizing textual evidence and historical research, and that therefore their interpretation is shaped by linguistic and cultural constraints – which include their reliance on a translation. Recognizing a text as translated and figuring this recognition into classroom interpretations can teach students that their critical operations are limited and provisional, situated in a changing history of reception, in a specific cultural situation, in a curriculum, in a particular language. And with the knowledge of limitations comes the awareness of possibilities, different ways of understanding the foreign text, different ways of understanding their own cultural moments.

Such a pedagogy would obviously force a rethinking of courses, curricula, canons, and disciplines. After all, translations are usually assigned as required readings because the foreign texts they translate are valued highly, not because of their own value – even if particular translations are undoubtedly selected over others according to various criteria. Addressing the issue of translation in the classroom makes these valuations problematic because it requires a double focus, encompassing not just the foreign text and culture, but the text and culture of the translation. Hence, the instructor must displace canonical texts and confront the concept of a canonical translation; revise syllabi and reapportion classroom time; develop course materials that cross disciplinary divisions between languages and periods. Not only Dante, but Dorothy Sayers must be taught, not only the lyrical precision of his Italian, but the late Victorian poeticism of her English, not only medieval Florentine culture, but Oxford literary culture before World War II (for a first step in

93

THE PEDAGOGY OF LITERATURE

reconstructing the context of Sayers's translation, see Reynolds 1989). A detailed and informed juxtaposition of selected Italian and English passages would illuminate the unique features of the two texts as well as their different cultural and historical moments. Yet students would also learn that the Great Books are only as Great as their translations permit them to be, that canonicity depends not simply on textual features, but also on forms of reception which reflect the values of specific cultural constituencies to the exclusion of others.

Because a pedagogy of translated literature aims to understand linguistic and cultural difference, it would exemplify Giroux's concept of a "border pedagogy," in which "culture is not viewed as monolithic or unchanging, but as a shifting sphere of multiple and heterogeneous borders where different histories, languages, experiences, and voices intermingle amid diverse relations of power and privilege" (Giroux 1992: 32). Teaching the issue of translation reveals how different forms of reception construct the significance of the foreign text, but also which of these forms are dominant or marginalized in the domestic culture at any historical moment. Such a pedagogy can intervene into the recent debates concerning multiculturalism, although in an unexpected way. It does not insist that European literary canons be abandoned: this would not be a strategic move, anyway, when contemporary culture continues to be at once deeply rooted in European cultural traditions and utterly dependent on translations of their canonical texts. The study of contemporary American literature that is considered exemplary of multiculturalism – for example, the Chicana writer Gloria Anzaldúa – in fact requires "not only the received canons of Spanish American and Anglo-American literatures [. . .], but a freshly elaborated setting that includes Whitman, José Vasconcelos, Vallejo, Mário de Andrade, Toomer, Nicolás Guillén, Alfonsina Storni, and Ginsberg" (Greene 1995: 152–153). Translation is unavoidable in understanding American ethnic literatures, and it will only complicate unreflective dismissals of canonical texts.

A pedagogy that addresses translation would likewise question any simple integration of these texts with those of excluded cultures, or in other words the notion of a multicultural canon. This would equalize by removing the historical specificity that distinguishes texts, creating what Giroux called "the horizon of a false equality and a depoliticized notion of consensus," ignoring the exclusions that enter into any canon formation and any educational institution (Giroux 1992: 32; cf. Guillory 1993: 53). Studying translation rather suggests that respect for cultural difference – a pedagogical goal of multiculturalism – can be learned by historicizing various forms of receiving the foreign, including the discursive forms applied in the translation of foreign texts, canonical and marginal.

A pedagogy of translated literature can thus serve the political agenda that Giroux conceived for border pedagogy. "If," he observed, "the concept of border pedagogy is to be linked to the imperatives of a critical democracy, as it

94

must be, educators must possess a theoretical grasp of the ways in which difference is constructed through various representations and practices that name, legitimate, marginalize, and exclude the voices of subordinate groups in American society" (Giroux 1992: 32). The mention of "American" suggests that Giroux was thinking only about varieties of English, not foreign languages, and not the question of translation; like other champions of multiculturalism, the only borders he conceives are those between American cultural constituencies. Yet current translation rates indicate that foreign cultures are certainly "subordinate" in such English-speaking countries as the United Kingdom and the United States. More fundamentally, translation effectively enacts a degree of subordination in any target language by constructing a representation of the foreign text that is inscribed with domestic cultural values. By bringing to light the domestication at work in every translated text and assessing its cultural and political significance, a pedagogy of translated literature, like Giroux's border pedagogy, can function as "part of a broader politics of difference [which] makes primary the language of the political and ethical" (ibid.: 28). When students see that translation is not simple communication, but an appropriation of the foreign text to serve domestic purposes, they can come to question the appropriative movements in their own encounters with foreign cultures.

Still, in the classroom this agenda can be served only by scrutinizing the peculiarly aesthetic or literary qualities of the translated text, locating difference at the level of language and style, dialect and discourse. Teaching the issue of translation requires close attention to the formal or expressive properties of literature, while demonstrating that these properties are always historically situated, laden with the values of the cultural constituencies by and for which the translation was produced. Here, learning respect for cultural difference involves a double operation: on the one hand, recognizing the distinctively domestic nuances that qualify foreign themes, what in the translation is not foreign and unavoidably alters the possible meanings of the foreign text; and, on the other hand, allowing those themes and meanings to defamiliarize domestic cultural values, revealing their hierarchical arrangements, their canons and margins.

A pedagogy of translated literature

Such a pedagogy, then, will examine differences not only between the foreign text and the translation, but within the translation itself. This can be done by focussing on the remainder, the textual effects that work only in the target language, the domestic linguistic forms that are added to the foreign text in the translating process and run athwart the translator's effort to communicate that text. An English-language translation will use a variety of dialects, registers, and styles that refer to various moments in the history of English, but are repressed whenever the translation is read as a transparent communication, or indeed as indistinguishable from the foreign text. Teaching the issue of

THE PEDAGOGY OF LITERATURE

translation means teaching the remainder in the translation, calling attention to the multiple, polychronic forms that destabilize its unity and cloud over its seeming transparency.

To exemplify this pedagogy, let us take Trevor Saunders's recent translation of Plato's *Ion*, a text that might appear on course syllabi at various levels, undergraduate and graduate, and in various academic departments and programs, English, comparative literature, philosophy, humanities. In this brief dialogue, Socrates argues that the rhapsode Ion performs and interprets Homer's poetry, just as Homer wrote that poetry, by virtue of divine inspiration, not knowledge. As the argument unfolds through Socrates's typical questioning, there is much irony at Ion's expense: he is portrayed as conceited and unthinking, occasionally unable to follow Socrates's reasoning. If we approach the English version reading for the remainder, what quickly becomes noticeable is that the ironic effects are linked to a strain of colloquialism, notably British, in a translation discourse that tends for the most part to adhere to the current standard dialect. The colloquialism doesn't simply support the irony; it also attaches a class significance to the argument of the dialogue.

Ion is given several colloquial idioms. One occurs near the end, at a point where he is speaking in a most conceited and unthinking fashion:

SOCRATES: Now then, are you, as a rhapsode, the best among the Greeks?
ION: By a long chalk, Socrates.

(Saunders 1987b: 64)

"By a long chalk," a distinctively British idiom meaning "to a great degree" (*OED*), renders *polou ge*, a Greek phrase which, in a version that sticks closer to standard usage, could be rendered as "very much so" (Burnet 1903: 541b). The colloquialisms appear not only in Ion's lexicon, but in his syntax too. At the beginning, Socrates points to the similarities among the Greek poets in an effort to show that Ion's enthusiasm for Homer alone is not based on any knowledge of poetry:

SOCRATES: What of the other poets? Don't they talk about these same topics?
ION: Yes – but Socrates, they haven't composed like Homer has.

(Saunders 1987b: 51)

A comparison with the Greek – *onch homoios pepoiekasi kai Omeros* – reveals the translator's hand, since it contains nothing that resembles Ion's use of "like" for "as" (Burnet 1903: 531d). The translator deliberately chose the colloquial syntax instead of a rendering in standard English, such as "not in the way that Homer has written poetry," or Benjamin Jowett's freer version, "not in the same way as Homer" (Jowett 1892: 499). The conjunctival use of "like" is conversational, of course, so that as a translation it can be viewed as appropriate to the genre of the Greek text, a dialogue. Yet the effect is nonetheless to brand Ion as a speaker of substandard English, perhaps implying a limited education, if not simply inferior social standing. In the words of the *OED*, which are later quoted by prescriptive stylistic manuals like Fowler's, this usage is "now generally condemned as vulgar or slovenly" (Fowler 1965: 334–335).

In the translation, the colloquial becomes a signal of Ion's dimwittedness. And Socrates often adopts such usages when he waxes ironic, in effect talking down to Ion, puffing up the rhapsode's pride while using language that suggests his pride is unwarranted. Usually, a brief phrase is enough to signify the irony. The translator has Socrates say "in a nutshell" for *en kephalaioi*, "to conclude," and "my dear chap" for *ophile kephale*, a salutation that means "dear friend" but refers to the friend metonymically by indicating the head (*kephale*) – clearly a wink at Ion's witless bafflement in the Greek text (Burnet 1903: 531e, d). Aside from these barbs, there is an extended passage at the opening of the dialogue in which the strain of British colloquialism is pronounced:

> I must confess, Ion, I've often envied you rhapsodes your art, which makes it *right and proper* for you to dress up and look as *grand* as you can. And how enviable also to have to immerse yourself in a great many good poets, especially Homer, the best and most inspired of them, and to have *to get up* his thought and not just his lines!
>
> (Saunders 1987b: 49; my italics)

None of the italicized words is so free as to be judged a mistranslation, even if none of their Greek counterparts can be called colloquial: the phrase "to get up," for example, renders *ekmanthanein*, "to know thoroughly, to learn by rote" (Burnet 1903: 530c). Still, the combined effect of the translator's choices is to give a peculiarly British informality to the language. The idea that Socrates is talking down to Ion in such passages becomes evident in the course of the dialogue, since Socrates speaks in other dialects: in the translation as in the Greek text, only his lexicon includes philosophical abstractions, and these repeatedly mystify Ion:

SOCRATES: It's obvious to everyone that you are unable to speak about Homer with skill and knowledge [*techne kai episteme*] – because if you were about to do it by virtue of a skill, you would be able to speak about all the other poets too. You see, I suppose, there exists an art of poetry as a whole [*olon*], doesn't there?
ION: Yes, there does.
SOCRATES: So whatever other skill you take as a whole, the same method

of inquiry [*tropos tes skepseos*] will apply to every one of them? Do you want to hear me explain the point I'm making, Ion?

ION: Yes, by Zeus, Socrates, I do.

(Saunders 1987b: 52–53; Burnet 1903: 532c, d)

In effect, the colloquialism in the translation inscribes a class code into the thematic hierarchies that inform the Greek text. The most conspicuous of these hierarchies is epistemological: Socrates aims to show that Ion neither possesses the skill or knowledge of performance and interpretation, nor understands the philosophical concept at issue, the notion that knowledge is systematic and specialized and enables the performance and evaluation of all practices within a particular field or discipline. Hence, Socrates argues, Ion should be able to perform and interpret all poets with equal success, not just Homer, whom he judges to be the best while failing to explain the grounds of his judgment. In setting Socrates above Ion as the position from which this argument becomes intelligible or obvious, the Greek text privileges philosophy over performance, theoretical over practical knowledge.

This epistemological hierarchy also carries political implications. In two passages, Ion's native city is identified as Ephesus, which he describes as "ruled [*archetai*] by you Athenians," and several topical allusions date his conversation with Socrates to a period before Ephesus revolted against Athenian domination (Moore 1974; Meiggs 1972). As a result, the dialogue seems to be offering a propagandistic representation of Athenians (in the person of Socrates) as intellectually superior to their colonial subjects, and Ion's ignorance legitimizes Athenian imperialism: dimwitted Ephesians require the guidance of the Platonic philosopher kings in Athens. In the translation, this ideological burden is brought into English and further complicated by the different dialects: the speaker of the standard dialect, educated and adept in philosophical abstraction, is valued over the speaker of colloquialisms, who lacks an education in philosophy and exhibits weak intellectual abilities – even if he is a very successful performer.

Teaching the remainder can thus illuminate both the Greek text and the English version. The dialectal difference, especially insofar as it is the vehicle of irony, is useful in drawing attention to the cultural and political hierarchies constructed in the Platonic argument and so to its historical specificity. But insofar as the dialects constitute a peculiarly English-language remainder, they also establish a contemporary, domestic relevance that exposes the hierarchical values in Anglo-American culture, in English. Teaching the remainder can make students realize that the translation enacts an interpretation, but also that this interpretation may be summoned to support or interrogate the representations of Socrates and Ion in the Greek text. Ion's dialect, for example, can seem right, revealing of his slow intellect and limited education; or it can seem stigmatized, expressive of cultural elitism and determined by class domination. In thinking through such possibilities, students can learn about the limits of their own interpretations. Whether they read the collo-quialism as a verification or a demystification of the Platonic argument, their reading will depend not merely on textual evidence and historical research (e.g. an informed answer to the question of whether Ion does in fact possess a kind of knowledge), but also on the cultural and political values which they bring to the translation.

Scrutinizing the remainder offers a productive method of teaching the issue of translation. In the classroom it can be done on the basis of brief, pointedly selected passages, and it need not involve an extended compari-son between the foreign and translated texts, even if such a comparison is extremely informative. The remainder is pedagogically useful because it can be perceived in the translation itself, in the various textual effects released in the target language. It enables a close reading of translations *as translations*, as texts that simultaneously communicate and inscribe the foreign text with domestic values. Hence, this reading is also historical: the remainder becomes intelligible in a translation only when its diverse discourses, registers, and styles are situated in specific moments of the domestic culture. In the class-room, discourse analysis of a translation must be combined with cultural history. The remainder is the eruption in standard usage of linguistic forms that are currently not standard, "the place of inscription of past and present linguistic conjunctures" (Lercercle 1990: 215).

The temporal aspect of the remainder is perhaps most dramatically revealed when several translations of a single foreign text are juxtaposed. Multiple versions bring to light the different translation effects possible at different cultural moments, allowing these effects to be studied as forms of reception affiliated with different cultural constituencies. A historical sampling can be especially helpful in demystifying a translation that has achieved canonical status in the domestic culture: when a translation comes to represent a foreign text for a broad audience, when in effect it comes to replace or be that text for readers, teaching the remainder can show that its cultural authority depends not simply on its superior accuracy or stylistic felicity, but also on its appeal to certain domestic values.

Take Richmond Lattimore's *Iliad* (1951), by far the most widely used English version since its publication, "the preferred text of more than three-fourths of the respondents" to an MLA survey of instructors in departments of English, classics, comparative literature, history, philosophy, and anthro-pology (Myrsiades 1987: x, 4). Lattimore's version is quite close to the Greek, adhering even to the Homeric line, yet not so close as to eliminate the remainder that links the English text to a specific cultural moment – despite the apparent transcendence of its accuracy and its sheer readability for contemporary English-language readers.

Consider these lines from a key scene in the first book: Achilles's surrender of his captive Trojan mistress, Briseis, to the leader of the Greek force, Agamemnon:

hos phato, Patroklos de philoi epepeitheth'h etairoi,
ek d'agage klisies Briseida kallipareion,
doke d'agein. to d'autis iten para neas Achaion.
he d'aekous'h ama toisi gune kien. autar Achilleus
dakrusas hetaron aphar ezeto nosphi liastheis,
thin'eph'alos polies, horoon ep'apeirona ponton.
polla de metri philei eresato chieras oregnus.
    (transcribed from Monro and Allen 1920: 13)

So he spoke, and Patroklos obeyed his beloved companion.
He led forth from the hut Briseis of the fair cheeks and gave her
to be taken away; and they walked back beside the ships of the
    Achaians,
and the woman all unwilling went with them still. But Achilleus
weeping went and sat in sorrow apart from his companions
beside the beach of the grey sea looking out on the infinite water.
Many times stretching forth he called on his mother:
    (Lattimore 1951: 68)

Lattimore's translation discourse is grounded in a very simple register of the standard dialect, what he called "the plain English of today" (ibid.: 55). As he himself pointed out, he followed Matthew Arnold's prescriptions in *On Translating Homer* (1860): "the translator of Homer must bear in mind four qualities of his author: that he is rapid, plain and direct in thought and expression, plain and direct in substance, and noble" (Lattimore 1951: 55). This is a scholarly reading of the Greek text, performed, in Arnold's words, by "those who both know Greek and can appreciate poetry," and although he had in mind such Victorian classicists as Jowett, this reading has clearly prevailed into the present, informing Robert Fagles's version of *The Iliad* as well as Lattimore's (Arnold 1960: 99; Fagles 1990: ix; Venuti 1995a: 139–145). Although Lattimore wrote a scholarly translation, he felt a need to revise Arnold's call for a "poetical dialect of English" because "in 1951, we do not have a poetic dialect," and any poetical use of archaism, "the language of Spenser or the King James Version," seemed inappropriate to Homer's plainness (Lattimore 1951: 55).

Yet, as the above passage illustrates, a strain of archaism can in fact be detected in Lattimore's discourse, partly lexical ("beloved," "led forth"), partly syntactic (inversions like "weeping went"), partly prosodic ("a free six-beat line" that imitates the Homeric hexameter – as Arnold had also recommended) (for a similar reading of Lattimore's *Odyssey*, see Davenport 1968). It is the archaism that gives the translation its poetic qualities, joining with the Greek and Latinate names and the close renderings of the epithets ("of the fair cheeks") to elevate the tone to a slight formality and make the verse seem "noble" or lofty. Where Lattimore departs from Arnold most tellingly is in keeping these qualities unobtrusive for a mid-to-late twentieth-century reader of English, restraining the remainder by minimizing the archaism. Although divided into poetic lines, Lattimore's version is cast in "the language of contemporary prose," which is to say the language of communication and reference, of realism, immediately intelligible and seemingly transparent, a window onto meaning, reality, the foreign text. In a most successful way, Lattimore's *Iliad* updated the scholarly, Arnoldian reading, establishing this reading as natural or true by drawing on the broadest register of English usage since the 1940s.

Thus, Lattimore was not so much bridging the linguistic and cultural differences that separated his readers from the Greek text, as rewriting it according to dominant domestic values. We can defamiliarize his translation by juxtaposing it with two others that also acquired significant cultural authority, although at earlier moments in literary history: the versions of George Chapman (1608) and Alexander Pope (1715). The historical distance will highlight the remainder in their translations, the English cultural values they inscribe in the Greek text, but it will also call attention to their remarkable differences from Lattimore.

> This speech usd, Patroclus did the rite
> His friend commanded and brought forth Briseis from her tent,
> Gave her the heralds, and away to th'Achive ships they went.
> She, sad, and scarce for griefe could go. Her love all friends
>   forsooke
> And wept for anger. To the shore of th'old sea he betooke
> Himselfe alone and, casting forth upon the purple sea
> His wet eyes and his hands to heaven advancing, this sad plea
> Made to his mother:
>
> (Chapman 1957: 33–34)

> *Patroclus* now th'unwilling Beauty brought;
> She, in soft Sorrows, and in pensive Thought,
> Past silent, as the Heralds held her Hand,
> And oft look'd back, slow-moving o'er the Strand.
>   Not so his Loss the fierce *Achilles* bore;
> But sad retiring to the sounding Shore,
> O'er the wild Margin of the Deep he hung,
> That kindred Deep, from whence his Mother sprung.
> There, bath'd in Tears of Anger and Disdain,
> Thus loud lamented to the stormy Main.
>
> (Pope 1967: 109–10)

If our reading focusses merely on the lexical differences (excluding the other features of these rich passages), the versions by Chapman and Pope reveal a marked anxiety about the gender representations in Homer's poem. For both translators, the fact of Achilles's weeping was so difficult to assimilate to early modern concepts of masculinity, that they needed not only to revise the Greek text, but to supplement their translations with explanatory notes. Chapman reduced the weeping to "wet eyes," to which he lent an air of normalcy by introducing "friends" who also "wept for anger" at Briseis's departure; Pope redefined the "Tears" by associating them with "Anger and Disdain." Chapman's comment on the passage typifies the pervasive syncretism in Renaissance culture, comparing the pagan hero to "our All-perfect and Almightie Saviour, who wept for Lazarus," but it also puts the gender issue in a distinctively masculinist form: "Who can denie that there are teares of manlinesse and magnanimitie as well as womanish and pusil-lanimous?" (Chapman 1957: 44). Pope's note rationalized his revision with the equally masculinist argument that "it is no Weakness in Heroes to weep" because "a great and fiery Temper is more susceptible" to "Tears of Anger and Disdain" (Pope 1967: 109 n. 458). Both translators regarded extreme emotion as feminine, so both altered the Greek text to portray Briseis as emotionally weak ("scarce for griefe could go"; "soft Sorrows") in contrast to the manly strength of Achilles's anger; Pope went so far as to increase her passivity and submissiveness by introducing the idea that she is "past silent." By the same token, both translators deleted the Greek *philo*, "beloved," in treating the relationship between Achilles and Patroklos, thus omitting the traditional theories of their homosexuality which emerged in Athenian literature during the fifth century B.C. (Williams 1992: 102–104).

These previous versions can challenge the cultural authority of Lattimore's by worrying his choices, showing that they too are laden with gender representations despite the seeming transparency of his English. Interestingly, the slight deviations from the standard dialect are the textual sites where Achilles deviates from the patriarchal concepts of masculinity that prevailed in Lattimore's cultural moment, as in Chapman's and Pope's. The archaisms – "beloved," "weeping went" – may produce an estranging effect upon the contemporary reader, fogging the transparent surface of Lattimore's translation: they allow for the possibility of a homosexual relationship between Achilles and Patroklos as well as an intense emotionalism on the part of the militaristic hero, and as archaisms they situate these cultural values in the past. Yet such effects remain merely potential in the translated text: they can only be released through a juxtaposition with other versions that teases out the remainder in Lattimore's, since the plainness of his discourse is designed to gloss over subtle nuances, to propel the narrative, and to envelop every scene in an elevated tone. The archaisms tend to be absorbed in the uniformity of the current standard dialect, shifting attention away from the remainder in English to the themes of the Greek text, concealing how the translation is shaping Achilles or Briseis and therefore any interpretation of them.

If the remainder can be useful in teaching the issue of translation, it will also establish new grounds for choosing one translation over another. In the overwhelming majority of cases – we know – translated texts appear on syllabi because the foreign text, in form or theme, is considered pertinent to a course topic or curriculum. The general practice in the United States and Canada, judging from the instructor surveys that accompany the MLA volumes on teaching world literature, is to choose a translation on the basis of a comparison to the foreign text, apart from extrinsic considerations like cost and availability. Accuracy is the most consistently applied criterion, even if canons of accuracy are subject to variation. Yet when the instructor plans to teach the issue of translation, accuracy is joined by other criteria that take into account the cultural significance and social functioning of a particular translation, both in its own historical moment and now. If a translated text, no matter how accurate, constitutes an interpretation of the foreign text, then the choice of a suitable translation is a question of picking a particular interpretation, one that offers an efficient articulation of the issues raised by translation, but also one that works productively with the critical methodologies applied to other texts in the course. Choosing a translation means choosing a text with a rich remainder, an especially suggestive translation discourse, for example, or a discourse that gained the translation a canonical or marginal position in the domestic culture. An instructor may also wish to include a contemporary version (or an excerpt from one) to engage students in a scrutiny of contemporary cultural values, which is to say a self-criticism.

In the end, teaching the remainder enables students to see the role played by translation in the formation of cultural identities. Of course all teaching is designed to form subjectivity, to equip students with knowledge and to qualify them for social positions. This is especially true of courses that teach cultural forms and values and often rely to an enormous extent on translations. Because the creation of subjects in the classroom is the creation of social agents, a course in literature comes to carry considerable linguistic and cultural capital, not accessible to everyone, capable of endowing agents with social power. "The literary syllabus," as Guillory has argued,

> constitutes capital in two senses: First, it is *linguistic* capital, the means by which one attains to a socially credentialled and therefore valued speech, otherwise known as "Standard English." And second, it is *symbolic* capital, a kind of knowledge-capital whose possession can be displayed upon request and which thereby entitles its possessor to the cultural and material rewards of the well-educated person.
> (Guillory 1993: ix)

Insofar as translated literature continues to be a medium for the transmission of linguistic and cultural capital (the standard dialect of English is currently the preferred language for the rendering of canonical texts), translation becomes a strategic means by which the identity-forming process of education can be studied – and changed.

For, as we saw in the previous chapter, at least two such processes operate simultaneously in translation. The cultural difference of the foreign text, when translated, is always represented in accordance with target-language values that construct cultural identities for both foreign countries and domestic readers. Pope, for instance, fashioned an elegant Enlightenment Homer for a male elite, both aristocratic and bourgeois, "who have at once a Taste of Poetry, and competent Learning" (Pope 1967: 23; Williams 1992). Intended for American college-level students in the post-World War II period, Lattimore's Homer joined the scholarly reading of the Greek text to the standard dialect of English, reinforcing cultural divisions and class distinctions while inculcating the nobility of an archaic aristocratic culture distinguished by its masculinity and its militarism. Studying translation can make students more aware of the domestic interests to which any translation submits the reader, as well as the foreign text. In a pedagogy of translated literature, learning respect for cultural difference goes hand in hand with learning the differences that comprise the cultural identity of the domestic reader. At a time when the global hegemony of English invites a cultural narcissism and complacency on the part of British and American readers, translation can illuminate the heterogeneity that characterizes any culture.

If translation is to function in this way, however, graduate education in literature will need to be rethought. The discipline of comparative litera-ture has begun this self-scrutiny, although for decades after World War II its "focus on national and linguistic identities" worked to discourage trans-lation studies (Bernheimer 1995: 40). The 1993 Bernheimer Report on Standards for the American Comparative Literature Association argued that "the old hostilities toward translation should be mitigated" because "trans-lation can well be seen as a paradigm for larger problems of understanding and interpretation across different discursive traditions" (ibid.: 44). In contrast, the British Comparative Literature Association has long regarded translation as a model of the field, encouraging a leading translation scholar to conclude that "We should look upon translation studies as the principal discipline from now on, with comparative literature as a valued but subsidiary subject area" (Bassnett 1993: 161). Although this view would be considered extreme by many comparatists in the United States, it is nonetheless a useful reminder that courses in translation theory and history remain relatively rare in American comparative literature programs.

In English departments, translation can generate interest only by breaking down the insularity (some would say, the xenophobia) that currently prevails in advanced literary study. Gone are the days when the foreign-language requirement for the doctorate supported research in British and American literature, whether at the dissertation stage or beyond. In many English

graduate programs, especially in the United States, foreign-language requirements have been curtailed, and foreign-language study rarely goes beyond
the rudiments necessary to render a brief excerpt into passably idiomatic
English. New doctorates are therefore not equipped to think about the
cultural and political issues raised by their dependence on translations in
research and teaching.

Yet the remedy, I suggest, is not to return to traditional requirements
that demand reading proficiency in two (or more) foreign languages. The
knowledge gained through such onerous requirements would be of limited
use in graduate curricula that are so firmly rooted in English-language literatures – not to mention the delay in progress toward the degree and the
continued search for shortcuts to pass language examinations. A much more
productive alternative would be to require superior knowledge of one foreign
language (certified by an examination that tests reading comprehension instead
of translation ability) along with an English course that considers the problem
of negotiating linguistic and cultural differences. This is precisely the problem that can be addressed in a historical survey of translation theory and
practice where the focus is on translating into English, on learning how to
read English-language translations as translations.

The twofold requirement I am proposing will enable doctoral candidates
to conduct research in a foreign language, to enter into contemporary critical
debates on the formation of cultural identities, and, perhaps most importantly, to confront the question of translation when teaching translated texts.
They will see that no national culture has ever developed without encounters
with the foreign, and their own courses in English-language cultures will
become more polylingual and transnational. Students at every level surely
have much to gain from putting translation on the pedagogical agenda.

6

PHILOSOPHY

Philosophy does not escape the embarrassment that faces contemporary academic disciplines when confronted with the problem of translation. In philosophical research widespread dependence on translated texts coincides with neglect of their translated status, a general failure to take into account the differences introduced by the fact of translation. The problem is perhaps most glaring in Anglo–American cultures, where native philosophical traditions from empiricism to logical semantics have privileged language as communication and therefore imagined the transparency of the translated text. But even in Continental traditions like existential phenomenology and poststructuralism, where language is viewed as constitutive of thought and translating can more readily be seen as determining the domestic significance of the foreign text – even here philosophical argument and speculation give only passing acknowledgement to their reliance on translations. Philosophy has long engaged in the creation of concepts by interpreting domestic versions of foreign texts, but for the most part these versions have been taken as transparent, and the concepts unmediated by the domestic language and culture that is their medium. This is never more true than on the rare occasions when a translation is actually noticed in reviews and studies: philosophers assume that transparency is an attainable ideal by evaluating the accuracy of the translation as a correspondence to the foreign text, chastising the translator for missing the foreign philosopher's intention or the full significance of the foreign philosophical terms. In such cases, translations are presumably adjusted, brought into a more adequate relation to the essential meaning of the foreign text, whereas the adequacy that is in fact established reverts to a domestic standard, usually a stylistic canon or a competing interpretation applied implicitly by the critic.

Translation exposes a fundamental idealism in philosophy by calling attention to the material conditions of concepts, their linguistic and discursive forms, the different meanings and functions they come to possess in different cultural situations. And in so doing translation offers philosophy an opportunity for self-criticism, a scrutiny of philosophical discourses and institutions and a rethinking of current practices in the interpreting and translating of philosophical texts. My aim here is to challenge the neglect of translation in academic philosophy by taking a materialist approach, one that doesn't abandon the philosophical project of concept formation, just grounds it in the difference that translating opens in the materiality of the philosophical text. The questions I want to address are both basic and practical: What does philosophy stand to gain from thinking about the domestic determinations and effects of translations? And how can this thinking contribute to the translating of foreign philosophies?

The gain of translation

The reception of Ludwig Wittgenstein's *Philosophical Investigations* is a remarkable example of the marginality of translation in the discipline of philosophy. When first published in 1953, the text was bilingual, with G.E.M. Anscombe's English version facing the German. Very few of the fifteen or so reviews that greeted it even mentioned the quality of her translating, and in these instances the comments were extremely brief, restricted to vague honorifics like "excellent," "well done," "on the whole very successful and reliable," "adequate and honest" (Nakhnikian 1954: 353; Workman 1955: 293; Hampshire 1953: 682; Findlay 1955: 179). Despite their brevity, such comments make clear that the translation was judged in terms of its correspondence to the German text, to Wittgenstein's unusual style of philosophizing, to the meanings of his concepts. Most reviewers tacitly assumed this correspondence by avoiding any reference to Anscombe's work at all and devoting their reviews to critical expositions of Wittgenstein's ideas and arguments. To document the latter, they quoted from the English version as if he wrote it, as if it were a simple communication of his intended meanings (e.g. Strawson 1954; Feyerabend 1955).

Because of the negligible attention paid to Anscombe's translation, criticisms were very slow in coming. But when they finally appeared, they continued to assume correspondence as the criterion of accuracy, an assumption that proved to be rather disingenuous because it concealed competing domestic interpretations of the German text. Saul Kripke questioned Anscombe's renderings of "*Seele* and its derivatives sometimes as 'soul,' sometimes as 'mind,' depending on the context" because he found a sentence in the German text where "'mind' might be a less misleading translation of *Seele*" (Kripke 1982: 49). If "soul" was "misleading," then it was a mistranslation, an inaccurate expression of Wittgenstein's concept. Yet Kripke's rationale for using "mind" ultimately had less to do with communicating the foreign text than with assimilating it to the domestic culture, to the secularism and anti-foundationalism that prevails in Anglo-American philosophy, and to Kripke's own investment in these values. "For the contemporary English speaking philosophical reader," he explained, "['mind'] is somewhat less loaded with special philosophical and religious connotations" (ibid.). This tendency to domesticate Wittgenstein's text, to assimilate it to domestic intelligibilities and interests, was strengthened in 1963, when *Philosophical Investigations* began to be published without the

German. Today the English-language philosophical reader first encounters Wittgenstein as an English-language philosopher, which for all intents and purposes he remains, given the virtual invisibility of translation in Anglo-American philosophy.

To make Anscombe's version visible, we must avoid the assumption that language, especially language with the conceptual density of philosophical discourse, can ever simply express ideas without simultaneously destabilizing and reconstituting them. Wittgenstein's own philosophy warns against this assumption by questioning the possibility of personal expression, arguing that statements of intentionality are matters of linguistic convention, not logical necessity. We will go further: any language use is prone to the unpredictable variation of the remainder, the collective force of linguistic forms that outstrips any individual's control and complicates intended meanings. The peculiarly domestic remainder that translating attaches to the foreign text increases this unpredictability, exceeding the foreign writer's intention and the translator's as well. Hence, no English translation can ever simply communicate Wittgenstein's German text without simultaneously inscribing it with English-language forms that destabilize and reconstitute his philosophy.

Consider a typical excerpt from Anscombe's version:

> Das Benennen erscheint als eine *seltsame* Verbindung eines Wortes mit einem Gegenstand. – Und so eine seltsame Verbindung hat wirklich statt, wenn nämlich der Philosoph, um herauszubringen, was *die* Beziehung zwischen Namen und Benanntmen ist, auf einen Gegenstand vor sich starrt und dabei unzählige Male einen Namen wiederholt, oder auch das Wort "dieses". Denn die philosophischen Probleme entstehen, wenn die Sprache *feiert*. Und *da* können wir uns allerdings einbilden, das Benennen sei irgend ein merkwürdiger seelischer Akt, quasi eine Taufe eines Gegenstandes. Und wir können so auch das Wort "dieses" gleichsam *zu* dem Gegenstand sagen, ihn damit *ansprechen* – ein seltsamer Gebrauch dies Wortes, der wohl nur beim Philosophieren vorkommt.

> Naming appears as a *queer* connexion of a word with an object. – And you really get such a queer connexion when the philosopher tries to bring out *the* relation between name and thing by staring at an object in front of him and repeating a name or even the word "this" innumerable times. For philosophical problems arise when language *goes on holiday*. And *here* we may indeed fancy naming to be some remarkable act of mind, as it were a baptism of an object. And we can also say the word "this" *to* the object, as it were *address* the object as "this" – a queer use of this word, which doubtless only occurs in doing philosophy.
>
> (Wittgenstein 1953: 19)

The translation is cast mostly in a plain register of the standard dialect of English, but the orthography is British, and Anscombe draws noticeably on British colloquialisms: the verb "fancy," the use of "holiday" and "queer" where American English would substitute "vacation" (or "day off") and "strange." The colloquialisms are heightened by the more educated strain in the lexicon ("innumerable," "as it were," "address," "doubtless"), which contains as well some philosophical abstractions ("object," "connexion," "relation," "philosophy").

This heterogeneous mix of Englishes is sufficient to cast doubt on any effort to evaluate the translation merely by comparing it to the German text. It might be thought, for instance, that the different dialects, registers, and discourses correspond to the most frequently remarked qualities of Wittgenstein's prose, "at once rhetorical and informal" (Hampshire 1953: 682). Any such correspondence, however, can hold only at the most general level: a comparison of the above excerpt with the German text immediately reveals points where Anscombe's version is deviant and excessive. Nothing in the German evokes a difference comparable to that between British and other forms of English, a difference that is national in scope. And nothing in the German quite matches the colloquial register hit by "fancy" and "holiday": the first avoids the customary English equivalent, "imagine," for the German "einbilden," while the second excludes the customary range of possibilities ("celebrates," "stops work," "idles") for the German "feiert." Anscombe's choices can't be classified as errors in the sense of ignoring the meanings assigned to these words in current dictionaries. Yet the effect of her choices undoubtedly goes beyond any equivalence based on lexicography.

In Anscombe's English, Wittgenstein acquired a British remainder that has exerted a powerful force in philosophical discourses and institutions. The thinking in *Philosophical Investigations* was itself eccentric, a departure from the logical positivism that dominated British philosophy during the 1930s and 1940s (Quinton 1967: 392). The diverse language of the translation, as well as the discontinuous and uncertain form of the text (discrete numbered sections that were in part assembled by Wittgenstein's editors), inevitably increased the contrast to current philosophical trends, where the style of writing was more formal and less familiar, more analytically precise and less metaphorically suggestive, more academic and less popular. Anscombe's translation can be said to have communicated Wittgenstein's ideas, even to have mimicked his style of writing. Yet in the process both were overlaid with a domestic remainder that also enabled them to be transgressive: the translation both marked and crossed the institutional boundaries of British philosophy, allowing the text to remain irreducibly foreign even as it entered the domestic culture. "Each sentence," wrote a reviewer of the translation, "is clear and almost colloquial," but "the cumulative effect of the sentences is peculiar" (Hamilton 1954: 117). This peculiarity hasn't vanished: although Wittgenstein's ideas have deeply influenced British philosophy (Quinton 1967: 393–396), the style of Anscombe's translation has not produced any imitators among British philosophers, and her "unusual" renderings continue to be revised by other commentators (Hanfling 1991: 117 n. 1; see also Hacker 1986: 113 n. 3 and Hintikka and Hintikka 1986: passim). Even the so-called "ordinary language" philosophers who, like Wittgenstein, analyze everyday speech write with an academic formality dotted with jargon (e.g. J.L. Austin's distinction between "performative" and "constative" utterances). The case of Wittgenstein shows that from reading the remainder in an influential translation, philosophy gains a historical knowledge of itself, of the hierarchical arrangement of discourses that exists in the discipline at any given moment and that variously affects the importation of foreign philosophies, admitting, excluding, and transforming them in accordance with domestic values.

The workings of the remainder are collective and therefore question any narrowly biographical understanding of the translation, any individualistic assumption that it somehow mirrors the intention or experience of the foreign writer (or the translator). It might be argued, for instance, that the British colloquialisms reflect Wittgenstein's own use of English. As a student who attended Wittgenstein's lectures in Cambridge and then as a friend and colleague who hosted him in the last years of his life, Anscombe would have been very familiar with his English conversation and writing. Her translation might be seen as adequate to his version of the text if he had written it in English. Norman Malcolm, another former student, recalled that Wittgenstein "spoke excellent English, with the accent of an educated Englishman," and was not averse to using colloquial expressions, some distinctly British, such as when he referred to his lectures as "a lot of rubbish" or described food as "grand" or mentioned his fondness for "detective mags" – a notable source of slang (Malcolm 1984: 24, 38, 96, 124). "One of Wittgenstein's favourite phrases," Malcolm observed, "was the exclamation, 'Leave the *bloody* thing *alone!*'" (ibid.: 69).

Nevertheless, the fact remains that Wittgenstein wrote *Philosophical Investigations* in German, not English. And he didn't choose the colloquialisms that appear in Anscombe's translation. In the specific case of the German word "feiert," her choice of "goes on holiday" has actually been criticized as inconsistent with his intention. The authors of a full-scale commentary on the text have asserted that Wittgenstein "preferred" a different rendering, "idles" (Baker and Hacker 1980: 221), although without providing any documentation, apparently on the strength of a later section where he makes a similar remark:

> Die Verwirrungen, die uns beschäftigen, enstehen gleichsam, wenn die Sprache leerläuft, nicht wenn sie arbeitet.

> The confusions that occupy us arise, as it were, when language idles, not when it is working.
>
> (Wittgenstein 1953: 51; my translation)

Another commentator has silently revised Anscombe's version according to Wittgenstein's undocumented preference: "'Philosophical problems', wrote Wittgenstein, 'arise when language is *idling*'" (Hanfling 1989: 51). But this rendering can be no more than another possible alternative, no closer to Wittgenstein's intention than the version made by his student and friend. Any translation can only submit the foreign text to a *domestic* interpretation, based on some sort of reconstruction – lexicographical, textual, biographical – that answers to the needs of a particular interpretive occasion.

The fascinating thing about Anscombe's version is precisely the interpretive richness of its remainder. A colloquialism like "goes on holiday," along with the vaguely metaphorical use to which it is put, is unexpected in Anglo-American philosophical discourse, even in a text as informally ruminative as Wittgenstein's. As a result, it stands out more conspicuously against the otherwise standard dialect in the translation and sets going an uncontrollable proliferation of English meanings.

The statement in which the phrase appears – "philosophical problems arise when language *goes on holiday*" – has usually been taken as Wittgenstein's criticism of certain kinds of philosophy, namely linguistic analysis that is either metaphysical, conceiving of meaning as a mental or spiritual essence, or positivist, reducing semantics to the formal rules of logic (e.g. Ambrose 1954: 111; Mundle 1970: 198; Hallett 1977: 114). In support of this reading, Wittgenstein's commentators have pointed out that he considered the meaning of a word to be contextually determined, not essential but conventional, a function of its use in a specific social practice or "language-game" (*Sprachspiel*). "Language goes on holiday," then, when metaphysical or positivist philosophers wrongly speculate on the meaning of a word apart from its practical application, its job. In one of Wittgenstein's recurrent examples, builders can meaningfully exchange terms for building materials because the terms are defined by their use on the job.

To communicate Wittgenstein's criticism of other philosophers, Anscombe's choice must signify the stoppage of work, which "holiday" definitely does. But the word also connotes playful activity that is performed within a conventionally defined period (a bank holiday, Christmas, summer vacation) and thereby suggests that the philosophical use of language participates in a language-game too, that when a word is discussed philosophically, detached from its practical use, it is merely doing a different kind of work, in a different language-game. Philosophy, it could be argued, is always taking language on a busman's holiday. This applies not just to metaphysicians and logical positivists, but to Wittgenstein as well. Doesn't his own use of the builders' terms depart from the work of building to do philosophical work, to create the concept of a language-game and thus resolve the philosophical problem of meaning?

The translation points to the conflicting possibilities in the German ("feiert" can be translated by "goes on holiday" as well as "idles") and opens up a contradiction in Wittgenstein's text that reveals the deep conservatism of his philosophy. He didn't see the methodological likeness between his and the other philosophies because he was more concerned with their impact on linguistic problems. Insofar as he dismissed philosophies that interrupt the practical application of language, he restricted the evaluation of language-games to their smooth functioning, their maintenance of the status quo. Wittgenstein's builders use language to build a project, not to conceptualize its status as a language-game, not to discuss their working conditions or their wages, the relationship of their work to other projects, other kinds of work, other people. He believed that "philosophy may in no way interfere with the actual use of language; it can in the end only describe it," not explain it, because explanation depends on theoretical assumptions that lead to mis-understanding (Wittgenstein 1953: 49). Yet any description that "leaves everything as it is," far from giving mere facts, effectively assumes a theory of ethical and political value wherein language-games are judged to be good and just, worth the effort to keep functioning. This value may be construed as a democratic ideal, since language-games theoretically lose their ability or right to dominate other games. Yet in practice they are always arranged hierarchically, whether according to the use at hand or their institutional function. Wittgenstein undoubtedly challenged the languages-games currently played in philosophy – yet with an alternative that would seem, paradoxically, to recommend a quietism toward them, toward the stylistic and discursive hierarchies in the discipline.

Anscombe's choice of "holiday" thus makes possible a competing reading of Wittgenstein's philosophy – but only when her translation is examined from a materialist perspective. Reading for the remainder means focussing on the linguistic and cultural differences that English inscribes in the German text and then considering their reconstitution of Wittgenstein's ideas. In effect, Anscombe's colloquialism establishes a metacommentary on key themes in the German, notably the language-game and the criticism of other philosophical concepts of meaning. But the comment I derived from her rendering was obviously against the grain of Wittgenstein's text: my materialist assumptions brought to light the determinations and effects, not only of the translation, but also of Wittgenstein's philosophy, the social conditions concealed by his conservative notion of the language-game. Reading for the remainder in a translation forces a self-awareness upon the interpreter, the knowledge that textual effects can be made intelligible and significant only from a specific theoretical orientation. Wittgenstein himself had this knowledge, even if he didn't apply it explicitly to translation: "The paradox disappears," he wrote, "only if we make a radical break with the idea that language always functions in one way, always serves the same purpose: to convey thoughts – which may be about houses, pains, good and evil, or anything else you please" (Wittgenstein 1953: 102). The same self-awareness is absent from the domi-nant reading of Anscombe's text, where the idealism of transparent translation is assumed, and the colloquial expression is interpreted in deference to

Wittgenstein's philosophy (or at least to the part of it that supports a particular commentary). Thus, an interpreter who noticed the peculiarity of Anscombe's choice – "If language goes on holiday during philosophical rumination, it is a working holiday" – nonetheless found it consistent with Wittgenstein's ideas: "the philosopher's conception of meaning accounts for his cavalier attitude toward context" (Hallett 1971: 101).

Which is to say that the remainder is unpredictable. The metacommentary it sets going in a philosophical translation will take different forms in different contexts, depending as much on the specific ideas under discussion as on the interpreter's assumptions. Consider another passage from Anscombe's translation, where the remainder leads not to an ideological critique, but to a more deferential exposition of Wittgenstein's philosophy:

Denk nur an den Ausdruck "Ich hörte eine klagende Melodie"! Und nun die Frage: "*Hört* er das Klagen?"

Think of the expression "I heard a plaintive melody". And now the question is: "Does he *hear* the plaint?"

(Wittgenstein 1953: 209)

The most striking feature of Anscombe's rendering is the archaism of key words. "Plaintive" is antique, even if still in some use, reserved for poetical expressions, whereas "plaint" is obsolete, recurring most frequently in British poetry of the seventeenth and eighteenth centuries, appearing, for example, in Milton's *Paradise Lost* and Goldsmith's *Deserted Village* (*OED*). The ordinary German words "klagende" and "Klagen" can easily be translated into current English equivalents that preserve the repetition, such as "lamenting" and "lament" or "complaining" and "complaint." Yet the archaisms are much more effective choices: they add another, poetical register to the fairly plain style and inscribe the German with a distinctively English significance that supports Wittgenstein's thinking. The passage, however oblique, seems to assume his concept of meaning as use in a language-game. Hence, the question "Does he *hear* the plaint?" is rhetorical: the person who uses the expression "I heard a plaintive melody" didn't hear any information communicated by the music, no complaint, but rather remembered previous musical applications of the word "plaintive" and therefore applied it to the sound he heard, his physical sensation, and perhaps to the emotion he felt upon hearing it, his psychological response. The language-game, for Wittgenstein, is primarily a social practice in which meaning is assigned to words according to certain conventions and circumstances. Anscombe's poetical archaisms in effect make this point because they illustrate the idea of conventionality, although in literature. Their resonance in English literary history transforms "Does he *hear* the plaint?" into "Does he *hear* the traditional applications of the poeticism 'plaintive' to music?" Here the metacommentary established

113

by the remainder can be seen as performative, enacting on the stylistic level the concept stated on the thematic level.

Of course the unpredictability of the remainder means that not all of its effects are so conspicuous or so significant as the examples I have chosen. Some are subtle, becoming visible only on a comparison to the foreign text – although a comparison that is willing to reflect on the deviations and excesses of the translation, that doesn't seek a correspondence so as to eliminate the remainder. The most subtle effects in philosophical translations are also the most powerful in assimilating the foreign text to the disciplinary discourses and institutions of the domestic culture. This domestication occurs with any translating and indeed is necessary if the foreign text is to become intelligible and interesting to domestic readers. It is also at work in Anscombe's version, despite the estranging heterogeneity of her language. When Wittgenstein discussed the act of defining of words by pointing to an object, "hinweisende Definition," she used the Latinate technical term "ostensive" for the German word "hinweisende," which can also be rendered as "pointing," "referring," "demonstrative," "indicative." Anscombe's choice follows Augustine's use of "ostendere," "to point at," in the excerpt from the *Confessions* that Wittgenstein quotes at the opening of his text: as a child, Augustine writes, he "grasped that the thing was called by the sound [his elders] uttered when they meant to point at it" ("tenebam hoc ab eis vocari rem illam, quod sonabant, cum eam vellent ostendere") (Wittgenstein 1953: 2). In choosing "ostensive" Anscombe was also manifesting the tendency of philosophy – including plain-style British traditions – to create technical terminologies, to increase the conceptual density of language and move it away from everyday speech. "Ostensive" was a term in British philosophical discourse from Francis Bacon to Bertrand Russell.

In other choices, Anscombe does in fact yield to the plain style that has dominated British philosophy since the seventeenth century, to its preference for current usage, continuous syntax, and univocal meaning and its suspicion of figurative language. In Wittgenstein's criticism of other linguistic philosophies, for example, she translated "wenn die Sprache leerläuft" ("when language idles") as "when language is like an engine idling," whereby she removed an elliptical metaphor and made the analogy more explicit for the English-language reader (ibid.: 51). Behind such choices we can ultimately perceive the long-standing dominance of fluent strategies in English-language translating, where the aim is immediate intelligibility and the absence of any linguistic or stylistic peculiarities that might preempt the illusion of transparency.

The remainder at once enriches and redirects the interpretation of philosophical translations. The sort of interpretation it demands continues to be philosophical, engaged in conceptual analysis, but now made more literary, concerned with the formal properties of language, and more historical, concerned with various domestic traditions, linguistic, literary, philosophical. The addition of effects that work only in the target language thickens the semantic

114

burden of the foreign text by posing the problem of their relation to its concepts and arguments, their potential articulation as a metacommentary. Understanding those effects also involves the problem of their relation to a range of domestic practices and institutions: the competing interpretations that domestic philosophers have put forward for the foreign text, the hierarchies of styles and discourses that characterize domestic academic philosophy, and the social functioning of philosophy among the other practices and institutions in its historical moment. The remainder in a translation demonstrates, with varing degrees of violence to the foreign text and the target language, that the philosophical project of concept formation is fundamentally determined by its linguistic and cultural conditions. Translation remains the dark secret of philosophy precisely because the remainder shatters the bedrock assumption of this project in its modern academic form: the stability and authority of the philosophical subject as the autonomous agent of reflection.

Strategies of philosophical translation

To be useful in translating foreign philosophies, the remainder requires a reformulation of the notion of accuracy, a broadening that takes into account both the foreign text and domestic readers. It would be more precise to reserve the term "accuracy" for lexicographical equivalence and rather refer to the translator's ethical responsibilities. Since translating can communicate only by reconstituting the foreign text, a translator can choose to judge a translation good when it signifies the linguistic and cultural difference of that text for domestic constituencies. The ethical value of this difference resides in alerting the reader that a process of domestication has taken place in the translating, but also in preventing that process from slipping into an unreflective assimilation to dominant domestic values. Foreign philosophies can retain their difference in translation when they differ to some extent from those that currently dominate the discipline at home, or when they are translated so as to differ from prevailing domestic interpretations of their concepts and discourses. The best philosophical translating is itself philosophical in forming a concept of the foreign text based on an assessment of the domestic scene. But if the philosophy of the translating values difference, the concept will be defamiliarizing, not based on a ratification of that scene.

The translator's responsibility is not just twofold, both foreign and domestic, but split into two opposing obligations: to establish a lexicographical equivalence for a conceptually dense text, while intelligibly maintaining its foreignness to domestic readerships. Translating motivated by an ethics of difference seeks to inform domestic readers of foreign philosophies, but also to provoke them into new thinking. It acknowledges that foreign concepts and discourses can change domestic institutions by forcing a self-criticism and by stimulating the invention of new philosophies, new philosophical canons and curricula, new qualifications for academic philosophers. And it takes responsibility for these possible consequences by manipulating the remainder, the target-language effects that signal the second-order status of the translation by distinguishing it from the foreign text.

Philosophical translating can of course assume another sense of responsibility. The translator may follow an ethics of sameness: choosing foreign texts and developing discursive strategies so as to shore up institutional limits, establishing a domestic equivalence for foreign concepts and discourses that minimizes their unsettling differences. This translating, although it may be considered accurate within the discipline, risks showing less regard for the foreign text than for the domestic status quo. And its efforts to strengthen reigning interpretations are not immune to the variations that accompany domestic dialects, discourses, institutions, and audiences. The linguistic peculiarities released by the remainder provide a textual basis for judging a philosophical translation because they constitute a means of gauging how much the foreign text has succumbed to or resisted the domestication performed during the translating process. It was in fact Anscombe's strikingly heterogeneous language that allowed her to preserve the eccentricity of Wittgenstein's philosophy – and attract the criticisms and revisions of more domesticating commentators.

English-language translators of philosophical texts have long shown an awareness of the remainder, of the irreducible difference introduced by the translation, but they have tended to restrain it by adhering to the Anglo-American preference for fluency, immediate intelligibility, the illusion of transparent communication. As a result, they have not been very critical of the domestic values that the remainder inscribes in the foreign text. Benjamin Jowett, the distinguished Victorian translator of Plato, asserted that a translation "should be based, in the first instance, on an intimate knowledge of the text," but also that "it should read as an original work," concealing not merely its status as a translation, but the translator's decision to "sacrifice minute accuracy for the sake of clearness and sense" (Jowett 1892: xv, xvi). To secure transparency, Jowett recommended a homogeneous English style that relies mostly on current usage, recognizable and therefore highly accessible: "no word, however expressive and exact, should be employed, which makes the reader stop to think, or unduly attracts attention by difficulty or peculiarity, or disturbs the effect of the surrounding language" (ibid.: xxii). Yet despite this effort to control the excesses of the remainder, Jowett's own literary and religious values visibly shaped his work. He allowed that "equivalents may be drawn from Shakespeare," provided that they are "used sparingly," and "a similar principle should be observed in the employment of Scripture" (ibid.). Jowett's version of Plato mixed Jacobean with later literary forms, especially the style of the King James Bible, producing a rich strain of archaism that Steiner has described as "the language of 1611 [. . .] filtered through that of the later seventeenth century and that of the Victorian poets" (Steiner 1975: 345–346). This translation aligned the Greek texts with dominant traditions in English culture, helping to ensure that Platonic philosophy would simultaneously lose some of its pagan unfamiliarity and retain its canonical status in academic institutions.

Trevor Saunders, the contemporary editor and translator of Plato's texts, has been deeply influenced by Jowett's recommendations, but he is much more self-conscious about translating for specific domestic readerships. Jowett set out from the populist belief that "an English translation ought to be idiomatic and interesting, not only to the scholar, but to the unlearned reader" (Jowett 1892: xiv), overlooking the fact that only a fairly educated reader could appreciate the literary and religious remainder in his Plato. Saunders similarly believed that the *Laws*, Plato's detailed plan for a utopian state, carried a broad appeal, potentially interesting "lawyers, sociologists, historians, philosophers, theologians, and many others" (Saunders 1987a: 160). Yet, in contrast to Jowett, he saw his translation as a scholarly project, a reformation of the academic canon of Platonic texts as it stood during the 1960s:

> The style of a version must, it is true, be determined partly by the nature and purpose of the original text; but it must be determined also by the current status of the text and the characteristics of the intended readership of the translation. What is the status of the *Laws*? It is Plato's bulkiest work, and probably his most neglected; it has few partisans, and the intended readership is indifferent or lukewarm. In that situation, the best service the translator can do for the *Laws* is to ensure that it shall be *read*.
>
> (ibid.: 157)

Saunders's "intended readership" consisted primarily of university-based scholars, teachers, and students where "partisans" of Platonic texts can usually be found. He was writing a translation that would appear in the Penguin Classics, the paperback series that was designed to bring entertaining versions of canonical texts to a mass readership, but that under the editorship of Betty Radice turned more academic and increasingly served university courses (Radice 1987: 21–22). Hence, while agreeing with Jowett that any translation "should read like an original composition" (Saunders 1987a: 155), Saunders deliberately relied on English dialects, registers, and discourses that made his version at once familiar and transparent to educated readers. And, as he himself admitted, the domesticating movement in his version was so strong as to result in mistranslation and anachronism. He explained, for example, that to render one Greek phrase (*kerdos kai rastonen*) he used a Shakespeareanism, "cakes and ale," instead of the accurate "profit and ease" because "the Shakespearean expression seemed to me to catch the tone of the remark so well that I deliberately jettisoned accuracy for readability" (ibid.: 158). The publishing history of Saunders's translation shows beyond a doubt that his strategies were effective in bringing Plato's *Laws* to the attention of English-language readers: it has remained in print for more than twenty-five years.

Nonetheless, Saunders definitely underestimated the workings of the remainder. In justifying his pursuit of readability, he argued that "a calculated and deliberate – and modest – exaggeration of certain relatively unimportant features of the text is a perfectly legitimate method of enticing readers" (ibid.: 157). But "exaggeration" doesn't begin to describe the metacommentary that might be constructed from his textual effects, wherein what seemed "unimportant" can assume considerable interpretive force – particularly from a materialist perspective.

In the *Laws* he felt that a close rendering of "xenoi" ("strangers," "foreigners") "would have jarred in modern English," so throughout he replaced it with English words like "sir" and "gentlemen," which appeared to "catch something of the three elderly speakers' staid formality" (ibid.: 158). "Strangers" is indeed jarring in modern English, an alienating way to refer to one's interlocutors, but only because it points to a historical difference: the issue of ethnic and political identity was of such central importance in ancient Greek culture that it could enter unoffensively into everyday conversation as well as become the basis of social oppression, including discrimination against non-Greeks and Athenian imperialism in the Peloponnesus. "Xenoi" ambiguously referred both to a "guest" and a "stranger" (or "foreigner"), although a stranger who might also be another Greek (Delacampagne 1983: 189; Liddell and Scott 1882). It appears in the opening sentence of Plato's *Laws*, where a character called the "Athenian Stranger" (variously taken to be Plato himself or Aristotle) greets the Cretan Cleinias and the Spartan Megillus with a question that resonates with ethnic and political rivalry. Saunders's version reads, "Tell me, gentlemen [*xenoi*], to whom do you give the credit for establishing your codes of law? Is it a god, or a man?" (Saunders 1970: 45). The choice of "gentlemen" removes any implication of rivalry while adding a politeness and mutual respect that are missing from both "xenoi" and "strangers." More than establishing a tone or manner of speaking, Saunders's version depicts Plato's dialogue as an exchange of ideas that is democratic, even if staidly formal, a "genial conversation" (Saunders 1987a: 155).

What is questionable about this effect is not so much that the Greek text suffers a loss – some loss is inevitable in translating – as that the loss is not supplied by a compensatory difference in the domestic culture: Saunders's is a deferential representation of Platonic philosophy, deferring both to modern English usage and to the modern canonization of Plato's work. Saunders knew quite well that any translation attaches a domestic range of reference to the foreign text. But because he cultivated this reference only to improve readability, he stopped short of figuring its impact on the thematic level of the text, its creation of new interpretive possibilities.

Continental philosophy has most inspired English-language translators to challenge the discursive regime of transparency and experiment with the remainder. And the experiments have often been successful in preserving the linguistic and cultural difference of this philosophy on the Anglo-American scene. Translators of Martin Heidegger's texts have been particularly effective in developing new translation strategies, not only because his neologisms and etymologies, puns and grammatical shifts demand comparable inventiveness, but also because his texts address translation as a philosophical problem, exploring its decisive role in constituting the meaning of concepts. With rare exceptions, these translators have been academic philosophers who allowed Heidegger's philosophy to increase their translatorly self-consciousness, as well as inform their own philosophical research. Even here, however, the pull of domestication hasn't diminished, just taken different shapes. John Macquarrie and Edward Robinson's version of *Being and Time* did more than enough to reproduce Heidegger's stylistic peculiarities, partly by finding English that is equally peculiar and partly by relying on various scholarly conventions, like a glossary of key terms and detailed footnotes that explain the limitations of particular renderings. All the same, the translators admitted to making "numerous concessions to the reader" that conform to current English usage and alter the conceptual density of the German – for instance, inserting "personal constructions where Heidegger has avoided them" (Heidegger 1962: 15) and thereby complicating his anti-individualistic concept of human subjectivity.

In 1962 such deviations proved to be inconsequential, too minimal to make Heidegger's philosophy any more accessible to English-language readers. The American pragmatist Sidney Hook wrote a mixed review that acknowledged Heidegger's enormous influence in Europe, but concluded that "few philosophers will find the rewards of discovery commensurate with the pains of diving into and dredging [his book's] murky depths" (Hook 1962: 6). The first step in preserving the foreignness of Heidegger's text was of course Macquarrie and Robinson's decision to translate it: Heidegger's essays had been translated throughout the 1950s, amid popularizations of existentialism by academic philosophers (e.g. Barrett 1947), but his style of thinking deviated so widely from the logical analysis prevailing in Anglo-American philosophy that he remained an alien figure in English deep into the 1970s. Today, when Continental philosophical traditions have gained greater acceptance in British and American universities and leading American philosophers like Richard Rorty feel they must take account of Heidegger's work (e.g. Rorty 1979), it's clear that his translators played a crucial role in reforming the canon of foreign philosophies in English.

For the translation of philosophy, the most important factor in this development is the experimentalism. Heidegger's translators created an equivalence that tampered with current usage, whereby they didn't just communicate his difficult concepts, but practiced them through various discursive strategies. David Farrell Krell's version of "The Anaximander Fragment" is a dazzling enactment of the translation theory that Heidegger himself at once expounded and enacted in translating Anaximander's Greek.

Following Schleiermacher's notion of translation as bringing the domestic reader to the foreign text, Heidegger argued that "our thinking must first, before translating, be translated to what is said in Greek" by abandoning modern "pre-suppositions" that are anachronistic and antithetical to the ancient experience of "Being" (Heidegger 1975: 19, 22). Because Anaximander was able to think of "Being" as the "presencing" of things, we must avoid assimilating the fragment to later metaphysical traditions that are positivist or idealist, that follow Aristotle or Plato in aiming to analyze or transcend existence, what Heidegger called the "collapse of thinking into the sciences and faith" (ibid.: 40). These traditions entered into the "standard translation" of the Greek text, where Anaximander's thinking is represented as a moral cosmology, a "philosophy of nature" in which "inappropriate moralisms and legalisms are enmeshed" (ibid.: 22). Heidegger cited the classicist Hermann Diels's close version, written in a modern German filled with moral and philosophical abstractions:

> es on de e genesis esti tois ousi kai ten phthoran eis tauta ginesthai kata to chreon. didonai gar auta diken kai tisin allelois tes adikias kata ten tou chronou taxin.

> Woraus aber die Dinge das Enststehen haben, dahin geht auch ihr Vergehen nach der Notwendigkeit; denn sie zahlen einander Strafe und Buße für ihre Ruchlosigkeit nach der festgesetzten Zeit.

> But where things have their origin, there too their passing away occurs according to necessity; for they pay recompense and penalty to one another for their recklessness, according to firmly established time.
>   (Heidegger 1972: 296; 1975: 13)

For Heidegger, the translation that best reproduces early Greek thinking is "poetizing": it does "violence" to everyday language by relying on German archaisms whose kinship to the Greek words he demonstrated in elaborate etymological interpretations (Heidegger 1975: 19). The essay concluded with his partial version of the fragment, a free rewriting that even involves a parenthetical insertion:

> . . . entlang dem Brauch; gehören nämlich lassen sie Fug somit auch Ruch eines dem anderen (im Verwinden) des Un-Fugs.

> . . . along the lines of usage; for they let order and thereby also reck belong to one another (in the surmounting) of disorder.
>   (Heidegger 1972: 342; 1975: 57)

Krell followed Heidegger's German closely and managed to find an English equivalent for at least one of the key archaisms. Whereas Heidegger resorted to two words from Middle High German, "Fug" and "Ruch," which he redefined as "order" and "care" on the basis of later variants, "Unfug" ("nonsense," "disorder") and "Ruchlos" ("reckless"), Krell used "reck," an Anglo-Saxon word that fell into disuse during the early modern period, was revived in the nineteenth century as a poeticism, and is currently obsolete (*OED*). The repetition of the unfamiliar "reck" throughout Krell's version works powerfully upon the English-language reader: it underscores the conceptual density that Heidegger assigns to the German *Ruch*, the archaic ontological value of the term, while calling attention to the foreignness of his thinking in relation to contemporary Anglo-American philosophy. The translation made reviewers aware that they were reading a translation, and a very accomplished one, not to be confused with the text that Heidegger wrote. Thus, they not only judged Krell's work successful because it was "faithful," but praised it for clarifying the German (Collins 1975: 2056; Caputo 1979: 759). "What more can one say about a translation," wrote John Caputo, "than that it helps one to understand the original?"

The unpredictability of the remainder, however, comes back to haunt the translations, Heidegger's as well as Krell's. Archaism is undoubtedly a very effective choice in translating an essay whose theme is ancient thinking and whose method is etymology. Krell peppered his version with other English archaisms to render German words that are not obsolete, but in common use. He translated "Graben" ("trench," "ditch") as "abyss"; "in ihrem täglichen niederen und hohen Gebrauch" ("in its daily low and high use") as "in common everyday parlance as well as in its learned employ"; "Beständigen" ("standing," "fixed," "enduring") as "perduring"; and "mächtiger" ("powerful," "potent," "mighty") as "puissant" (Heidegger 1972: 303, 313, 328, 341; 1975: 19, 28, 42, 55). In making these choices, Krell was clearly answering Heidegger's call for a poetizing translation of philosophical texts, yet the poeticisms tend to be linked to early modern English literature, to the work of Sidney, Shakespeare, and Milton, among others. This is most obvious in Krell's translation of "aus den Fugen" as "out of joint," where Heidegger's concern with the disappearance of Being gets refracted through Hamlet's anxiety about the moral chaos of the Danish court: "The time is out of joint," says Hamlet, "O cursed spite / That ever I was born to set it right!" (Heidegger 1972: 327; 1975: 41). Krell's translation subtly links Heidegger's philosophy to canonical texts and traditions in English, helping in some small degree to situate him in the English-language canon of foreign philosophies. Yet this literary allusiveness questions Heidegger's belief that poetizing translation is somehow more "faithful" to early Greek philosophy because "its terms are words which speak from the language of the matter itself" (Heidegger 1975: 14). On the contrary, Krell's version shows that translation, even when it experiments to preserve the linguistic and cultural difference of the foreign text, is likely to contain anachronisms, deviations and excesses, because it releases a domestic remainder. Krell's archaisms communicate Heidegger's philosophical theme and imitate his peculiar style, but they suggest that the ancient Greek experience of Being isn't disclosed but displaced in translation, that it can never be more than the historical variations of the translating language, and these can only be glimpsed when contemporary linguistic practices are disrupted (cf. Benjamin 1989: 31–38).

The translation of philosophical texts can be improved, and the issue of translation productively introduced in philosophical interpretation, if translators take a more experimental approach to their work. Current translation practices show that translators' prefaces, glossaries, and annotations are helpful in clarifying the conceptual density of key terms and in indicating their foreignness among domestic philosophical trends. But any such apparatus can only gesture at the effects of the remainder, its literary and historical resonances in the target language and the metacommentary they make possible. This means that philosophical translation must become more literary so as to release an appropriate domestic remainder for foreign concepts and discourses. However unpredictable the remainder may ultimately be, it nonetheless requires translators to respond creatively to the stylistic pressures exerted by the philosophical project of concept formation.

Deleuze and Guattari commented on the "element of style" in philosophical writing:

> some concepts must be indicated by an extraordinary and sometimes even barbarous or shocking word, whereas others make do with an ordinary, everyday word that is filled with harmonics so distant that it risks being imperceptible to a nonphilosophical ear. Some concepts call for archaisms, and other for neologisms, shot through with almost crazy etymological exercises [. . .] The concept's baptism calls for a specifically philosophical *taste* that proceeds with violence or by insinuation and constitutes a philosophical language within language – not just a vocabulary but a syntax that attains the sublime or a great beauty.
>
> (Deleuze and Guattari 1994: 7–8)

By developing a philosophical language, then, the philosopher faces a choice between maintaining or varying the major language – i.e., the standard dialect, the philosophical canon, the dominant concepts and discourses. The taste that the philosopher exercises is not simply literary, but social, having some bearing upon institutional limits: a style of philosophical writing may insinuate itself among or violate the philosophies that currently hold sway in the discipline, adhering to the major language or admitting the minor linguistic forms that it excludes (e.g. the "shocking word," archaism, neologism) and thus creating what Deleuze and Guattari elsewhere call a minor literature (see Deleuze and Guattari 1987, especially chap. 4). A stylistic innovation in a philosophical text might indeed be too esoteric, too discipline-bound, for the "nonphilosophical ear"; yet if it is drawn from minor forms, from linguistic and literary traditions that deviate from the dominant philosophical discourses, then it might indeed reach nonspecialist readers. If philosophy is practiced as a minor literature, it marks and crosses the current limits of the academic institution.

For the translator, a more literary approach turns the philosophical translation into a minor literature within the literature of philosophy. The experimental translation is minoritizing: it creates a philosophical language that challenges the domestic hierarchy of philosophical languages. The translation that in contrast avoids stylistic innovation will have an insinuating impact on the domestic discipline, assimilating the foreign text to the standard dialect, the dominant philosophies, the prevailing interpretations. Only the experimental translation can signify the linguistic and cultural difference of the foreign text by deterritorializing the major language and opening the institution to new concepts and discourses. By taking account of translation, philosophy doesn't come to an end, doesn't become poetry or history, but rather expands to embrace other kinds of thinking and writing.

7

THE BESTSELLER

Among the decisive factors in the current marginality of translation is its tenuous economic value. Quite simply, publishers keep the volume of translations low because such books are financially risky: they are so costly to produce, requiring a significant initial outlay for translation rights, the translator's fee, and marketing, that publishers generally regard them as inevitable losses, possessing only cultural capital, useful as a means "to enhance the variety and appeal of their lists" (Purdy 1971: 10). Since the 1970s, furthermore, the drive to invest in bestsellers has become so prevalent as to focus the publisher's attention on foreign texts that were commercially successful in their native cultures, allowing the editorial and translating process to be guided by the hope of a similar performance in a different language and culture. And yet translations that reward investment, especially those that become bestsellers, risk the stigma of scholars and critics who possess the cultural authority to shape taste and affect long-term sales. The appeal of translations to a mass readership invites the cultural elite to dismiss them as "popular" or "middlebrow," "as failed attempts to approximate the achievement of the best books" according to the judgment of the literary press and academic institutions (Radway 1989: 260). Translation is thus squeezed in a double bind, both commercial and cultural, which threatens to restrict access to foreign literatures and to reduce them to the status of domestic ephemera, passing with the changing interests of the broadest possible audience, falling out of print when sales diminish.

It is this very predicament, of course, that enables translation to expose the scandalous conditions under which publishing decisions and literary evaluations are made with foreign texts. Since "bestsellers have been books which address major concerns of a population" (Dudovitz 1990: 25), publishing a translation can be highly profitable only when it meets expectations that currently prevail in the domestic culture. The publisher's approach to the foreign text, then, is primarily commercial, even imperialistic, an exploitation governed by an estimate of the market at home, whereas the approach of the domestic reader is primarily self-referential, even narcissistic, insofar as the translation is expected to reinforce literary, moral, religious, or political values already held by that reader (this expectation is certainly held by some publishers). A bestselling translation tends to reveal much more about the domestic culture for which it was produced, than the foreign culture which it is taken to represent. These revelations include the dubious but inescapable fact that the foreign text has been made to serve domestic interests, and therefore neither sales projections nor reviews can be seen as true and objective assessments of its value.

On the contrary, the foreign text that achieves bestseller status in translation becomes a site where values proliferate unexpectedly. Translations exemplify Pierre Nora's category of the "bestseller *inattendu*," the book whose success is unforeseeable (Ozouf and Ferney 1985: 67). His examples include Françoise Sagan's 1955 novel *Bonjour Tristesse*, which was a bestseller in French and in many other languages worldwide. The "rule" that defines this sort of bestseller, says Nora,

> is transgression, a violation of its natural sociological space, its explo-
> sion among publics for which it was not intended. The prof at the
> Collège de France that starts to be read in thatched cottages. The
> left-wing book [. . .] whose anti–intellectualism fragments the right;
> or the right-wing book that starts to be read by a left shaken out
> of its maoist cult.
>
> (ibid.)

Nora's view of the bestseller is obviously based on a diagnosis of a peculiarly French cultural and political situation. Nonetheless, it implicitly describes the cultural conditions in which any book, translated or not, becomes a bestseller. Nora assumes that the reading audience consists of several distinct constituencies, each characterized by specific values. Since a bestseller by definition reaches a mass readership, it must appeal to different constituencies, and so it inevitably crosses the cultural borders between them. When the bestseller is also a translation, the border crossings increase. A translation reaches the bestseller list when it is capable of supporting values and performing functions for which neither the foreign text nor the translation itself was intended. The shift from the foreign to domestic culture detaches the foreign text from the linguistic and literary traditions where it draws its significance, ensuring that it will be interpreted and evaluated differently in translation. And as the translation circulates within the domestic culture, it will lead multiple lives among various social groups. Since the bestseller treats issues that are of interest and concern to the broadest segment of the reading audience, the treatment offered by a bestselling translation must be intelligible within the different, potentially conflicting codes and ideologies that characterize that audience. Hence, the translation will put to work discursive strategies that facilitate its appeal to a mass readership.

The bestseller is a cultural form that hews to the popular aesthetic. Here every element is based on the affirmation of continuity between art and life, which implies the subordination of form to function, [. . .] a refusal of the refusal which is the starting point of the high aesthetic, i.e., the clear-cut separation of ordinary dispositions from the specifically aesthetic disposition.

(Bourdieu 1984: 32).

Bestsellers blur the distinction between art and life by sharing a specific discourse: although cast into various genres – fiction and nonfiction, novel and history, romance and memoir, horror and self-help – they favor melo-dramatic realism that solicits the reader's vicarious participation (Cawelti 1976; Radway 1984; Dudovitz 1990). This is perhaps most clear with best-selling fiction, which depends for its success on the reader's sympathetic identification with characters who confront contemporary social problems. In Resa Dudovitz's anatomy of novels addressed to women,

the narrative strategy is twofold: on the one hand, if the text is to speak to current issues, the novelist must create a world the reader recognizes. On the other, the escapist nature of the fiction demands a certain degree of fantasy. Simplicity of language, reliance on stereo-typical and trite images, the absence of psychological subtlety, and readily identifiable characters permit the reader easy access to the imaginative world because the values these characters represent are obvious and well known to the reader.

(Dudovitz 1990: 47–48)

Since identification is the characteristic experience produced by bestselling novels, the pleasure they give can be compensatory: a realistic narrative addressing contemporary problems presents imaginary solutions in terms of dominant cultural and political values. To give this pleasure, moreover, the narrative must be immediately comprehensible, and so the language must fix precise meanings in simple, continuous syntax and the most familiar lexicon. The emphasis on function, on communication and reference instead of the high aesthetic appreciation of form, makes the language seemingly transparent, thereby producing the illusion of reality that invites the reader's identification.

The realism typical of the popular aesthetic dictates parallel strategies for bestselling translations. Not only are publishers more inclined to choose real-istic foreign texts for translation, neglecting foreign literatures distinguished by formal experiments that frustrate the "deep-rooted demand for partici-pation" (Bourdieu 1984: 32), but they also insist on fluent translations that produce the illusory effect of transparency, of seeming untranslated. Fluent strategies pursue linear syntax, univocal meaning, current usage, lexical consis-tency; they eschew unidiomatic constructions, polysemy, archaism, jargon, any linguistic effect that calls attention to the words as words and therefore preempts or interrupts the reader's identification. In fluent translating the emphasis is placed on familiarity, on making the language so recognizable as to be invisible. This guarantees not only that the foreign text will reach the widest possible domestic audience, but that the text will undergo an extensive domestication, an inscription with cultural and political values that currently prevail in the domestic situation – including those values according to which the foreign culture is represented. To enable the foreign text to engage a mass readership, the bestselling translation must be intelligible within the various domestic identities that have been constructed for the foreign culture, often stereotypes that permit easy recognition. In the mirror of the bestselling translation, domestic readers who adopt a popular approach are likely to take a realistic representation inflected with their own codes and ideologies for an immediate encounter with a foreign text and culture.

To document and develop these observations, I want to consider the English-language translations from the work of Giovanni Guareschi, an Italian writer who was an international bestseller for more than two decades after World War II. Guareschi (1908–68) wrote comic fiction with a sharp satiric edge. His most popular books featured Don Camillo, a priest in a northern Italian village who engages in amusing ideological skirmishes with the Communist mayor, Peppone, and always comes out the victor. Guareschi was translated during the Cold War, the political and economic struggle between the Western democracies and the Communist bloc, so that his worldwide popularity stemmed in large part from his recurrent theme of anti-Communism. Yet in order to achieve bestseller status in translation, Guareschi's books had to meet cultural expectations that were necessarily diverse, appealing to different domestic constituencies, and these expectations necessarily deviated from the ones he met in Italy.

Guareschi's success in English illuminates the place of the bestselling translation in the political economy of Anglo-American culture during the postwar period. We can see how the choice of the foreign text, the development of a discursive strategy to translate it, and the reception of the translation are each inscribed with codes and ideologies that support political agendas in the domestic culture, while constructing a cultural identity for the foreign country. With Guareschi, as with most bestselling translations, the popular aesthetic forges a broad cultural consensus that conceals the contradictions among domestic tastes and interests, but also between them and contemporary developments in the foreign culture.

The reception

Between 1950 and 1970, twelve English translations of Guareschi's writing were issued in the United States, and most of them were enormous bestsellers. The first, *The Little World of Don Camillo* (1950), became an immediate success, landing on bestseller lists in several magazines and newspapers, including the *Chicago Tribune* and the *New York Times*, and gaining national distribution through mail-order book clubs like the Book-of-the-Month Club and the Catholic Digest Book Club. Within two years the book sold roughly a quarter of a million copies, and it set a pattern that would be followed by other Guareschi translations. The second, *Don Camillo and His Flock* (1952), sold 185,000 copies within a comparable period. The third, a collection of autobiographical stories entitled *The House That Nino Built* (1953), the fourth, *Don Camillo's Dilemma* (1954), and the fifth, *Don Camillo Takes the Devil by the Tail* (1957), all sold over 25,000 copies within a few months of publication. Not only did Guareschi's books sell briskly in large initial printings, but since they were continuously in print over two decades, their sales were sustained in successive reprintings and paperback editions.

They repeated this performance, furthermore, in many other countries. Every Guareschi translation published in the United States later became a best-seller in England, and many were also distributed through book clubs. In 1955, an omnibus volume containing the first three Don Camillo books was adopted by the British-based Companion Book Club, whose membership was approximately a quarter of a million. At the same time, Guareschi's books were being translated into twenty-seven languages worldwide, achieving similar success in other Western European nations (the first Don Camillo sold 800,000 in France), but also reaching countries in the Communist bloc or under Communist domination, including Czechoslovakia, Hungary, Poland, Korea, and Vietnam. The global figure for the sale of Guareschi's books was estimated to be 20 million in 1957, when he had a decade of writing ahead of him. [1]

Guareschi's anti-Communism was undoubtedly a key factor in his popularity. In the United States, the Don Camillo books hit an exposed nerve among readers – a national fear of Communism – and numbed it. *The Little World of Don Camillo* was published in August of 1950 when this fear reached a high point. American involvement in the Korean War was entering its second month amid the threat of a Chinese Communist intervention. Campaigns for the fall congressional elections were filled with "unusual amounts of scurrility, distortion, and redbaiting," in which candidates claimed to present evidence of their opponents' Communist sympathies (Fried 1974: 219). Congress was debating the Internal Security Act, legislation that would identify "Communist organizations" and brand them as political conspiracies, and the press joined politicians in fabricating an underground network of Communist subversives, which only seemed to be confirmed by the Rosenbergs' arrests for espionage in July and August (Caute 1978: 38–39, 446–449).

Many of Guareschi's reviewers glanced at this tense, maniacal situation and welcomed the utopian comfort provided by Don Camillo's humorous victories over the Communist mayor. At the *Saturday Review of Literature*, the first volume was featured on the cover, and one of the editors wrote an article that made explicit the political terms of Guareschi's reception:

Here is a book for what ails you. Whether you are suffering from the heat, a case of sunburn, or an overdose of newspaper headlines about Korea, Giovanni Guareschi's bright, enchanting little book will cure it. This is all the more remarkable because although *The Little World of Don Camillo* on the surface merely reports a series of altercations between the parish priest and the mayor of an Italian village, it actually has some sage things to say about the huge and grim problem that haunts us all today: the battle of the free world against Communism.

(Walters 1950)[2]

Although Guareschi contributed a preface to the English translation that described the "background of these stories [as] my home, Parma, the Emilian plain along the Po" (Guareschi 1950: 8), the reviewer read them as an allegory of current international politics. And the code for this allegorical reading was the Truman Doctrine, the foreign policy whereby the United States set out to contain Soviet expansion by assisting foreign countries who were perceived to be threatened by it. The reviewer was echoing Truman's 1947 message to Congress, which argued that "totalitarian regimes imposed upon free peoples, by direct or indirect aggression, undermine the foundations of international peace and hence the security of the United States" (Truman 1963: 176). Guareschi's writing articulated a worldwide concern about Communism during the 1950s, but in the United States the prevalent response assimilated the Italian text to distinctly American codes and ideologies, in response to a distinctly American cultural and political situation.

This domestication signals the importance of the popular aesthetic to understanding Guareschi's success. American reviewers tended to treat his writing as a topical allegory because they assumed a continuity between art and life. They voiced the popular demand for vicarious participation in a narrative that offers some moral application (Bourdieu 1984: 4–5). The Don Camillo books were so warmly received because they invited a deep readerly involvement in their entertaining solution for the most alarming American "problem." This too is clear in the *Saturday Review* article:

In all probability as you read Mr. Guareschi's delightful book, you will start identifying yourself with Don Camillo in his battle in behalf of the free world against Communism. If we of the free world will only fight with the courage, strength, faith, – yes, and good humor – of Don Camillo, his victories will surely be ours.

(Walters 1950)

An occasional reviewer found Guareschi's solution not entirely acceptable because too utopian, too implausibly "romantic" in its depiction of Communists (Paulding 1952: 6). But even such skeptics took the popular approach of the enthusiastically rapt majority by asking that this Italian writer perform an ethical function in American culture, establishing an ideal of conduct, however unattainable: "They are all nice people in Don Camillo's little world and it is a pity that there is not much chance that ours can be made to resemble it" (ibid.).

Guareschi's Don Camillo books achieved bestseller status in the United States not simply because they were anti-Communist, but because, under the aegis of the popular aesthetic, their version of anti-Communism was agreeable to familiar, domestic values. These values included ethnic stereotypes for Italy. Reviewer after reviewer praised Guareschi for his peculiarly "Italian" point of view, an ethnicity that was defined as antithetical to Communism on various grounds, biological, psychological, moral, religious. "In his books," wrote the reviewer for the Catholic magazine *Commonweal*, "the Communists, for all their roaring, are not monsters. Underneath their big talk they are still emotionally charged Italians whose first love is the Church" (Gable 1952: 492). *Life* made the same equation of "Italian" with emotion and Catholicism in a long profile of Guareschi. The magazine performed a popular reduction of a cultural form (here opera) to Italian "life," creating an ethnic psychology to explain the contest between Don Camillo and Peppone: "Such is the operatic nature of the Italian temperament that the sharp edges of ideological issues are continuously blurred by intrigue, compromise, drama, confusion and emotion" (Sargeant 1952: 125). The Book-of-the-Month Club, in line with its popular view of fiction as "a tool for enabling its reader to move about more effectively in the world" (Radway 1989: 278), saw Guareschi expressing "that mixture of tragic acceptance of destiny and philosophic laughter which we regard as characteristically Latin" (*Book-of-the-Month Club News* 1950: 8). Yet "this familiar national trait," although attributed to Italy, was comparable to "the manner of Charlie Chaplin," culture that was not Italian, but recognizable to Americans, if not recognized as American (ibid.: 6).

Guareschi's writing also fed into an American stereotype for Italy that was profoundly masculinist. *Commonweal* opened its review of *The Little World of Don Camillo* by asserting that

> Guareschi's book confirms the general idea of Italy, land of stocky olive-skinned men with black mustaches and impetuous gestures. The people are poor, eat tremendous amounts of *pasta*, and drink tolerable red wine. The families are large, the wives submissive, and the children impertinent. They are good people, *brava gente*.
>
> (Hughes 1950: 540)

While Guareschi's writing confirmed an American stereotype for Italians, it was also reinforcing a value that dominated American culture during the 1950s, the patriarchal family, wherein the masculine ideal was represented

as physical and moral strength (May 1988). This ideal carried political implications: it defined the loyal American citizen, whereas subversive Communist
sympathizers and spies were seen as weak, effeminate, homosexual (Edelman
1993; Savran 1992). In *The Vital Center: The Politics of Freedom* (1949), the
historian Arthur Schlesinger Jr. described the American "fellow traveler" as
"soft, not hard" and argued that Communism "perverts politics into something secret, sweaty and furtive like nothing so much, in the phrase of one
wise observer of modern Russia, as homosexuals in a boys' school"
(Schlesinger 1949: 36, 151). What American readers saw in Guareschi was
a writer who substantiated the ideological link between the power of male
heterosexuality and anti-Communism.

Guareschi himself, his own physical appearance, called forth these terms.
An interviewer for the *New York Times Book Review* remarked that he looked
"formidable":

A man of about 40, of medium height and built like a wrestler, he
has enormous scraggy black mustachios, an unexplored jungle of
black hair, and a suit of clothes that looks as if it had been slept
in. Behind this formidable exterior are a gentle, sensitive spirit, a
maddeningly perverse sense of humor and a personal integrity which
has often gotten him into hot water. The sense of humor, politically applied, won him in 1948 the accolade of public denunciation
by the chairman of the Italian Communist party.

(Clark 1950: 13)

Guareschi's anti-Communism expressed a virility that was both physical and
moral, a rugged individualism ("personal integrity") that would be especially
congenial to American readers absorbing the Cold War representation of
Communism as totalitarianism, a threat to individual autonomy. But the
interviewer went further in taking a popular address toward Guareschi's
masculine image: he was associated with familiar Hollywood film characters
and actors ("the hard-boiled police reporter in an Italian production of *The
Front Page*"; "the movie tough guy," Humphrey Bogart), and the emphasis
on his dishevelled look positioned him in the working class, where "aesthetic
refinement, particularly as regards clothing or cosmetics, is reserved for
women by a representation, more strict than in any other class, of the sexual
division of labour and sexual morality" (Bourdieu 1984: 382). Guareschi's
neglect of his hair and clothing was laden with political significance:
"Guareschi," wrote the interviewer, "just can't be bothered about his personal
appearance. In fact, he can't be bothered about much of anything except
the Communist party, which he loathes" (Clark 1950: 13).

It was this ideological configuration, fashioning a particular gender, class,
and national identity, that characterized the American reception of Guareschi's
writing. His autobiographical stories about his family charmed American

readers among whom "husbands, especially fathers, wore the badge of 'family man' as a sign of virility and patriotism" (May 1988: 98). *The House That Nino Built* (1953) represented Guareschi as the breadwinner whose patriarchal authority underwent comical challenges from his wife, Margherita, and his two children, challenges which, although never decisive, were occasionally formulated in political terms. "If I did not have such great respect for Margherita," sighs Guareschi's stand-in Giovannino, "I would say that her tactics are typically Communist" (Guareschi 1953a: 85). The Don Camillo books spoke directly to the American link between masculinity and anti-Communism because the conflicts always involve extremely physical male characters and sometimes take violent forms. When Don Camillo hears Peppone's Communist propaganda, "the veins in [his] neck [are] very soon swelled to the size of cables" (Guareschi 1950: 89). Don Camillo tends to intimidate his political opponents by punching or kicking them. In a story entitled "The Avenger," he even masquerades as a boxer so that he can defeat the local Communist champion by a knockout.

The success of the Don Camillo books depended on their assimilation to highly charged American values, and the values they supported were diverse, even contradictory. One of the paradoxes in Guareschi's reception is that the ethnic stereotyping coincided with a humanism that erased all difference, ethnic, religious, political, national. The popular aesthetic that seeks some moral application in narrative transformed his anti-Communism from a peculiarly Italian characteristic to a universal truth about "humanity." The reviewer for the *New Republic* rehearsed the familiar Italian stereotype: "Although Peppone and his 'gang' mouth the usual Stalinist clichés, they are basically far too Italian and too Catholic to feel morally clothed without the presence of the Church" (Cooperman 1952: 23). But to account for Guareschi's best-seller status, the reviewer abandoned these distinctions:

> The secret of Guareschi's success, of course, is the complete and irresponsible humanity of his cast. Don Camillo may be a priest, but a big-fisted, broad-chested and delightfully mercurial man all the same. And Peppone, the Communist mayor of the village and Don Camillo's chief antagonist, is equally human – a far cry from the demoniac political caricatures which seem to be rushing about everywhere.
>
> (ibid.)

Guareschi's books were able to remove the threat that Americans perceived in an opposing ideology – namely Communism – by suggesting that there was no opposition. Peppone is the same as Don Camillo: "human." Yet the concept of "humanity" assumed by the reviewer indicates that this solution was itself ideological. The human was defined as uniquely individual: Don Camillo and Peppone each possess a complex personality that deviates from the roles fixed for them by social institutions (the Catholic Church, the Communist party) and by ideological abstractions ("political caricatures"). The reviewer's humanism was thus liberal and democratic, based on a notion of personal autonomy that all enjoy ("equally human"). It was also, of course, anti-Communist: as the reviewer for the *Baltimore Sun* put it, "by developing the human side of these men and women, Guareschi points up the incompatibility of Red ideology and practice with the Italian's fundamental humanity" (Gallagher 1952: 30). In the United States, the reception of the Don Camillo books was marked by a liberal humanism that simultaneously concealed its own ideological status and excluded political opponents from its definition of humanity.

To highlight the distinctly American nature of this reception, we need only glance at Guareschi's very different impact in Italy. He began publishing the Don Camillo stories in 1946 in the magazine he edited, *Candido*, a mass-audience weekly (circulation: 400,000) devoted to humor and political satire. The ideological standpoint of this magazine was rabidly anti-Communist, but it was also staunchly monarchist, so that Guareschi was addressing a divided readership: in a popular referendum, a narrow margin had chosen a republic over the Savoy monarchy as the form that the Italian government would take in the postwar period (Vené 1977: 43–44). The magazine definitely swayed public opinion, particularly through Guareschi's cartoons: his most bitterly satiric drawings depicted Communists as inhuman, ape-like creatures with three nostrils ("trinariciuti"); his illustrations for the amusing Don Camillo stories defused the ideological conflict by reducing it to a quarrel between two children, making the Christian Democrat a cute angel and the Communist an impish devil. The party that benefited most from Guareschi's popularity was actually not the monarchists, but the Christian Democrats: he contributed to their victory over the Communists in the 1948 elections and was publicly denounced by the Communist party chairman (Guareschi 1950: 7). All the same, Guareschi cannot be described as a propagandist for or even a member of the Christian Democratic Party. In 1954, after a trial that received international attention, he was convicted of libelling a Christian Democrat who had recently served as premier.

Since the opposing political ideologies and parties were woven deeply into Italian social life, supported by a network of very active cultural organizations, Guareschi's writing did not encounter in Italy the same paranoiac fear of Communism that existed in the United States and stigmatized membership in any left-wing group. On the contrary, the local governments in such northern Italian cities as Bologna were controlled by Communists who earned a reputation for improving administrative efficiency and stimulating the regional economy (Ginsborg 1990: 184, 296). In Italy's political culture, the humanistic slant of the Don Camillo books ultimately helped the left to gain power in national coalition governments (Vené 1977: 8). *Mondo Piccolo: Don Camillo*, first published in 1948, had gone through fifty-two printings by 1975, when the Communist party constructed a "historic compromise" with the Christian Democrats and controlled 34 percent of the vote (Ginsborg 1990: 354–358). Guareschi himself anticipated this development as early as 1952, when he told the interviewer for *Life*, with typical irony, that "I am doing something exceptional, something that is prodigious, something that no other writer has ever done: I have succeeded in making a Communist sympathetic" (Sargeant 1952: 125). In Italy, Guareschi's mostly middle-class readers saw the resemblances between Don Camillo and Peppone, especially their Catholicism, as signs that Christian Democrats could collaborate with Communists, whereas in the United States the "humanity" of the characters indicated the "incompatibility" of liberal democracy with Communism.

The various codes and ideologies that figured in Guareschi's American reception were shared by a broad range of readers from different cultural constituencies. The largest segment of his audience can be described as "middlebrow," educated but not intellectual, interested in reading fiction and viewing films for entertainment but unlikely to "make their living producing, analyzing, and distinguishing among cultural products" (Radway 1989: 261). This was the audience served by the Book-of-the-Month Club, which sold five of Guareschi's books: a 1958 club survey showed that most members had attended college, but only 13 percent were themselves teachers (Lee 1958: 149).

The Don Camillo books were particularly well received among college students, including those at private institutions. In 1953 the Cornell Drama Club staged readings of *The Little World of Don Camillo* (Pat MacLaughlin to Laura Lee Rilander: 30 November 1953). And as soon as *Don Camillo's Dilemma* was shelved at Barnard College Library, it was withdrawn continuously between October 1954 and December 1955. Guareschi's Don Camillo stories also circulated widely in anthologies that were used as textbooks in colleges and secondary schools.[3] In 1962, Herman Ward, professor of English at Trenton State College and consultant to the English Department of Princeton High School, went so far as to recommend that Guareschi replace Dickens and Eliot in the secondary school curriculum. In an article for the *New York Times Magazine*, Ward argued that the "fossilized classics" discouraged students from developing an interest in reading, unlike "the hundreds of lesser greats who excite them now" because "these books are for our times" (Ward 1962: 79). Interestingly, this view amounted to a pedagogy of the popular aesthetic, turning students into readers who seek a continuity between art and life by concentrating on the contemporary, the topical, the immediately identifiable. Ward did not in fact want to abandon the "classics," but to prepare students for a vicarious reading of them by constructing "a childhood and a youth in which books were as interesting as life itself" (ibid.).

Ward is evidence that Guareschi's American audience included the intellectual elite, readers whose livelihood involved teaching and criticizing cultural products. Whereas in Italy Guareschi was neglected by contemporary intellectuals, omitted from literary histories and curricula, in the United States he was read in schools, reviewed by respected writers and academics, included in a comprehensive anthology and discussed in a scholarly monograph (Vené 1977: 22–25; Slonim 1954; Heiney 1964: 104–105). Here the Don Camillo stories were installed in the canon of Italian literature, juxtaposed to the work of Verga, Pirandello, and Moravia, associated with the neorealist movement in fiction (Slonim 1954: 230–231).

Remarkably, American intellectuals also took the popular approach to Guareschi, abandoning the critical appreciation of form that distinguishes the high cultural aesthetic and assimilating his writing to the codes and ideologies that were then dominating American culture at large. For Donald Heiney, professor of English at the University of Utah, "it was a peculiarity of [Guareschi's] talent that he was able to make Peppone, the Communist mayor of the *Don Camillo* sketches, seem both totally human and completely wrong-headed" (Heiney 1964: 112). Eudora Welty, who by the 1950s had been recognized as a leading fiction writer, favorably reviewed *Don Camillo and His Flock* for the *New York Times*, where her remarks displayed the same humanism, ethnic stereotyping, and anti-Communism that generally characterized Guareschi's reception: "The difference between adversaries so evenly matched – who seem really inclined to like each other in their warm, Italian way – is in their backing. Stalin is too far away to do Peppone any good" (Welty 1952: 4). For a reviewer like William Barrett, professor of philosophy at New York University and editor of the highbrow journal *Partisan Review*, Guareschi's autobiographical book *The House That Nino Built* presented an occasion to affirm the patriarchal family as part of the familiar Italian stereotype:

> only an Italian, certainly no American, could have written it. When comparable stories of family life appear here in magazines like *The New Yorker*, there is always the skeleton of some neurosis in the closet or some attendant irony of sophistication. And when the fiction in our ladies magazines gets around to the family, usually there is breast-thumping self-consciousness. The Italian can escape such awkward self-consciousness because he takes the family for granted in a way that we do not.
>
> (Barrett 1953: 49)

Barrett was assuming a Cold War concept of the American family, wherein "the self-contained home held out the promise of security in an insecure world" (May 1988: 3). He also left unstated the ideological reasons why Americans could not take the family for granted: its stability was regarded as an important means of combating Communist infiltration and subversion, a domestic form of the global containment announced in the Truman Doctrine. Barrett valued Guareschi because his writing provided the middlebrow pleasure

135

of reader identification with this concept of the family, in contrast to the skeptical detachment provoked by other treatments, whether the unhealthy "irony" of the *New Yorker* or the melodramatic "self-consciousness" of "ladies magazines." Barrett's review dissented from the contemporaneous debates conducted by fellow intellectuals like Leslie Fiedler and Dwight MacDonald, who sought to reinforce their cultural authority by attacking "midcult" for leveling class-based distinctions in taste (Ross 1989: 56–61). Instead, Barrett positioned *The House That Nino Built* above elite and mass culture (exemplified here by the *New Yorker* and "ladies magazines") and revealed an investment in the characteristic terms of Guareschi's middlebrow reception: his representation of the family was defined as peculiarly Italian, male, and yet somehow universal, "all broad and simple humanity" (Barrett 1953: 49).

The wide appeal of Guareschi's writing, its ability to cross the boundaries between American cultural constituencies and to elicit a popular response from the intellectual elite, was engineered to some extent by his publishers, Pellegrini and Cudahy. This small husband-and-wife firm developed a promotion campaign that brought the first two Don Camillo books to a diverse national audience. They published excerpts and bought advertising in a variety of periodicals, newspapers as well as magazines, both elite and mass-audience, including the *Chicago Tribune, Colliers, Harper's*, the *New York Times*, the *New Yorker*, the *San Francisco Chronicle*, and the *Saturday Review of Literature*. Sheila Cudahy, the editor who acquired and oversaw the publication of Guareschi's books for some fifteen years, wrote the cover letter sent with the review copies of *The Little World of Don Camillo*, offering a description that both anticipated and shaped the responses of reviewers: "The priest and the mayor," it read, "meet head-on in a series of funny and typically human predicaments" (11 July 1950).

Sheila Cudahy particularly cultivated the Catholic market through religious book clubs and periodicals. She placed excerpts and advertisements in magazines like *Books on Trial, Our Sunday Visitor*, and *The Sign*, but she also tested whether the response would be favorable by submitting the first Don Camillo book to Catholic editors before publication. In 1949 the manuscript of the translation was sent to Harold C. Gardiner, S.J., literary editor of the national Catholic weekly *America*, who found it "a most delightful piece of work" and recommended a "foreward":

> Just what form this would take I don't know, but I should think that an explanation of the Italian background of the book plus something of a reminder that though many simple people were rather naively deceived by Communist propaganda the instigators of the propaganda were and are by no means naive, would serve to offset any impressions that Communism is being treated as a rather laughable business.
>
> (Gardiner to Cudahy: 15 August 1949)

Cudahy followed Gardiner's advice. "The author," she responded on 31 August, "is prepared to write a new introduction along the lines you suggest," and Guareschi produced an autobiographical text that made clear his opposition to the Italian Communist party, compensating for the American reader's unfamiliarity with his cultural and political impact in Italy (Guareschi 1950: 7).

Cudahy's promotion of the Don Camillo books implicitly invited readers to domesticate the translation by assimilating it to prevailing American values. Yet she could not control the domesticating process entirely because she could not anticipate every form it would take: different cultural constituencies put the books to different uses; and even within a particular constituency the uses were varied and conflicting. Although Welty's review of *Don Camillo and His Flock* does contain the critical appreciation of literary form that we might expect from a sophisticated writer like her – she makes the cutting comment that "the stories are all brief, around six pages long, and are cheerfully alike in nearly every other way as well" – she finally set aside the high cultural aesthetic to articulate the popular response: "Their pleasure for the general reader is likely to lie in the warmth with which they are written" (Welty 1952: 4). *The New Yorker*, however, took a characteristically highbrow approach filled with acid wit, mocking the formulaic quality of Guareschi's writing and questioning its ideological standpoint. Here the humanism was found to be repressive:

> Mr. Guareschi again presents his pet clown, Don Camillo, in a series of whimsical incidents designed to prove that people who do not agree with us are wrong but that even though they are wrong they are human, and if we treat them good-naturedly they will come around to our way of thinking, and then we will all be right.
>
> (*New Yorker* 1952: 89)

Among the cultural elite Guareschi's reception was mixed, ranging from sheer neglect to satire to reasoned approval. Yet it was also mixed among Catholics, whose approach to the Don Camillo books was partly intellectual, an evaluation according to Church orthodoxy, and partly popular, an emotional engagement with the narratives and an assessment of their value as a source of moral guidelines. On 3 October 1950, a pastor from Cortland College in New York wrote to Pellegrini and Cudahy to request the use of Guareschi's illustrations for a brochure, adding that "the basic ideas of [*The Little World of Don Camillo*] are sound, yet presented in a delightful and sophisticated manner." The Chicago-based Thomas More Book Club thought differently: the editors were scandalized. They rejected the book as "objectionable," and when Sheila Cudahy sought an explanation, the vice president of the club complained that "the priest acts in a manner unworthy of the priesthood," and, more grievously, his conversations with Christ "bordered on irreverence" (Dan Herr to Cudahy: 19 and 27 June 1950).

Guareschi's humanism, furthermore, was judged to be a morally questionable attitude toward Communism:

> We were disturbed by the underlying theme of the book – at least in our minds – that there is not too much difference between good Christians and good Communists and that Communists are ridiculous and not to be taken seriously. I realize this is a satire but when the Church is suffering so tragically throughout the world, Communists no longer seem amusing.

The aspects of Guareschi's writing that drew criticisms from some conservative segments of the Catholic audience found favor with others who were more liberal, particularly those who adopted a more high cultural approach by situating the Don Camillo books in the history of religious art. Anticipating the response of readers "who may possibly be offended by these Christ-centered chats," the reviewer for *Catholic World* remarked that "sometimes, indeed, they achieve the simple innocence of the early songs and plays of the Middle Ages" (Sandrock 1950: 472).

Guareschi's American publishers could not have controlled the heterogeneity of his reception particularly because it far exceeded their own approach to his writing. George Pellegrini, an Italian who emigrated to the United States in 1940, and Sheila Cudahy, the daughter of a leading Chicago meat packer, were college-educated publishers with advanced degrees: he studied at the universities of Florence and Oxford, she at Barnard, and then both did graduate work in literature at Columbia. Their publishing drew on their high cultural interests, but for the most part it was commercial and middlebrow in taste. Between 1946, when they brought out their first books, and 1952, when George's early death precipitated a merger with Farrar, Straus, their list included such books as a memoir by the British painter Augustus John, a novel by the Italian writer Ennio Flaiano, and *The Complete Canasta* by the syndicated bridge columnist Charles Goren. Pellegrini and Cudahy issued Goren's book in 1949, joining at least three other publishers who aimed to exploit a national fad for the card game (Goulden 1976: 195–196).

Cudahy's interest in Guareschi was indicative of the firm's entrepreneurial approach. Attracted by the commercial success of the first Don Camillo book in Italy, she located a translator who was known to have done a complete English version (telephone interview: 3 March 1995). She and Pellegrini treated it as a lucrative property: they purchased the world English-language rights from Guareschi and developed aggressive promotion and marketing campaigns.

Not only did they invest what was then considered an enormous sum in advertising, $10,000, but they quickly sold a wide range of subsidiary rights in the translation.[4] They licensed it to the British publisher Victor Gollancz for a modest advance (£175 for the first book, £500 for the second) against a large royalty (15 percent), shrewdly anticipating Guareschi's huge sales in the United Kingdom. And since the American demand was so great, they published their own hardback edition in substantial printings (55,000 copies within two years), while selling licenses for hardback editions both to the Book-of-the-Month Club (for an initial order of 100,000 copies) and to Grosset and Dunlap (who printed 40,000 copies of the first two Don Camillo books). Then in 1953 Pocket Books purchased the paperback rights for a $10,000 advance against royalties. At the same time, Guareschi's popularity ensured that editors of anthologies and textbooks would want to buy reprint rights, whose price depended on the nature of the publication, whether educational or commercial, and the size of the printing. The average price ranged from $35 to $150 per story, although the mass-audience magazine *Colliers* paid $750 for an excerpt. No record of Pellegrini and Cudahy's return on their investment survives, but some sense of their profit can be gauged from Guareschi's income: between 1950 and 1954, for instance, *The Little World of Don Camillo* earned the author over $17,600 in subsidiary rights sales (which he shared fifty-fifty with the publishers) and over $29,400 from royalties (6 percent of the $2.75 retail price for the first 5,000 copies, 7.5 percent for the second 5,000, and 10 percent thereafter).

To Guareschi's American publishers, however, the capital produced by his writing was not simply economic, but cultural as well. Pellegrini and Cudahy were undoubtedly guided by a profit motive, yet they seem to have shared the same middlebrow approach to the Don Camillo books as the broadest segment of their readers. This is clear in Cudahy's letter to the vice president of the Thomas More Book Club, where she describes her response:

> I wonder if you could let me know on what grounds you found *The Little World of Don Camillo* unsuitable. The reason I ask is because as a Catholic I naturally feel a publishing responsibility and would not want this book to be interpreted either as disrespectful or as in some way too sympathetic to Communism. If some of your readers found it objectionable on such grounds I would like to know this because actually the author is a devout Catholic and has done possibly more than any journalist in Italy and at the risk of his life to fight Communism. Therefore it would be a pity to have it misunderstood here and possibly there is something we can do in our presentation of the book to the public to dispel any confusion.
>
> (Cudahy to Dan Herr, 21 June 1950)

Cudahy's response dissolved the distinction between Guareschi's writing and the values that were then dominating American culture. More, she conceived of her role as publisher in moral terms, wherein she sought to serve readers by taking the clearest and strongest stand on urgent contemporary issues.

This necessitated an adherence to the popular aesthetic, explaining the work of author and publisher alike by reference to their lives and editing the book to emphasize its ethical and political content. The content was of course a domestic inscription: Cudahy read the Don Camillo stories in accordance with the same ideological configuration that shaped Guareschi's American reception as a whole – anti-Communistic and humanist, although here the humanism took an explicitly religious form.

Guareschi was so successful in the United States because his writing carried the same meanings for readers from varying social groups. Don Camillo consolidated codes and ideologies that were truly national in scale, but without restricting the diverse uses to which different cultural constituencies might put them: religious, pedagogical, commercial, political, propagandistic. The broadcast rights, for instance, were avidly pursued by film and television producers as well as the State Department, which requested international radio use on the Voice of America (Evelyn Eisenstadt to Pellegrini and Cudahy, 16 February 1951). A mass readership emerged because these diverse uses shared a particular approach to culture, the popular aesthetic, so that Don Camillo constituted a pleasurable collective fantasy, an imaginary resolution for a tense social situation. And this fantasy worked for both producers and consumers of Guareschi's books. Nearly fifty years later, Sheila Cudahy recalled only the pleasure: she declined to link *The Little World of Don Camillo* with one of the most inflammatory periods of the Cold War and believed she was attracted to the book because it was very entertaining, with illustrations that were charming and to the point (telephone interview: 3 March 1995).

The scandal of Guareschi's American reception is not that it rested on the popular aesthetic (this would be scandalous only from a more elite cultural position), but that it fostered questionable domestic values. The Don Camillo books at once managed and sustained an American paranoia about Communism, along with the various ethnic and gender stereotypes that were intertwined with it, while distorting the cultural and political situation in Italy.

Editing and translating

The key factor in Guareschi's success was the production of the translations, a complicated process that comprehended various editorial moves and is documented to some extent in the publishers' archive.[5] The Italian texts were deliberately edited and translated so as to cross linguistic and cultural boundaries, not just between Italy and the United States, but between different English-language constituencies, British as well as American.

The production process for *The Little World of Don Camillo* got underway in the summer of 1949, as soon as Cudahy received an English-language translation prepared from the first Italian collection of Guareschi's stories, *Mondo Piccolo: Don Camillo* (1948). The translation was a complete version of the Italian text, but Cudahy cut it down, omitting sixteen stories and an elaborate autobiographical preface, some 180 pages of the Italian edition. This was a decisive domesticating move: the cut made the book easier to digest for most American readers since the omitted material contained topical satire filled with references to contemporary Italian political figures and developments, including a specific parliamentary bill. Following the advice of the Catholic literary editor whom she asked to evaluate the translation, Cudahy got Guareschi to write a much briefer preface (seven pages) that was likewise autobiographical, but that provided basic information about the author's life and work for the American reader. This new preface consisted of details that Guareschi's sizeable Italian readership would already know about him, but it suppressed others that would be equally familiar in Italy: he presented himself as strongly anti-Communist, although without any reference to the monarchist sympathies evident in his magazine.

The translation of the new preface, furthermore, was directed to an American audience. The language generally adhered to current English usage while cultivating a strain of colloquialism that would be immediately intelligible to a broad segment of American readers, if not simply recognizable as an American dialect of English. This is borne out by the choice for the title. The Italian title, "Io Sono Così" (in a close version, "I Am Like This"), was initially translated as "This is the Way I Am," but was finally rewritten as "How I Got This Way" (Guareschi 1950: 3). The first rendering is correct, yet the syntax, although informal, is a bit lumbering; the revision is a much freer interpretation and noticeably more fluent, even colloquial in its use of "got," which gives it a wry quality.

The English version of the preface also reveals the pressure of contemporary American values, notably the high esteem for the patriarchal family that distinguished the post-World War II period. In the Italian text Guareschi described himself as a son, husband, and father, a member of an extended family whose influence reaches deeply into his life. And he treated these relationships in an affectionately humorous way. In one passage, however, while pursuing the sort of non sequitur that characterizes the humor of the piece, he apparently offered a representation of the family that Cudahy found unacceptable since she deleted it from the translation. The English version reads: "I have a motorcycle with four cylinders, an automobile with six cylinders and a wife and two children" (Guareschi 1950: 4). Yet the Italian text continued:

una moglie e due figli dei quali non sono in grado di precisare la cilindrata, ma che mi sono assai utili in quanto io li uso come personaggi in molte delle storie.

a wife and two children whose cylinders I am not in a position to describe precisely, but who are very useful to me inasmuch as I use them as characters in many of my stories.

141

Depicting the family as one among the patriarch's mechanical posses-
sions – Cudahy's edited version – might well have been amusing to American
readers, a wittily unexpected turn on dominant cultural values, not just the
nuclear family, but more fundamental ideologies like possessive individualism, especially as materialized in automotive vehicles, signs of economic
stability that carry the promise of mobile independence. Yet since the Italian
text developed a rather different metaphor, reducing Guareschi's wife and
children to objects of paternal exploitation that are purely utilitarian, whether
mechanical or literary, the passage was deleted: it ran the risk of seeming
irreverent to readers for whom the family also symbolized emotional fulfill-
ment and security. The deletion preempted such responses; whether or not
this was Cudahy's conscious intention, the effect of her revision answered
to values that dominated postwar American culture.

She similarly revised the ending of the preface to bring it in line with
reigning gender roles. The Italian text concludes with another example of
Guareschi's zany humor: "Oltre a una statura ho anche un peso. Spero di
poter avere anche una cane" ("In addition to height, I have weight. I hope
to be able to have a dog too"). The English version deletes "weight" and
"dog" and rewrites the passage to refer to the most striking feature of
Guareschi's masculine appearance: "In addition to 5'10" I have all my hair"
(Guareschi 1950: 9).

As these choices suggest, the translation discourse involved a thorough-
going domestication guided by the popular aesthetic: the aim was to produce
an extreme fluency that invited readerly participation in the realist illusion
of the narrative, while inscribing the Italian text with American codes and
ideologies. This aim becomes clear in a comparison of the Italian text to
two English translations, the version published by Pellegrini and Cudahy
and the initial draft prepared by the British translator Una Vincenzo
Troubridge. Only fifteen pages of this draft are extant, but they do indicate that Cudahy heavily revised Troubridge's work, removing most of her
Britishisms and inserting American colloquialisms. The British dialect was
present at every level, in Troubridge's lexicon, syntax, orthography. Wherever
she rendered "canonica" as "presbytery," Cudahy changed it to "rectory."
Similarly, "half a metre" was replaced by "two feet," "liberally daubed" by
"plastered," "constables" by "men," "parcels" by "baskets," "a considerable
weight" by "pretty heavy," and "tyre" by "tire" (Troubridge 1949: 77, 79,
80, 222; Guareschi 1950: 67, 69, 70, 187). Troubridge also used some colloquialisms, but they were typically British and unfailingly blue-pencilled by
Cudahy, who provided American counterparts that she considered necessary
to match Guareschi's Italian. "I should have liked to box their ears," a free
rendering of "prenderei volentieri a sberle" ("I would have gladly slapped
them"), was turned into "I would have preferred smacking them between
the eyes" (Troubridge 1949: 55; Guareschi 1948: 49; 1950: 49). "I must
have got up quite two hundred lotteries" (for "avrò combinato [arranged]

duecento lotterie") was recast as "I must have organized two hundred bazaars" (ibid.).

Cudahy felt that her responsibility as editor of the translation was to be as true as possible to Guareschi's text (Cudahy to Timothy Gillen, Farrar, Straus and Giroux, May 1997). The result of this view was to incline the language toward the colloquial register while avoiding any sophisticated literary or rhetorical effects that would interfere with immediate intelligibility. Cudahy even revised passages in Troubridge's translation that were not noticeably British, but merely formal or educated, indicative of an acquaintance with a wide English lexicon. Troubridge sometimes put Guareschi's rather simple Italian –

> la crepa non si allargava, ma neppure si restringeva. E allora perdette la calma, e un giorno mandò il sagrestano in comune.
>
> (Guareschi 1948: 31)

– into more elevated, Latinate English:

> The crack [in the church tower] had not increased in width, but neither had it diminished. Finally he lost his composure, and there came a day when he dispatched the sacristan to the headquarters of the Commune.
>
> (Troubridge 1949: 43)

The American version returned to Guareschi's simplicity, but was also Americanizing:

> the crack got no wider but neither did it get smaller. Finally he lost his temper, and the day came when he sent the sacristan to the Town Hall.
>
> (Guareschi 1950: 37)

Troubridge didn't translate "comune," an Italian term for municipal government that would be known to English-language readers who travelled in Europe, especially British expatriates like Troubridge herself. Cudahy, however, replaced it with a term closer to American usage: "Town Hall."

The editorial insistence on colloquial English supported the popular demand that artistic representation be indistinguishable from everyday life, and that therefore the Italian text be assimilated to familiar American values. Although Cudahy favored colloquialisms current in both British and American English at the turn of the twentieth century, she included many that were specific to the United States during the postwar period, when the Don Camillo books first appeared. And, most important for Guareschi's bestseller status, these American colloquialisms were comprehensible across different cultural constituencies (the following lexical analysis relies on Partridge 1984, the *OED*, and Wentworth and Flexner 1975). "Campione federale" ("federal champion") was translated as "champ" (Guareschi 1948: 126; 1950: 106), a term that originated in American sports, particularly boxing. "Bravo, bravo!" was translated as "Swell!" (Guareschi 1948: 320; 1950: 198), an informal expression of approval or satisfaction that occurred in prewar British writing – for example, P.G. Wodehouse's comic novels – but that later became a chiefly American usage, appearing in journalism from national news agencies like Associated Press, as well as more elite literary and dramatic forms: "We're eating at the lake," says a character in Arthur Miller's play *All My Sons*, "we could have a swell time" (Miller 1947: 62). "Uno importante" ("an important man") was translated as "big shot" (Guareschi 1948: 55; 1950: 57), a term for a successful and influential person that was used in popular fiction, like James M. Cain's Hollywood-inspired novel *Mildred Pierce* (1941), but also in scholarly research, like H. L. Mencken's lively articles for the journal *American Speech* (1951). Such colloquialisms made *The Little World of Don Camillo* highly readable for a wide spectrum of Americans, regardless of the diverse interests, educational backgrounds, and social positions that would ordinarily distinguish their cultural practices.

Editing according to the popular aesthetic achieved an easy readability that would elicit a participatory response. The narrative was made to unwind faster by omitting Italian passages that are obviously repetitive or convoluted; phrases were inserted and passages rearranged to improve the continuity (e.g. Guareschi 1948: 58, 60, 78, 92, 96; 1950: 61, 67, 70, 74). Sometimes the insertions were explanatory, intended precisely for the English-language reader. When Don Camillo woke one morning to find "Don Camalo" painted on the rectory wall, the Italian text merely reported the event, but the English version added an explanation that shows the unusual spelling of the name to be a pun, and that connects it to the preceding story: "*Don Camalo*, which means stevedore and which undoubtedly referred to a feat of strength and daring which Don Camillo had performed a few days before" (Guareschi 1948: 78; 1950: 66–67).

The concreteness of the language was increased through the addition of details that neither advance the plot nor carry any symbolic significance – "any characterial, atmospheric, or sapiential signified," as Barthes puts it (Barthes 1986: 145) – but work only to strengthen the realist illusion. Thus, Cudahy retained Troubridge's vivid renderings of "una pedata fulminante" ("a violent kick") as "a terrific kick in the pants," of "arrivò il treno" ("the train arrived") as "the train steamed in," and of "alle fine perdette la calm" ("finally he lost his calm") as "by now [he] was almost frothing at the mouth" (Guareschi 1948: 92, 152, 168; 1950: 69, 136, 153). The narrative was also made more engaging through idioms and clichés that heightened its suspensefulness or introduced a note of melodramatic exaggeration. "Pigiava sui pedali" ("pressing on the pedals") became "pedaling away for all he was worth"; "Ormai la

voce si era sparsa" ("by now the word had spread") became "the story of
Peppone's feat spread like wildfire"; "scalpitava come un cavallo" ("pawing
the ground like a horse") became "like a restive horse"; a "pugno" ("fist")
was "clenched"; a "mormorio" ("murmuring") became an "audible whisper";
"Deve andar via come un cane!" ("He must leave like a dog!") became "And
we will let him slink away like a whipped cur" (Guareschi 1948: 47, 56, 60,
61, 94; 1950: 48, 58, 63, 64, 72).

A most effective move in enabling the American reader's vicarious participation was the revision or deletion of discursive features that emphasized cultural differences, including those that were specific to Italy. References to
Italian newspapers (*Milano Sera*, *Unità*) were removed, and brand-name products were made generic: "Wolsit" was rendered as "racing bike," "cartucce
Walstrode" as "cartridges" (Guareschi 1948: 29, 33, 298; 1950: 29, 40). A
mention of "reticelle," the net rack for luggage in Italian train compartments,
underwent a domesticating clarification as "the baggage racks overhead," and
a peculiarly Italian metaphor for a refined use of language, "appena vendem-
miate nella vigna del vocabolario" ("scarcely harvested in the vineyard of the
dictionary"), was replaced by a commonplace English expression, "newly
minted" (Guareschi 1948: 95, 97; 1950: 73, 75). Cudahy yielded to the
American indifference toward soccer by replacing the Italian term for it ("cal-
cio") with the English for another sport entirely, a "race"; and in a story where
such a revision was impossible because the plot hinged on an important soccer match, she nonetheless deleted the name of a noted Italian goalie
(Guareschi 1948: 112, 180; 1950: 91, 167). In a remarkable effort to mini-
mize the American reader's potential confusion with the Italian language,
Cudahy even simplified the characters' names (or allowed Troubridge's sim-
plifications), replacing three names ("Brusco," "Gigotto," "Sghembo") with
the same one in several different passages: "Smilzo" (Guareschi 1948: 62, 92,
103, 104, 144, 168; 1950: 65, 70, 81, 82, 83, 127, 153).

The generalizing tendency behind some of these translation choices would
have encouraged the humanist response to Guareschi's writing that was articulated in the reviews, the perception that Don Camillo and Peppone represent
an essential human nature transcending time and place. Not only did the
narrative seem to provide evidence for their fundamental sameness, despite
their political differences, but the removal of cultural markers in the translation, coupled with the extensive use of colloquialisms, made these characters
appear to be the same as the American reader, despite their Italian origins. Yet
the choices also demonstrate that the editing and translating process never
escaped the cultural constraints of its moment: the Italian text was rendered
into a prevailing humanism that was firmly anti-Communist.

This is perhaps most clear in the influence of Cold War political termi-
nology on the lexicon of the translation. Guareschi referred to Italian
Communists in neighboring villages as "frazioni" ("fractions," "sections") of
the Party, but in the English version they were called "cells," a term that

from the 1920s onward was used for a small unit of a Communist group engaged in subversive activity (Guareschi 1949: 32, 55; 1950: 38, 57). The term "satellite" was put to similar uses. In both British and American English, it came to signify a country or state under the political or economic domination of another, principally Germany and Italy during World War II, then the Soviet Union during the postwar period. Yet in *The Little World of Don Camillo* "satellite" translated a range of very different Italian words and phrases, all applying to Peppone and other members of the Communist Party: "gli uomini del suo stato maggiore" ("the men of his general staff"), "la banda dei fedelissimi di Peppone" ("the group of men most loyal to Peppone"), even a pejorative, "mercanzia" or "riff-raff" (Guareschi 1948: 61, 157, 184; 1950: 65, 141, 170). In these instances, "satellite" referred not to countries or states, but to fictional characters, turning them into personifications of the contemporary geopolitical situation.

The inscription of the political code in the translation thus invited the American reader to turn the ideological rivalry between Don Camillo and Peppone into an allegory for the Cold War. And since the English terms carried negative connotations of domination and subversion, they inevitably stacked the deck against Peppone and Communism. The English version does in fact display a marked effort to stigmatize the mayor and his political affiliates by characterizing them as criminal or at the least socially undesirable. Where Guareschi referred to Peppone's "banda" ("group") or "squadra" ("squad"), Troubridge and/or Cudahy repeatedly used "gang"; expressions like "gli altri capoccia rossi" ("the other red leaders") and "fedelissmi" ("the most loyal men") were rendered with "henchmen"; and an apparently neutral demonstrative like "quelli" ("those men"), when applied to Peppone's affiliates, became "those ruffians" (Guareschi 1948: 32, 98, 146, 173; 1950: 38, 76, 129, 159).

At the same time, some translation choices reveal a tendency to whitewash Don Camillo by revising or deleting details that question the morality of his actions. With "Don Camillo rise perfidamente" ("Don Camillo laughed treacherously"), the word "perfidamente" was replaced by the less sinister "unpleasantly"; and Christ's warning that Don Camillo consider himself right "fino a quando non farà qualche soperchia" ("only so long as he doesn't commit some outrage") was mitigated through a more positive rephrasing: "just as long as he plays fair" (Guareschi 1948: 21, 143; 1950: 29, 125). The translation entirely omitted many sentences in which Don Camillo displays an awareness of his own guilt or performs some unethical act: for example, "Gli dispiaceva di essersi dimostrato così maligno" ("He was sorry to have shown himself to be so evil"); or "di' al Bigio che se non mi ripulisce, e gratis, il muro, io attacco il vostro partito del giornale dei democristani" ("tell Bigio if he doesn't clean up my wall, gratis, I'll attack your party in the Christian Democratic newspaper") (Guareschi 1948: 27, 186). Even when Cudahy substituted "bazaars" for "lotteries" in one of Don

Camillo's conversations with Christ, she in effect decriminalized the priest for American readers: lotteries were legal institutions in Italy, but in 1950s America the term might be confused with a criminal activity (namely the numbers racket); her use of "bazaars," events designed to raise funds for charitable purposes, constituted a rewriting of the Italian text, but the term also carried an innocuous significance appropriate for a priest.

The most remarkable thing about the translation, of course, is that the inscription of domestic codes and ideologies was invisible to American readers. This was so partly because the Italian text was edited and translated according to the popular aesthetic: the high degree of fluency, underwritten by the adherence to current American usage and by a rich vein of colloquialism, resulted in the realist illusion, the effect that the text is a transparent window onto the world, a true representation and therefore not a translation, a second-order image. Not surprisingly, then, the translation was rarely mentioned by reviewers; even when the review appeared in a more high-brow periodical like the *New York Times Book Review* or the *Saturday Review of Literature*, it included no comments on the quality of the translation because the popular aesthetic prizes the informative function of any text over the subtle appreciation of formal elements like a translation discourse. One of the few comments occurred in *Catholic World*, and it confirmed the effect of transparency: "The translation is such that one never adverts to the fact that this is one" (Sandrock 1950: 472).

Yet the domestic inscription at work in the production process was also invisible because it was domestic, familiar. Under the aegis of the popular aesthetic, American readers looked into the translation to find themselves, their own dialect of English, the values that were then dominating their country, and any imaginary solutions that might be applied to their own cultural and political problems. The editing and translating answered to a deep-seated cultural narcissism by maintaining it. This was evident in the general reception of *The Little World of Don Camillo*, but also, perhaps more explicitly, in a letter to the publisher from an appreciative reader in Ohio. Admitting that "I do not read Italian," he nonetheless went on to praise the translator's work: "she not only kept the elusive essence but, at times, refined it into current American English so deftly that it lands like one of the Don's great fists" (Deac Martin to Pellegrini and Cudahy, 9 February 1951).

The editing and translating process for *The Little World of Don Camillo* set the pattern for all of the Guareschi translations that followed. Cudahy assembled most of the Don Camillo books from Italian texts that Guareschi had published in his magazine but had not yet collected in Italian editions. In some cases, he sent her a complete book-length typescript, in others a series of partial drafts, and she would "start to work going through the Italian text," as she once described the process, "selecting the stories, and doing my usual shifting together" (Cudahy to Victor Gollancz, 6 November 1956). The editing aimed to keep the books topical, evidently to capitalize on international political developments. While at work on *Don Camillo Takes the Devil by the Tail* (1957), Cudahy wrote to the translator Frances Frenaye that "I have just received and enclose quite a nice story from Guareschi written apropos of the Hungarian Revolution," adding that "I think we should include this" (27 December 1956).

In Frenaye, who did six of Guareschi's books, Cudahy found a resourceful *American* translator whose work didn't need further editing to remove Britishisms. On the contrary, Frenaye easily turned the Italian texts into the most readable, occasionally racy, colloquialism. Her translating was confidently free, but accurate. She rendered "imbrigliarono" ("they harnessed") as "lassooed," "Perché mi avete fatto fare questo?" ("Why did you make me do this?") as "Why did you rope me into this?" and "l'ha saputo" ("he learned of it") as "[he] got wind of it" (Guareschi 1953b: 117, 118; 1981: 9; 1952: 9, 32). Her lexicon also assimilated the Italian text to domestic values, cultural and political: "comune" was translated as "town hall," while both "henchmen" and "gang" became routine epithets for Peppone's fellow Communists (Guareschi 1981: 39; 1952: 165; 1957: 11, 12, 15, 16). And the domestication at work in the English versions continued to be concealed by Frenaye's fluent, transparent discourse. Harold Gardiner, the literary editor of *America* who enjoyed the first Don Camillo, was less enthusiastic about the second because Guareschi's "comic-opera buffoons" didn't adequately take into account that "Communism is a much more sinister thing" (Gardiner 1952). Yet Gardiner felt that "it would be ungracious not to give special notice to the smooth and unnoticeable translation by Frances Frenaye."

Just as Guareschi's American success was due in large part to the Americanizing editing and translating, he sold equally well in Britain because the English version was put through an Anglicizing process. Pellegrini and Cudahy and later Farrar, Straus had the Italian texts translated in the United States and then licensed the British rights to Gollancz, who edited the translations for a British readership. Not only were spellings altered to reflect differences between British and American English, but the translation was substantially revised to conform to British usage. Thus, in *The Little World of Don Camillo* "big bruisers" was replaced by "rodomontades," "swimming pool" by "bathing pool," "soccer" by "football," "locker rooms" by "pavilion," and "flashlight" by "electric torch" (Guareschi 1950: 83, 87, 92, 120; 1951: 96, 99, 100, 106, 138). American colloquialisms, both lexical and syntactical, were changed to British equivalents or removed altogether: a "licking" became a "drubbing," "champ" became the more literal "federal champion," "it was me that did him in" became "it was I that did him in," "kick his backside to a pulp" became "kick his backside to a jelly" (Guareschi 1950: 88, 98, 106, 109; 1951: 101, 113, 123, 126). The British editing made the translation more accurate, restoring passages that had been deleted intentionally or accidentally from the American version. These restorations included the various names of the Italian characters as well as a long paragraph on unexploded bombs, which would have special significance among British readers who suffered from the German blitzes during World War II (Guareschi 1951: 74–75).

The marketing was likewise directed to a distinctly British audience. In 1962 the jacket copy for the first mass-market paperback edition from Penguin installed Guareschi in a pantheon of humorists who were popular in England and Europe but virtually unknown in the United States – except perhaps among more elite readers and film viewers: Richard Gordon, Tony Hancock, Peter Sellers, Jacques Tati, Kingsley Amis (Guareschi 1962). This jacket copy showed, however, that Guareschi's British success hinged on the same Cold War oppositions, and the same ideological standpoint, that figured in his American reception: the topic of the book was described as "the running fight between the honest village priest and his deadly opponent, Peppone, the Communist mayor."

Throughout the roughly two decades that Guareschi remained the best-selling Italian writer in English, the production process was unwavering in its adherence to the popular aesthetic. None of the editors and translators involved ever regarded the Italian texts as literature in a modern sense, as the unique work of an authorial intention. Hence, they translated with latitude, according to their own sense of accuracy. They were most interested in the functions of the text – informative, didactic, commercial – and therefore focussed on the effects of the translation, developing a fluent discourse that was readily assimilable to prevailing domestic values and eminently marketable. And all of Guareschi's editors and translators were aware that they were shaping the Italian texts for mass consumption.

Troubridge believed that a writer like Colette, whom she also translated, deserved to be treated with uncompromising literalism because "Colette is a great artist, [. . .] the greatest of French writers, perhaps the greatest of living writers" (Troubridge to Cudahy, 17 September 1950). For the translator, this meant a careful effort to reproduce the distinctive literary features of the French text. "For many years," Troubridge wrote to Cudahy, "I have waited in hopes of eventually giving the real Colette to the English-speaking public," since "she is *not* easy, having a terrifically big vocabulary & an immensely personal style." When Gollancz suggested that one of her texts "was to be blue-pencilled to make it 'milder,'" presumably because of the sexual material, Troubridge "refused" to undertake the translation. Yet from the very beginning she was willing to revise Guareschi's *Mondo Piccolo: Don Camillo* because "here and there it might have offended Anglo Saxon religious susceptibilities, and I omitted one small section which was a bit callous about cruelty to an animal for our tastes" (Troubridge to Cudahy, 14 June 1949). When Troubridge sold the rights in her English version to Pellegrini and Cudahy, through her agent she explicitly agreed to a further domesticating revision, "with a view to the American audience" (M.G. Ridley to Cudahy, 26 July 1949).

Some twenty-five years later, as Farrar, Straus and Giroux prepared to publish Guareschi's memoir *My Home, Sweet Home* (1966), editor Harold Vursell gave similar instructions to another British translator, novelist Gordon Sager (8 and 10 March 1966). Admitting that "Mr. G. ain't Dante," Vursell advised Sager

> not to condescend to the material; nor need you do it literally. What you will need to do is to abandon your own personality, and take on his, making the book as agreeable to the general reader as is humanly possible.

Sager himself seems to have regarded translating as a second-rate activity, hack writing, a financial necessity that might hurt his reputation as an author with literary ambitions: he translated under a pseudonym, Joseph Green. Yet he apparently believed that translating a popular writer like Guareschi was even more damaging, since he did a second book, the whimsical fable *A Husband in Boarding School* (1967), but published the translation anonymously.

If the editing and translating of Guareschi's books seem dubious today, it is not because their American publishers treated them as lucrative properties instead of unique literary works. As popular writing these books resisted elite modes of appreciation, and like other popular cultural forms they turned out to be ephemeral, too closely tied to a social function in their historical moment and so doomed to be forgotten once the concerns of that moment passed. The scandal is rather one of self-contradiction, wherein the publishers lose cultural credit: they themselves drew the highbrow distinction between the aesthetic and the functional, preferring to be known for their support of literary value, not for their pursuit of commercial interest. This is particularly clear in the case of Farrar, Straus and Giroux: they have acquired considerable cultural authority as the publishers of major contemporary writers, including many Nobel Laureates (T.S. Eliot, Isaac Bashevis Singer, Joseph Brodsky, Derek Walcott, Seamus Heaney), and have come to be viewed as an independent literary house, one of the last, who resists the profit orientation driving the lists of publishers now owned by transnational corporations (e.g. Simon and Schuster, HarperCollins). By 1980, when the mergers had dramatically changed American publishing, and Guareschi was long out of print, Roger Straus was presenting his firm in these elite terms, often in combative exchanges with more commercial publishers, like Richard Snyder of Simon and Schuster (Whiteside 1981: 119, 121–122). Straus, who personally secured some of the large subsidiary rights sales for the Guareschi translations, later protested the revision of the industry's national book awards to include popular genres, like westerns and mysteries: the new award categories, he felt, were "another ratification of the bestseller lists," one that "reflect[s] an emphasis on marketing and industry public relations offensive to anyone concerned with the disinterested recognition of literary merit" (ibid.: 94).

The editing and translating of Guareschi constitute a skeleton in the Farrar, Straus and Giroux archive, a commercial deviation from their allegiance to the high aesthetic. The commercialism represented by projects like the Guareschi translations did in fact finance other, more literary books that proved less profitable, as Straus later suggested, books by "young or beginning writers of talent," both American and foreign (ibid.: 103). Nonetheless, it exemplifies the very reduction of aesthetic to economic value that is denied by the publisher's self-presentations and avoided elsewhere in the Farrar, Straus and Giroux list. Between 1946 and 1996, they published a significant number of literary translations, including roughly sixty from the Italian; their most frequently published Italian author was actually not Guareschi (who ranks second at twelve books), but the highbrow novelist Alberto Moravia with twenty-six books (see Williams 1996: 537–578). The Guareschi translations expose not simply this publisher's inability to honor the high aesthetic and run a profitable business at the same time, but also the inability of an elite concept of literature to attract a mass audience – unless, of course, an author is ratified by the Nobel Prize.

What really rattles the skeleton, however, is the translators' systematic exclusion from the profits. Guareschi's American reception coincided with the gross exploitation of the translators who played a crucial role in his success.[6] By contract the publishers held the dominant position in all bargaining with translators: Pellegrini and Cudahy and later Farrar, Straus owned the exclusive right to produce and sell English-language translations of Guareschi's writing throughout the world, and they treated the translators, in the terms of copyright law, not as authors of their texts, but as workers-for-hire, writing in the service of their employer. In the routine arrangement, the translators were paid a flat fee per thousand English words with no share of the income from royalties or subsidiary rights sales. Since the Guareschi translations were international bestsellers, published in the United States but licensed to publishers in Canada, Britain, and Australia, the enormous income they generated makes the translators' exclusion seem all the more egregious.

The pattern of exploitation began with the first Don Camillo book. Una Troubridge (1887–1963) was an experienced translator living in Florence: during the twenty-year period before the Guareschi project, she had published six translations from French and Italian, histories and biographies as well as novels. Her rate, which her agent proposed to Pellegrini and Cudahy, was quite low by current New York practices, 30 shillings per thousand English words. For *The Little World of Don Camillo*, at 37,000 words, she received $125.20. Not only was this amount a tiny fraction of the value that accrued to her translation on the American and British markets – Guareschi's royalty earnings between 1950 and 1954 were $29,275.68 – but the publishers charged her ($30.20) for retyping a manuscript that they themselves had extensively revised. They were also reluctant to honor her agent's later request for an "ex gratia payment additional to the low price she charged [them] for the translation of Don Camillo in view of the great success of the book" (Cyrus Brooks, A.M. Heath and Company, to George Pellegrini, 21 November 1950). Ultimately, George Pellegrini paid Troubridge another $100, the fee he received from placing her translations of two omitted stories in a magazine.

Frances Frenaye (1908–96) too was an experienced translator, but her accomplishments carried greater literary significance than Troubridge's. In a career that lasted about fifty years, she produced over forty translations from the work of important contemporary Italian writers, including Ignazio Silone's *The Seed beneath the Snow* (1942), Carlo Levi's *Christ Stopped at Eboli* (1947), Natalia Ginzburg's *The Road to the City* (1952), and Anna Maria Ortese's *The Bay Is Not Naples* (1955). For her first Guareschi translation, *Don Camillo and His Flock* (1952), she received a New York rate, $10 per thousand words for a total of $808. Yet within two years Guareschi had earned $25,705.76 in royalties and subsidiary rights income from her work. Since Frenaye translated so many of Guareschi's books, she was gradually able to command a higher fee. But these increases did nothing to alter the fundamental inequity in the financial arrangements. For *Comrade Don Camillo* (1964), for example, her rate was $15 per thousand words, yet since it was a shorter book, she received a fee of $721.50. Farrar, Straus, who were entitled to 50 percent of subsidiary rights sales, licensed the translation to the Book-of-the-Month Club for $30,000 and to the Catholic Digest Book Club for another $3,000, while selling their own edition of 50,000 copies. Within six months of publication, Guareschi was paid $29,856.91. Given these earnings, Frenaye's fee appears a minimal production cost, but it was further reduced in subsidiary rights deals. Pellegrini and Cudahy and Farrar, Straus developed an unusual arrangement with Gollancz: after the first Don Camillo book, the British publisher was required to pay half of the translation fee, in addition to an advance against royalties. The only party not to benefit from Guareschi's commercial success in English was the translator – except perhaps by receiving a series of translation commissions.

The highbrow bestseller

Since Guareschi's first publication in English, some four decades ago, cultural changes in the United States have created the conditions for a different kind of translated bestseller, especially in the case of fiction. The mergers that made the publishing industry more profit-oriented have certainly led publishers to focus on foreign texts that were bestsellers in their native countries, more often than not with mixed results. But the commercialism has also sought to capitalize on existing domestic markets, locating foreign texts that already possess the potential for a large readership in English because they have been recently adapted in other forms of mass culture, particularly films, plays, and musicals. This strategy of investing in tie-ins has resulted most noticeably in the proliferation of cheap paperback editions of classic foreign novels, such as *Dangerous Liaisons*, *Les Misérables*, and *The Phantom of the Opera*. In these cases, a foreign text normally reserved for elite modes of appreciation, mainly academic study and research, is made available for the popular aesthetic, for a participatory and moralistic response guided by a pleasurable experience with another popular form, the adaptation. The translation, then, in the asymmetry between its commercial production and its varieties of reception, becomes a hybrid object, a highbrow bestseller.

The electronic media have been most effective in creating highbrow bestsellers in translation. The emergence of film and television as potent commercial forces has enabled the engineering of bestsellers before publication through elaborate promotion and marketing schemes (Dudovitz 1990: 24–25), so that in some cases the foreign text need not address urgent public issues to stimulate the sale of the translation. Here readers are attracted by the form of the foreign text, its resemblance to popular fiction genres in the domestic culture. The electronic media have shaped such reading practices by eliciting "a fascination for the medium" in preference to "the critical exigencies of the message" (Baudrillard 1983: 35), making popular formulae instantly recognizable through multiple reproduction, while effecting the realist illusion at its most mesmerizing.

At the same time, these media have influenced elite fiction by increasing the writer's self-consciousness about the forms of literary representation, encouraging a narrative experimentalism that involves the imitation of popular genres. The blurring of the divisions between high and low culture is a hallmark of the international tendency in contemporary fiction known as "postmodernism" (McHale 1992). Thus, foreign texts that display formal self-consciousness and would therefore seem to be too highbrow to appeal to different cultural constituencies, even in their native countries, have achieved commercial success in translation because their experimentalism allows them to be assimilated to current popular fiction. Bestselling foreign novels such as Umberto Eco's *The Name of the Rose* (1983), Patrick Süskind's *Perfume* (1986), and Peter Høeg's *Miss Smilla's Feeling for Snow* (1993) are distinguished by varying degrees of formal complexity joined to a conventional murder mystery plot. As a result, they can repay detached critical appreciation while inviting an unreflective identification. Some highbrow foreign texts are no doubt more inviting than others, which prove too resistant to the popular aesthetic and ultimately go unread by a mass audience. Still, the affiliation with domestic popular culture, foregrounded through promotion and marketing, can be visible enough to ensure that such translations are widely bought, even if unread.

This trend of highbrow bestsellers has been sustained by strongly domesticating translations that increase the readability of the foreign text. What has not changed since the 1950s is the prevalence of fluent, transparent discourse in English-language translating. The highbrow bestsellers are rendered into the most familiar dialect of English, the standard, although with a colloquial register and relatively few expressions peculiar to Britain or the United States. Even when the foreign text is set in a foreign country during a remote historical period, like the medieval Italy of Eco's novel or the eighteenth-century France of Süskind's, the translation adheres to current English usage, avoiding any archaism that would prove incomprehensible or too strange for the broadest segment of English-language readers. And highbrow foreign texts, even though written with a refined sense of literary form and received as works of high literature by the domestic elite, nonetheless undergo revision to make them more amenable to the popular aesthetic.

William Weaver's version of *The Name of the Rose* omits more than twelve pages of the Italian text, including lengthy catalogues of medieval terms and Latin passages (Chamosa and Santoyo 1993: 145–146). Such revisions seem designed to improve intelligibility and narrative continuity for the English-language reader by removing discursive features that would call attention to themselves and so interfere with the realist illusion. Other revisions constitute a more decisive domestication by removing linguistic and cultural differences, including passages where the difference is explained. The following sentence is omitted from Weaver's translation:

> E ai Fondamenti di santa Liperata uno gli disse: "Sciocco che sei, credi nel papa!" e lui rispose: "Ne avete fatto un dio di questo vostro papa" e aggiunse: "Questi vostri paperi v'hanno ben conci" (che era un gioco di parole, o arguzia, che faceva diventare i papi come animali, nel dialetto toscano, come mi spiegarono): e tutti si stupirono che andasse alla morte facendo scherzi.
>
> (Eco 1980: 241)

> And at the Convent of St Liperata, one man said to him: "Fool that you are, you believe in the Pope!" and he answered: "You've made a god of this your Pope" and added: "These geese [*paperi*] of yours are really cooked" (which was a play on words, or witticism, that likened the popes to animals, in the Tuscan dialect, as they explained to me): and they were all astonished that he would go to his death making jokes.

This deletion, besides avoiding the difficulty of translating an Italian pun (*papa/paperi*), simplifies the narrative, saving the English-language reader the intellectual effort of puzzling out the joke. At the same time, however, the reader loses a glimpse of a difference within Italian culture, the regional dialect. Since the passage criticizes the papacy, the deletion also suppresses a more sensitive, religious difference that may seem too irreverent to Catholic readers. The English translation has also been described as "target reader orientated" since certain choices seem to involve ethnic stereotyping: "the translated comments about Italy fit in with commonly held English beliefs" (Katan 1993: 161–162).

No translation can anticipate every possible response, of course, and this seems to be all the more true since the 1970s, when the American reading audience grew more heterogeneous, served by a widening range of small presses with diverse, special interests. Consequently, the success of highbrow foreign bestsellers has coincided with a more fragmented pattern of reception, even though they have been translated for a mass audience in much the same domesticating way as Guareschi's popular writing. The Guareschi translations consolidated American cultural and political values on a national scale, supporting the same meanings for different constituencies who took the same popular approach. The translation of Eco's novel, in contrast, maintained cultural and political divisions by supporting different meanings for different constituencies in accordance with different approaches, elite and popular.

These divisions were evident in the reviews. *Harper's*, for example, applied the high aesthetic by admiring the witty generic intricacies of Eco's narrative, calling it "an antidetective-story detective story" and "a semiotic murder mystery," while the *Hattiesburg American* made the middlebrow judgment that "Eco tells a good story and has a lot to say about such things as intellectual freedom and truth" (Schare 1983: 75; McMurtrey 1983: 2D). Both responses were domesticating to some extent, assimilating the foreign text to American codes and ideologies, but they each located a different source of domestic interest in it. Remarkably, the interest had little to do with Italy or Italian literature, but a great deal to do with recent developments in American academic culture, especially the importation of foreign critical methodologies (semiotics, poststructuralism), and even more with the popular tendency to provide domestic allegories for foreign texts. "We come away from *The Name of the Rose*," wrote one reviewer, "enriched by seeing contemporary questions unraveled through a parallel, but distinctive, historical period" (Weigel 1983).

The success of a highbrow novel in translation, then, should not be taken as a new sophistication in American literary taste or reading practices, one that indicates a greater openness to cultural difference or an increased awareness of contemporary foreign literatures. On the contrary, the foreign text becomes a translated bestseller because it is not so foreign as to upset the domestic status quo: the production process, from editing and translating to promotion and marketing, shapes the text for mass consumption by addressing dominant values in the domestic culture. The globalization of American popular culture has helped this process by enabling American publishers to pick foreign texts that reveal American cultural infiltrations. The popular aesthetic continues to be a key factor in producing a translated bestseller today, but it cannot be applied to such an extent that elite modes of appreciation are preempted. The translated bestseller must now be all things to many readers by permitting them to make what domestic use they will of it.

The question that remains is whether the fragmentation of the reading audience can be effective in changing the regime of domestication fostered by current publishing practices. The fragmented audience can definitely be utilized to increase the number of highbrow foreign texts made available in translation, provided that they are as "polyvalent or overdetermined" as a novel like Eco's, synthesizing elite and popular interests (Rollin 1988: 164). And this increase in volume can bring about a revision of domestic expectations for the foreign culture without risking the loss of intelligibility (and capital), provided that the production and reception establish a context in which the text can be understood. Of course another risk emerges here: will the focus on the foreign highbrow eventually rigidify domestic expectations? Or will an established track record of highbrow bestsellers create the conditions for another bestseller *inattendu*, a different foreign literary form whose very difference happens to answer to contemporary domestic interests?

Notes

My account of Guareschi's books in English translation relies on unpublished documents and editorial correspondence in the Farrar, Straus, and Giroux Archive, Rare Books and Manuscripts Division, New York Public Library.

1 The publishing history is drawn from Donald Demarest to Van Allen Bradley, 5 September 1950; "PW Forecasts," *Publishers Weekly* 19 July 1952: 261; Roger W. Straus Jr. to Herbert Alexander, 19 November 1959; Victor Gollancz to Roger Straus Jr., 4 December 1953; Hilary Rubenstein to Roger W. Straus Jr., 11 January 1955; Sheila Cudahy to Silvio Senigallia, 20 January 1958; Sheila Cudahy to Victor Gollancz, 6 May 1957; Obituary for Giovanni Guareschi, *New York Times* 23 July 1968: 39.

2 This article was not published. The *Saturday Review of Literature* ran a review of *The Little World of Don Camillo* by another writer who likewise sounded the political note and even repeated some of the wording of the unpublished article: see Sugrue 1950: 10.

3 Textbook and anthology publications are documented by subsidiary rights correspondence: Joseph Bellafiore to Pellegrini and Cudahy, 7 February 1953; Harcourt Brace to Farrar, Straus and Young, 19 November 1954; Beverly Jane Loo to Very Reverend Vincent J. Flynn, 13 March 1956; Kathy Connors to Scott, Foresman, 2 January 1957.

4 The publishers' entrepreneurial approach to Guareschi's writing is documented by contracts, letters, and income schedules: Memoranda of Agreement between Giovanni Guareschi and Pellegrini and Cudahy, 24 June 1949 and 14 August 1951; Donald Demarest to Chandler Grannis, 3 August 1950; George Pellegrini to Giangerolamo Carraro, Rizzoli, 20 November 1950; Sheila Cudahy to Sheila Hodges, Victor Gollancz Ltd., 4 June 1952; Victor Gollancz to Pellegrini and Cudahy, 27 August 1952; Cudahy to Herbert Alexander, Pocket Books, 22 April 1953; Robert Freier and Arnold Leslie Lazarus to Farrar, Straus and Young, 19 November 1954; Guareschi's Royalty and Subsidiary Rights Income Schedule from August 1950 to June 1954.

5 Various documents offer glimpses of the production process for the Guareschi translations: Giovanni Guareschi, "Io Sono Così," and an unattributed English version, "This is the Way I Am," both in typescript; fifteen non-consecutive typescript pages from Una Vincenzo Troubridge's translation of *The Little World of Don Camillo* (cited as "Troubridge 1949" in my text); Mary Ryan, In-House Memo, Pellegrini and Cudahy, 2 August 1949; Sheila Cudahy to Giovanni Guareschi, 18 March 1954; Cudahy to Frances Frenaye (Mrs. A. C. Lanza), 23 November 1959; Harold Vursell to W. J. Taylor-Whitehead, Macdonald and Co., Ltd., 3 May 1966; Vursell to Gordon Sager, 10 March 1966 and 23 January 1967; Andrée Conrad to Livia Gollancz, 17 September 1969.

6 Details concerning the translators' agreements with the publishers are drawn from correspondence and contracts: Sheila Cudahy to Cyrus Brooks, A. M. Heath and Company, 27 February 1950; Brooks to Cudahy, 10 March 1950; Cudahy to Una Vincenzo Troubridge, 12 April 1950; George Pellegrini to Brooks, 5 February 1951; Cudahy to Frances Frenaye (Lanza), 3 June 1952 and 27 April 1960; Cudahy to Victor Gollancz, 6 February 1957; Frenaye to Cudahy, 27 November 1959; Farrar, Straus and Giroux Contract with Gordon Sager, 10 March 1966; Sager to Harold Vursell, 8 April 1966; Vursell to Sager, 11 April 1966. Details concerning *Comrade Don Camillo* (namely printings, subsidiary rights sales, author's income) are drawn from the following correspondence: Milo J. Sutcliff, Catholic Digest Book Club, to Roger Straus Jr., 9 December 1963; In-House Memo, Farrar, Straus and Giroux, 10 December 1963; Straus to Herbert Alexander, Pocket Books, 13 December 1963; Lester Troob, Book-of-the-Month Club, to Straus, 23 December 1963; Robert Wohlforth to Giovanni Guareschi, 22 September 1964.

8

GLOBALIZATION

Translation is uniquely revealing of the asymmetries that have structured international affairs for centuries. In many "developing" countries (a term that will be used here to indicate a subordinate position in the global capitalist economy), it has been compulsory, imposed first by the introduction of colonial languages among regional vernaculars and later, after decolonization, by the need to traffic in the hegemonic lingua francas to preserve political autonomy and promote economic growth. Here translation is a cultural practice that is deeply implicated in relations of domination and dependence, equally capable of maintaining or disrupting them. The colonization of the Americas, Asia, and Africa could not have occurred without interpreters, both native and colonial, nor without the translation of effective texts, religious, legal, educational (see Rafael 1988; Cheyfitz 1991; Niranjana 1992). And the recent neocolonial projects of transnational corporations, their exploitation of overseas workforces and markets, can't advance without a vast array of translations, ranging from commercial contracts, instruction manuals, and advertising copy to popular novels, children's books, and film soundtracks.

The functionality of translation has worked just as well in initiatives mounted from subordinate positions, some directed against empire, others in complicity with globalized capital. Translations of foreign texts contributed to the militant nationalism of anticolonial movements. Between 1955 and 1980 the most frequently translated author in the world was Lenin, according to UNESCO statistics. In the developing countries, translations have played a crucial role in enriching indigenous languages and literatures while supporting reading and publishing. For oral cultures, translations are among the first books on the scene. For literate cultures with advanced or fledgling communications media, translations have accompanied lucrative deals with transnational publishers and film and television companies, sustaining industrial development by building native-language audiences for the cultural products of the hegemonic countries.

Since translating is always addressed to specific audiences, however vaguely or optimistically defined, its possible motives and effects are local and contingent, differing according to major or minor positions in the global economy. This is perhaps most clear with the power of translation to form cultural identities, to create a representation of a foreign culture that simultaneously constructs a domestic subjectivity, one informed with the domestic codes and ideologies that make the representation intelligible and culturally functional. Within the hegemonic countries, translation fashions images of their subordinate others that can vary between the poles of narcissism and self-criticism, confirming or interrogating dominant domestic values, reinforcing or revising the ethnic stereotypes, literary canons, trade patterns, and foreign policies to which another culture may be subject. Within developing countries, translation fashions images of their hegemonic others and themselves that can variously solicit submission, collaboration, or resistance, that may assimilate dominant foreign values with approval or acquiescence (free enterprise, Christian piety) or critically revise them to create domestic self-images that are more oppositional (nationalisms, fundamentalisms).

Translation can produce this range of possible effects in subordinate cultures because cultural domination doesn't necessarily entail a homogenizing process of identity formation. Of course the globalization of culture can't occur without "the use of a variety of instruments of homogenization," such as "advertising techniques" and "language hegemonies"; but "at least as rapidly as forces from various metropolises are brought into new societies they tend to become indiginized in one way or another," "absorbed into local political and cultural economies" (Appadurai 1996: 42, 32). In the multilingual cultures of Africa, Asia, and the Caribbean, translation forms identities marked by disjunction, hybrid formations that mix indigenous traditions with metropolitan trends. Although capable of diverse and contradictory effects, the cultural hybridity released by translation has been put to strategic uses in domestic literary styles and movements (switching between English and African languages in the West African novel); in commercial ventures (transnational advertising campaigns); and in government policies (the legislation of official languages that often do not include regional vernaculars).

The status of translation in the global economy is particularly embarrassing to the major English-speaking countries, the United States and the United Kingdom. It calls attention to the questionable conditions of their hegemony, their own dependence on the domination of English, on unequal cultural exchange that involves the exploitation of foreign print and electronic media and the exclusion and stereotyping of foreign cultures at home. At the same time, the globalization of English, the emergence of a world market for English-language cultural products, ensures that translations don't merely communicate British and American values, but rather submit them to a local differentiation, an assimilation to the heterogeneity of a minor position. Developing countries have been the sites of translation strategies and cultural identities that assimilate those prevailing in Anglo-American cultures and yet deviate from them in remarkable ways, some with greater social impact than others. In what follows I want to consider, first, the asymmetries that have long characterized translation relations in the global cultural economy, and then the forms of resistance and innovation that translation has taken under colonialism and in our own postcolonial era, where the imperialist project has not so much vanished as assumed the guise of transnational corporatism (Miyoshi 1993).

Asymmetries of commerce and culture

Translation patterns since World War II indicate the overwhelming domination of English-language cultures. English has become the most translated language worldwide, but despite the considerable size, technological sufficiency, and financial stability of the British and American publishing industries, it is one of the least translated into.

UNESCO statistics, incomplete because countries fail to report data and inconsistent because they follow different definitions of what constitutes a book, can still be useful for indicating broad trends. In 1987, the last year for which the data seems comprehensive, the global translation output was approximately 65,000 volumes, more than 32,000 of which were from English. These figures have probably not changed much over the past decade because international publishing has not increased dramatically, despite the widespread use of computers to generate camera-ready composition (Lofquist 1996: 557). The number of translations from English towers over the number of translations made from European languages: around 6,700 from French, 6,500 from Russian, 5,000 from German, 1,700 from Italian. In the geopolitical economy of translation, the languages of developing countries rank extremely low: for 1987 UNESCO reports 479 translations from Arabic, 216 from Chinese, 89 from Bengali, 14 from Korean, 8 from Indonesian. English also prevails over the other languages translated within these countries. In Brazil, where 60 percent of new titles consists of translations (4,800 out of 8,000 books in 1994), as much as 75 percent is from English (correspondence with Arthur Nestrovsky, 15 November 1995).

British and American publishers, in sharp contrast, translate much less. In the United States, 1994 saw the publication of 51,863 books, 1,418 (2.74 percent) of which were translations. This figure includes 55 translations from Chinese and 17 from Arabic, compared to 374 from French and 362 from German (Ink 1997: 508). Translation undoubtedly occupies a marginal position in Anglo-American cultures. Yet among the foreign texts that do enter English, writing in African, Asian, and South American languages attracts relatively little interest from publishers (for a similar situation in Germany where the number of translations is higher, see Ripken 1991).

These grossly unequal translation patterns point to a significant trade imbalance between the British and American publishing industries and their foreign counterparts. Quite simply, a lot of money is made from translating English, but little is invested in translating into it. Since the 1980s, sales of foreign rights for English-language books have become highly profitable, earning their publishers millions of dollars annually and in some cases earning more in foreign markets than at home (Weyr 1994; Tabor 1995). The foreign rights for an English-language "blockbuster" can fetch $500,000 in South America and from $10,000 to $200,000 in newly industrialized Asian countries like Taiwan, South Korea, and Malaysia (Weyr 1994: 33, 38). In Brazil, the rights to translate an English-language book start at $3,000 (Hallewell 1994: 596). According to UNESCO, 1987 saw Brazilian publishers bring out over 1,500 such translations, including not only highbrow literary works still under copyright (Samuel Beckett, Margaret Atwood), but also multiple titles by bestselling novelists who command higher fees: 25 books by Agatha Christie, 13 by Barbara Cartland, 9 by Sidney Sheldon, 7 by Harold Robbins, 5 by Robert Ludlum, 2 by Stephen King. In the same year, British and American publishers together issued only 14 translations of Brazilian literature (Barbosa 1994: 18). The enormous earnings from foreign rights sales don't increase the number of translations into English because British and American publishers are keen on financing domestic bestsellers, a trend that has continued unabated since the 1970s (see Whiteside 1981). In the words of Alberto Vitale, the chief executive officer of Random House, "foreign rights are the necessary income to compensate for the high advances we often pay in the U.S." (Weyr 1994: 34).

International copyright law favors British and American publishers in this trade imbalance by reserving for the author (or the publisher as the author's assignee) the right to license translations of a work. Even though the Berne Convention recognizes the translator's copyright in the translation, it still protects the author's exclusive ownership of the original work and derivatives made therefrom.

In the 1960s developing countries sought legal modifications to give them more freedom in using copyrighted works, especially where indigenous publishing was stymied by intractable problems: high rates of illiteracy, paper shortages, obsolete printing technology, minimal distribution, government control, and the fragmentation of the potential book market into numerous linguistic communities (for an overview of these problems, see Altbach 1994). Beginning with the Stockholm Revision (1967), the Berne Convention has included a "Protocol Regarding Developing Countries" that allows – much to the consternation of Western authors and publishers – compulsory licensing of their works for publication and translation in those countries.

Yet the protocol is actually a compromise that satisfies neither side in the conflict. It has not significantly improved indigenous publishing or affected the unequal patterns of cultural exchange because various conditions restrict compulsory licensing. Translations of Western books so licensed cannot be published in a developing country until three years after the publication of the original work, and they must be intended solely for the purposes of teaching, scholarship, and research – two conditions that prevent a publisher from capitalizing on the international popularity of a foreign work or author and increasing the size of the domestic audience (Berne, Appendix C: II(2)(a), (5)). In fact, Western publishers customarily avoid issuing compulsory licenses by exporting a low-priced edition of their own or by selling reprint or translation rights to an indigenous publisher within the allotted period (Gleason 1994: 193).

In the case of China, international copyright law does not merely support a trade imbalance, but imposes a different set of cultural and political values. China lacked a comprehensive copyright code until 1991 largely because Chinese thinking about the ownership of intellectual works has long been collective and not commercialistic, whether based in patrilineal tradition or in socialist ideology; it therefore differed radically from the individualistic concepts of private property that characterize Western law (Ploman and Hamilton 1980: 140–147). To Western publishers, unauthorized translations constitute a copyright infringement, if not sheer piracy, whereas in China they were a routine publishing practice and have only recently been made illegal (Altbach 1987: 103).

China's signing of the Berne Convention in 1992 has brought the Chinese publishing industry in line with most of the world, at least in the terms of copyright law. Yet it has actually decreased the volume of Chinese translations, since the government is now required to exercise greater control over publishing and is better able to exclude foreign works judged to be threats to the socialist order (Wei Ze 1994: 459). Translations have also declined because Chinese publishers are not able to pay high fees in hard currency for foreign rights. The profit motive of Western publishers, especially as expressed in the furor over copyright infringement, ultimately overrides the Western concern with the abuse of human rights in China.

For developing countries, the trade imbalance in translation publishing carries negative consequences, cultural as well as economic. Indigenous publishers invest in British and American bestsellers because they are much more profitable than domestic literary works, which lack wide recognition and so require more aggressive promotion and marketing to reach a large audience. As a result, domestic works go undersubsidized, and the development of domestic languages, literatures, and readerships is limited. Within multilingual countries, the unequal translation patterns reinforce existing hierarchies among linguistic and cultural constituencies. Foreign texts are rendered mostly into government-designated official languages or into the native language that dominates the publishing industry, and this practice deprives vernaculars of the linguistic and literary enrichment that translation can work on them. Inevitably, if the translation of English-language bestsellers attracts investment away from domestic literatures, it also preempts the translating between regional languages that can stimulate "a wider sharing of national problems and concerns" (Singh 1994: 467).

Because the English-language books selected for translation tend to be in popular genres like the romance and the thriller, which invite the pleasures of imaginative identification instead of the critical detachment of the high aesthetic, the translations allow Anglo-American values to cultivate an elite Westernized readership, unconcerned with domestic cultures. By the mid-1970s, for example, Bengali versions of "spy stories and crime thrillers" by British writers like Edgar Wallace and Ian Fleming – narratives that unfold in colonial situations (West Africa, the Caribbean) – had created "a wholly new class" of Indian reader, a popular audience for whom the books were objects of "sheer entertainment" as opposed to reflection on their post-colonial situation (Mukherjee 1976: 68–69).

In India and anglophone African countries, where the colonial language has been designated official or else become the language of publishing, transnational publishers maintain a neocolonial grip on local English-speaking minorities by exporting translations originally addressed to British and American audiences. These publishers also reach beyond the elite minority to more popular readerships because they (with their indigenous counter-parts) exploit indirect translation from English: they issue indigenous-language versions of English versions of foreign texts, so that English-language values mediate the reception of foreign cultures (for "indirect" or "second-hand" translation, see Toury 1995: chap. 7). In Indian publishing, where trans-lations of foreign literary texts represent "the most common and commercially most viable" form of translating, the canonical European works have been generally rendered from English versions of non-English originals (Mukherjee 1976: 68–69). The Indian translations are inevitably shaped by Anglo-American canons for foreign literatures, as well as the discursive strategies that prevail in English-language translating.

With school textbooks, the largest and most profitable category of publishing in developing countries, transnationals have issued translations or reprints in official languages without concern for their pedagogical value or their relevance to the domestic cultural situation. For decades after World War II American publishers seeking a foothold in the Brazilian market trans-lated textbooks that "had been prepared for their Hispanic American subsidiaries" (Hallewell 1994: 599), just as British publishers in Africa imported "either those used in Britain or those developed in India and the Far East" (Rea 1975: 145). Even when a British textbook was written precisely for an African audience, the author might ignore cultural differences by adhering too closely to British values. In 1932, for instance, Longmans published an elementary school geography in two versions, the original English and a Swahili translation, both designed for use in East Africa. Yet a contemporary reviewer who praised the British author "for providing a valuable textbook" nonetheless faulted him for complicating the translating process: he hadn't "written in the first instance with more sympathetic regard for Bantu metaphor" (Rivers-Smith 1931: 208).

Commercial translations have sought to create foreign markets for transnational corporations by taking advantage of language hegemonies in advertising campaigns. American-based Parker Pen recently ran a number of full-page advertisements in various mass-circulation magazines around the world, including versions in English (*Newsweek*, the *New Yorker*), French (*L'Express*), Italian (*L'Espresso*), and Brazilian Portuguese (*Veja*). The layout of the page is a striking juxtaposition of two vertical images. The left side contains a black-and-white photo of a performer standing upright – usually a ballerina or a jazz trumpeter – next to the caption, "Born to Perform." The right side contains a color photo of a very ornate fountain pen (gold trim, lacquer and pearl finishes) pointed downward toward the caption, "Just Like A Parker." The advertisement works by constructing a simple analogy, which transfers the prestige that invests certain cultural forms (ballet, jazz) to a luxury item (the "suggested retail price" for the pen is several hundred dollars). The Brazilian version turns this analogy into a locally effective marketing tool by translating the captions into more heterogenous language. It pictures the jazz musician and renders "Born to Perform" as "Nascido Para Performance" (*Veja* 26 July 1995: 6). A Portuguized English word of recent derivation, "performance" is widely used in Brazil to describe cultural forms or presentations, such as when a sports journalist or football fan assesses "a performance do time," the performance of a team (with "time" representing another Portuguized formation from English).

This translation at once exploits the polylingualism of Brazilian Portuguese and the divisions among Brazilian cultural constituencies. The English embedded in the advertisement, both the Portuguized form of "performance" and the brand name ("Como uma Parker," reads the caption), makes a subtle appeal to the anglophone elite who compose a significant segment of the readership for the relatively expensive magazine (the Parker advertisement is wedged between others that featured glossy color images of IBM laptop computers and BMW autos). Although "performance" is recognized as Portuguese by most Brazilians and has even passed into colloquial usage, educated readers of *Veja* would be aware of its English derivation. Hence, the advertisement not only trades on the prestige that American products have acquired in Brazil; it also plays to the prestige that the major language may hold for the anglophone elite by using a Brazilian Portuguese word borrowed from English. For the elite readers, the translation makes the pen desirable by setting up a hierarchy between the two languages (English as the origin of the Brazilian Portuguese word) to reinforce the hierarchy among Brazilian constituencies.

If translation reveals the cultural and economic dependence of developing countries on their hegemonic others, its many ramifications also make clear that this dependence is in various ways *mutual*, even if unequal. African, Asian, and South American countries look to the West for translations and imports of scientific, technical, and literary texts, even for school books at every educational level. Writers in the anglophone cultures of Africa and India look to the United Kingdom and the United States for critical and commercial success, seeking the approval of metropolitan intellectuals and preferring to publish their books with the transnationals instead of indigenous presses struggling with financing (Gedin 1984: 102; Singh 1994: 467). In some cases, the value of this writing is judged by indigenous critics according to whether it can be translated into the hegemonic languages and thereby gain international recognition for the subordinate culture (Barbosa 1993: 729; Dallal 1998).

At the same time, the practices of British and American publishers, their investment in English-language bestsellers and their cultivation of foreign rights and export markets, have made them increasingly dependent on income from developing countries. In the early 1970s, Longman "obtained 80 percent of its turnover from abroad" (Mattelart 1979: 147–148). A similar point can be made about the electronic media. Not only do Western news agencies and American film and television companies dominate the global flow of information and entertainment, whether in English or in translated and dubbed versions, but their profit margins can't be maintained without their continued domination. Between 1960 and 1980, according to UNESCO statistics, Walt Disney Productions ranked consistently within the top five "authors" most frequently translated in the world. Here, of course, the term "author" designates corporate publications drawn from films. Transnationalism depends not only on foreign markets, but on the effectiveness of local translations to compete in those markets, a cultural dependence that enforces new forms of authorship (corporate) and of publishing (tie-ins) to strengthen the bottom line.

Transnational identities

The translation practices enlisted by transnational corporations, whether publishers, manufacturers, or advertising agencies, function in the same fundamental ways as those that underwrote European colonialism. The main difference is that translation now serves corporate capital instead of a nation state, a trading company, or an evangelical program. What remains unchanged is the use of translation practices that establish a hierarchical relationship between the major and minor languages, between the hegemonic and subordinate cultures. The translations enact a process of identity formation in which colonizer and colonized, transnational corporation and indigenous consumer, are positioned unequally.

Although the history of colonialism varies significantly according to place and period, it does reveal a consistent, no, an inevitable reliance on translation. Christian missionaries and colonial administrators, with the help of educationalists and anthropologists, typically composed dictionaries, grammars, and orthographies for indigenous languages and then set about translating religious and legal texts into them. In the Philippines during the sixteenth century,

Spanish priests delivered sermons in Tagalog to convert the indigenous population. Translation enabled conversion and colonization simultaneously: the believer who acknowledged the Christian God also submitted to the divinely anointed Spanish king, especially since the missionaries linked political submission on earth to salvation in the hereafter (Rafael 1988: 168). Yet their preaching also invested colonial languages with awful authority and charisma because they left key terms in Latin and Castilian (*Doctrina Christina, Dios, Espíritu Sancto, Jesucristo*), indicating the doctrinal dependence of Tagalog on Castilian and Latin, as well as the proximity of Castilian to the language of the Bible and therefore to the Logos (ibid.: 20–21, 28–29, 35).

In the late nineteenth century, similarly, British missionaries in Nigeria rendered the Bible and devotional works like John Bunyan's *Pilgrim's Progress* into such indigenous languages as Yoruba, Efik, and Hausa (Babalolá 1971: 50–51, 55). Government-funded translation bureaux were subsequently established to provide vernacular versions of British textbooks (*Oversea Education* 1931: 30–33; Adams 1946: 120). The practice of the Hausa Bureau was to retain untranslated any "English term which has not yet passed into colloquial usage," even though the director acknowledged that "to an African who has only been taught to read in the vernacular the sudden appearance of an unknown and unpronounceable word is very disconcerting" (East 1937: 104). Yet the effect was likely to be mystifying as well: the unknown words implicitly marked English, not Hausa, as the source of knowledge and therefore the superior language, particularly since the text was a translation from English.

Colonial governments strengthened their hegemony through translations that were inscribed with the colonizer's image of the colonized, an ethnic or racial stereotype that rationalized domination. Sir William Jones, the eighteenth-century scholar and judge in the service of the East India Company, translated Sanskrit legal texts because he suspected the reliability of Indian interpreters and sought to restore Indian law to its ancient purity – which, it turned out, supported the Company's commercial ventures (see Said 1978: 77–79; Niranjana 1992: 12–20). He hoped that his translation of Manu's *Institutes* would be imposed as "the standard of justice" to "many millions of *Hindu* subjects, whose well-directed industry would add largely to the wealth of *Britain*" (Jones 1970: 813, 927). Jones's imperialist stereotyping influenced many subsequent British scholars and translators, so that after the introduction of English education in India, Indians came to study Orientalist translations of Indian-language texts and acceded both to the cultural authority of those translations and to their discriminatory images of Indian cultures. "Even when the anglicized Indian spoke a language other than English, 'he' would have preferred, because of the symbolic power conveyed by English, to gain access to his own past through the translations and histories circulating through colonial discourse" (Niranjana 1992: 31).

Because translation can influence the course of literary traditions, it has been deliberately used by colonial governments to create indigenous literary cultures that favor foreign domination. In the first decades of the twentieth century, the Dutch elicited the political consent of educated Indonesians through a competitive publishing program that featured translations. Instead of censoring the fiction and journalism of radical nationalists, the government-directed publisher Balai Pustaka issued cheap Indonesian versions of European romantic novels "devoid of political content," mainly adventure fantasies riddled with racist stereotypes and Orientalist exoticism, including the work of Rider Haggard, Jules Verne, and Pierre Loti (Watson 1973: 183–185). Haggard's novels in particular would be useful to this publishing strategy: they represent Africans as either submissively child-like or savagely violent and therefore in need of guidance by the white characters; and the narratives unfold in imperial settings while entirely omitting any representation of British imperialism (David 1995: 188–92).

Not only did such translations help undermine the Indonesian nationalist movement by decreasing the readership for radical writing; they also encouraged Indonesian novelists to produce conservative imitations of European romances. Abdoel Moeis's 1928 novel *Salah Asuhan* (*A Wrong Upbringing*) insists on the inferiority of Indonesians by warning them away from Dutch education and marriage with Europeans. And it couches this insistence in a melodramatic plot that emphasizes the "psychological incompatibilities" of the characters instead of the ethnic and political divisions they live out in their relationships (Watson 1973: 190–1).

Balai Pustaka's translations and indigenous novels disseminated literary and social values that aided the Dutch suppression of Indonesian radicalism – just as today the translated bestsellers issued by British and American publishers have created a global readership fascinated with hegemonic values, including literary forms (the romance, the thriller) that often glamorize metropolitan consumerism. Transnational publishers enjoy a hegemony that is not political, but cultural and economic, not repressive of dissent, but constitutive and exploitative of a market. Yet insofar as they don't reinvest income from foreign rights sales in translations from African, Asian, and South American literatures, their publishing strategies remain distinctly imperialist.

Over the past forty years the interest shown by British and American publishers in these literatures has achieved mixed results, mainly because they have created canons that offer a limited representation of the writing. The transnational venture that has achieved the greatest success, in critical as well as commerical terms, was undoubtedly Heinemann's African Writers Series, which published 270 literary texts between 1962 and 1983 (Currey 1985: 11). Heinemann profited hugely from the series, which was initially directed from London but eventually involved branch offices in Nigeria and Kenya. African countries adopted the books as school texts after independence, giving them an academic authority that ensured wide circulation. In 1976, when Nigerian law restricted Heinemann to 60 percent ownership, the sales of the Ibadan branch alone reached £2.38 million; in 1982, when Heinemann's share was reduced to 40 percent, this branch still yielded the London office a profit of £60,800 (St. John 1990: 477).

The editors were highly selective, so the series could not avoid being unrepresentative. Approximately twenty titles were published annually, chosen from a pool of 300 manuscripts (Currey 1979: 237). The first bestseller, a reprint of Chinua Achebe's novel *Things Fall Apart* (1962), set the standard by which subsequent books would be judged, especially since Achebe served as adviser for the first decade. By the 1980s, however, African readers found the series too "preoccupied with the clash of cultures between Africa and the West," the main theme of Achebe's novel (Chakava 1988: 240). In focussing on African literature that displayed this preoccupation, Heinemann neglected the latest developments in urban writing, popular novels that lacked the academic imprimatur of course adoption and aimed rather for a realistic depiction of Africa after decolonization: "these expressed the dreams and ambitions of a new generation looking for their fortune in the cities and putting education and material success higher than traditional rural life," evoking comparisons to Dickens and Balzac (Gedin 1984: 104). In a move that decisively reinforced language hegemonies, Heinemann excluded translations from African languages, devoting the series to anglophone and francophone texts.

The resulting canon reflected a distinctively European image of the "Third World" current among left intellectuals during the Cold War – when the concept of the Third World was first formulated. Seeking a "third way" in international relations, independent of both American capitalism and Soviet communism (the "First" and "Second" Worlds), these Europeans saw their wish for nonalignment realized in the anticolonialism of African, Asian, and South American nationalists (Worsley 1984: 307). Heinemann similarly created an image of African literature that was anticolonial, in emphasizing cultural confrontation, and nationalist, in questioning the impact of modern metropolitan cultures on ethnic traditions. The series defined its Western publishers, readers, and teachers as politically engaged intellectuals in solidarity with militant African writers whose goal was national self-determination. Alan Hill, the chairman of Heinemann who initiated the series and set up the African branches, saw his publishing strategies as a contribution to the decolonizing process. Describing his motivation as "my radical, nonconformist, missionary ethos," he criticized other British publishers for profiting from the sale of English textbooks in Africa but "putting nothing back" through investment in indigenous authors (Hill 1988: 122–123). And he recalled that "I gave [the directors of the local offices] dominion status instead of the colonial subordination preferred by some of our competitors" (quoted in St. John 1990: 477).

The case of the Heinemann series shows that Western canons of minor literatures have not only created specifically Western representations of those literatures, but enabled the construction of cultural identities for metropolitan intellectuals. The canons resulted from a process of identification with an ideal figured in the anglophone text or translation, a set of distinctively domestic values that are linked to cultural and political projects as well as sheer commerce. At Heinemann, Hill saw his radical missionary ethos realized in the independence he allowed the African branches – provided, of course, that their publishing was in line with Heinemann's competition against other transnationals.

In the United States, the so-called "boom" in South American literature during the 1960s and 1970s was fostered by publishers, novelists, and critics who valued its fantastic experimentalism over the realistic narratives that have always dominated American fiction. The boom was not a sudden increase in South American literary output, but primarily a North American creation, a sudden increase in English-language translations supported by private funding (Barbosa 1994: 62–63; Rostagno 1997). Publishers issued a wave of translations from the work of such authors as the Argentines Jorge Luis Borges and Julio Cortázar and the Columbian Gabriel García Márquez, forming a new canon of foreign literature in English as well as a more sophisticated readership.

This trend continued partly because the translations were profitable, as the economic metaphor ("boom") suggests. Gregory Rabassa's 1970 version of García Márquez's novel *One Hundred Years of Solitude* was a notable success, a bestseller in paperback and ultimately a textbook adopted in colleges and universities (Castro-Klarén and Campos 1983: 326–327). Yet the influx of South American writing was also altering contemporary fiction in the United States, encouraging writers like John Barth to develop related narrative experiments. Barth felt that South American writers provided a remedy for the "exhaustion" of traditional forms of storytelling, a "replenishment" in the shape of "magic realism" and a greater generic self-consciousness (Payne 1993: chap. 1). English-language fiction recreated itself in a particular image of South American writing premised on a diagnosis of the North American literary scene.

The resulting canon, however, excluded writing that evidently could not help in this recreation. The boom was largely an increase in translations of Hispanic literatures which neglected contemporary Brazilian developments: between 1960 and 1979, British and American publishers brought out 330 translations from Spanish, but only 64 translations from Brazilian Portuguese (Barbosa 1994: 17–19). The focus on Spanish reflected the international attention paid to South America after the Cuban Revolution in 1959, but especially the interest of North American intellectuals who viewed Hispanic cultures as "sources of political energy in a generalized struggle for a just society" (Payne 1993: 20; see Fernández Retamar 1989: 7, 30–31).

Yet the boom also involved a marked emphasis on male writers. This perhaps answered to a masculinist concept of authorship in American culture, an equation of radical experimentation with masculinity, and so the comparable achievement of an Argentine writer like Silvina Ocampo was obscured.

Her fantastic fiction was just as relentlessly innovative as that of her collaborators, Borges and her husband Adolfo Bioy Casares, but it wasn't translated into English until the late 1980s (see Ocampo 1988). It was during the same period that the much acclaimed work of the Brazilian Clarice Lispector began appearing in English, with six translations published in a three-year period (Barbosa 1994: 2). Her writing, which eschews fantasy for a more realistic evocation of female subjectivity, did not attain the canonical status it now enjoys in Anglo-American culture, especially in the academy, until it was championed by the French feminist theorist Hélène Cixous (who first read Lispector's work in French translation). The canonization of Lispector constructed a different cultural identity for the metropolitan intellectuals who studied her, at once feminist and poststructuralist: they found in her work a critique of patriarchal values expressed through the discontinuous textuality that Cixous theorized as *écriture féminine* (Arrojo 1997).

Metropolitan intellectuals have looked to developing countries as sources of cultural and political values that are useful in devising projects at home and indeed in fashioning domestic subjects, their own intellectual identities as well as the ideas and tastes of their audiences. These appropriations can't be simply dismissed as self-serving because the projects have included complicated challenges to dominant domestic values (e.g. colonial, masculinist), but also because they have brought international attention to subordinate cultures, installing certain literary texts and traditions in a widely recognized canon of world literatures. Yet insofar as the motives of metropolitan intellectuals have been informed by domestic interests and debates, even when expressed as a counter-hegemonic internationalism, they have inevitably developed selective representations of the subordinate cultures in which they made their investments, cultural and commercial, political and psychological. Translation patterns have created and consolidated the terms of cultural recognition for both hegemonic and certain developing countries, but without in any way diminishing the linguistic and cultural hierarchies in which those countries continue to be positioned.

Translation as resistance

And yet a subordinate position in the global economy must not be seen as passive submission. Under colonizing regimes the functions of translation are extremely diverse and unpredictable in effect, always allowing the colonized the discursive space to evade or tamper with the discriminatory stereotypes imposed on them. The possibilities for resistance are inherent in the fundamental ambivalence of colonial discourse: it constructs an identity for the colonized that requires them to mimic colonial values but is simultaneously a partial representation, incomplete and prejudiced, a resemblance that is nonetheless treated as an inappropriate difference, a hybrid necessitating surveillance and discipline, potentially menacing (Bhabha 1994: 86). The ambivalence discredits colonial authority by demonstrating that the evangelical program and the civilizing mission constitute forms of political domination, so that the religious and national symbols put before the colonized are eventually reduced to empty signs, apprehended as impurely ideological (ibid.: 112). Translating is uniquely effective in exacerbating the tensions of colonial discourse because the move between colonial and indigenous languages can refigure the cultural and political hierarchies between them, upsetting the identity-forming process, the mimicry of hegemonic values on which colonization relies.

Hence, translation was a recurrent worry in the discourse of British imperialism, where monumental projects (Jones's versions of Hindu legal texts) and key debates (on the language of colonial education) were concerned with its policing and regulation. When in 1835, as a governing member of the East India Company, Thomas Macaulay argued that the introduction of the English public-school curriculum was essential for British rule in India, he imagined it creating an elite corps of indigenous translators, "a class who may be interpreters between us and the millions whom we govern" (Macaulay 1952: 729). And he viewed these translators as racially suspect even though Anglicized, "a class of persons, Indian in blood and colour, but English in taste, in opinions, in morals, and in intellect," who had to be stopped from studying native languages like Arabic and Sanskrit to avoid "the influence of their own hereditary prejudices" (ibid.: 726).

For Macaulay, the English-educated interpreters would eventually build an indigenous national culture. Their knowledge and translations of English books would enable them to "refine the vernacular dialects" and "enrich those dialects" both "with terms of science borrowed from the Western nomenclature" and with a national literary tradition: "what the Greek and Latin were to the contemporaries of More and Ascham," wrote Macaulay, "our tongue is to the people of India. The literature of England is now more valuable than that of classical antiquity" (ibid.: 729, 724). Obviously the nationalism fed by this translation program would be British, a reverence for British literary traditions (at least initially, before inspiring Indian counterparts), and so it mystified the imperial function that Macaulay's translators served.

In the colonial project, translating takes so many forms and puts to work so many tools (grammars, dictionaries, language textbooks) that very few of their effects can be anticipated or controlled. The colonized, moreover, might have no economic incentives or support to learn the colonial language or might simply refuse to learn it; they might also teach it to one another as a means of negotiating and circumventing the colonizers' presence. In 1903, after almost four centuries of Spanish rule, only 10 percent of the Filipino population understood Castilian (Rafael 1988: 56). The first book written by a Filipino, the seventeenth-century printer Tomas Pinpin, was in fact a Tagalog manual for learning Castilian. Pinpin didn't set out to teach fluency in the colonial language, but rather a use of it for "pleasure and protection" against Spanish oppression – which of course could never be discussed in a book published by the Dominican press (ibid.: 56–57, 65). To his readers Pinpin presented the study of Castilian in terms of colonial mimicry, implicitly acknowledging that the Spanish presence had introduced an alien process of forming Tagalog identity. And he undoubtedly appealed to their anxiety about dealing with the colonizer:

> Di baquin ang ibang manga caasalan at caanyoan nang manga Castila ay inyong guinalologdan at ginagagad din ninyo sa pagdaramitan at sa nananandataman at paglacadam at madlaman ang magogol ay uala rin hinahinayang cayo dapouat macmochamocha cayo sa Castila. Ay aba itopang isang asal macatotohanan sapangongosap nang canila ding uica ang di sucat ibigang camtam? [. . .] Di con magcamomocha nang tayo nila nang pagdaramit ay con ang pangongosap ay iba, ay anong darating?

> No doubt you like and imitate the ways and appearance of the Spaniards in matters of clothing and the bearing of arms and even of gait, and you do not hesitate to spend a great deal so that you may resemble the Spaniards. Therefore would you not like to acquire as well this other trait which is their language? [. . .] if we look like them in our manner of dressing but speak differently, then where would things come to?

> (Rafael 1988: 57–58)

Pinpin didn't detail many of these unpropitious "things," the consequences of the Tagalogs' miscomprehension or mispronunciation of Castilian. But he did make clear that it could provoke scornful laughter from a Spanish interlocutor or even physical violence (ibid.: 72–73). To speak Castilian differently was to underscore the hybridity that escapes colonial power, the cultural difference that the mimicry of colonial values is designed to erase but only exaggerates, provoking repression.

In Pinpin's pedagogy, the differences between Tagalog and Castilian received the most attention, and perhaps nowhere to greater effect than in the macaronic songs he inserted between the lessons. Here Tagalog lines are followed by Castilian renderings, so that Tagalog is represented as the prior or "original" language displaced by a belated Spanish translation:

> Anong dico toua, Como no he de holgarme;
> Con hapot, omaga, la mañana y tarde;
> dili napahamac, que no salio en balde;
> itong gaua co, aqueste mi lance;
> madla ang naalman; y a mil cossas saben;

nitong aquing alagad, los mios escolares;
sucat magcatoua, justo es alegrarse;
ang manga ama nila, sus padres y madres;
at ang di camuc-ha, pues son de otro talle;
na di ngani baliu, no brutos salvages.
[. . .]
O Ama con Dios, o gran Dios mi Padre;
tolongan aco, quered ayudarme;
amponin aco, sedme favorable;
nang mayari ito, porque esto se acabe;
at icao ang purihin, y a vos os alaben.

Oh, how happy I am, why shouldn't I make merry,
when afternoon and morning, morning and afternoon,
no danger occurs, it was not in vain,
this work of mine, this my transaction.
So much will be known, and a thousand things will be known
by my followers, those my students.
Such is their joy, they do right to rejoice,
their parents, their fathers and mothers,
and even those not like them, for they are of another kind
they are not crazy, not savage brutes.
[. . .]
O God my Father, O great God my Father;
help me, please help me;
adopt me, be favorable to me;
that this be accomplished, so that this can be finished;
and you will be praised, and you will be glorified.

(Rafael 1988: 60–62)

The prosody of the song equalizes Tagalog and Castilian by submitting both to the regular rhythm and the assonantal rhyme scheme. As a result, the colonial language loses the privileged position it occupied in the Tagalog sermons delivered by the Spanish priests. The song makes the two languages "refer neither to a master language such as Latin nor to a single message such as the promise of salvation, but to the persistence of rhythm and rhyme" (ibid.: 62).

There is, moreover, a slippage of meaning in the move from Tagalog to Castilian that threatens to reduce the prayer-like song to a wry parody of Christian hymns. In the Tagalog, Pinpin's project might encounter ominously unspecified "dangers" in trying to attract "followers" whom he defends as "not crazy" for studying the Spaniards' language, whereas in the Castilian rendering his project might be "in vain" if he attracted no "students" whose desire to study the language distinguishes them from "savage brutes." In the

Tagalog, divine protection is sought for language learning and use that appear suggestively agonistic, possibly a betrayal of Tagalog autonomy or a means of resisting the Spanish colonizer, whereas in the Castilian God is asked to bless a more narcissistic submission to colonial authority, an identification with its civilizing language. Pinpin's textbook offers no explicit attack on the Spanish regime. But it constantly reminds his Tagalog readers of the hierarchies – linguistic, cultural, and political – in which they are subordinated.

The imposition of colonial languages led eventually to the emergence of hybrid literary forms wherein native authorship encompasses subversive varieties of translation. In West Africa, Europhone novels have occasionally been characterized by a "translingualism," in which traces of the indigenous language are visible in an English or French text through lexical and syntactical peculiarities, apart from the use of pidgins and the sheer embedding of indigenous words and phrases (Scott 1990: 75; see also Ashcroft, Griffiths and Tiffin 1989: 59–77; Zabus 1991: 3–10). Early in the 1950s the Nigerian Amos Tutuola began writing English-language narratives that synthesize Yoruba folklore and literature with several canonical European texts, notably *The Pilgrim's Progress* and Edith Hamilton's 1940 retelling of Greek and Roman myths, *Mythology* (Zell and Silver 1971: 195). Yet Tutuola cast his narratives in an eccentric prose that reflects a recurrent but unsystematic process of translating Yoruba into English. The eccentricities were due partly to his limited English-language education, roughly middle school level, and partly to his reliance on close English renderings of Yoruba expressions, in many cases calques that twist the English into unusual shapes (Afolayan 1971; Zabus 1991: 113). In this typical excerpt from Tutuola's first book, *The Palm-Wine Drinkard* (1952), the "drinkard's" supernatural quest to find his deceased tapster leads to an encounter with Death, who invites him to stay the night:

> when I entered the room, I met a bed which was made of bones of human-beings; but as this bed was terrible to look at or to sleep on it, I slept under it instead, because I knew his trick already. Even as this bed was very terrible, I was unable to sleep under as I lied down there because of fear of the bones of human-beings, but I lied down there awoke. To my surprise was that when it was about two o'clock in the mid-night, there I saw somebody enter into the room cautiously with a heavy club in his hands, he came nearer to the bed on which he had told me to sleep, then he clubbed the bed with all his power, he clubbed the centre of the bed thrice and he returned cautiously, he thought that I slept on that bed and he thought also that he had killed me.
>
> (Tutuola 1952: 13–14)

The passage contains non-standard usages and errors that point to Tutuola's imperfect schooling, his shaky command of English. At least one error – "I lied down there awoke" – shows Tutuola struggling with linguistic differences, overcompensating for the lack of morphological inflections in Yoruba by marking them in English where they don't belong: after "lied" the verb "awake" becomes "awoke" (Afolayan 1971: 51). Several other peculiarities – "I met a bed," "two o'clock in the mid-night," "to my surprise was that" – are direct translations of Yoruba words and phrases (ibid.). "I met a bed" renders *mo ba béèdé*, in which the verb *ba* can variously mean "to find," "to encounter," "to discover," "to overtake," as well as "to meet" (Zabus 1991: 113). Similarly, Tutuola used the odd English construction, "we were travelling inside bush to bush," confusing two idiomatic phrases ("inside the bush" and "from bush to bush") because he was translating closely from the Yoruba, *láti inú igbo dé inú igbo*, literally "from inside the forest to inside the forest" (Tutuola 1952: 91; Zabus 1991: 114–115).

This calquing sometimes occurs in second-language acquisition, producing the sort of "interlanguage" that is used by minorities with weak competence in the major language or the standard dialect – immigrants, for instance (Ashcroft, Griffiths and Tiffin 1989: 67). Under a colonial regime, the practice can't fail to take on a political dimension. Tutuola's translating imprinted English with Yoruba, forcing the colonial language in its very structures to register the presence of an indigenous language which, although spoken by a significant population (approximately 13 million), was reduced to minority status by British imperialism.

Because the translingualism of colonial and postcolonial writing redefines authorship to embrace translation, it issues an implicit challenge to the concept of authorial originality, a hallowed tenet of European romanticism that continues to prevail regardless of where a culture is positioned in the global economy. Not only are Tutuola's narratives fundamentally second-order, employing African and European cultural materials as well as English renderings from an African language, but the calquing isn't intentional. It occurred inadvertently during the composition process, owing to the diglossia of his colonial situation, and the striking neologisms and non-standard constructions were left virtually intact by his London publisher, Faber and Faber (a lightly edited manuscript page is reproduced in Tutuola 1952: 24).

The translating involved in Tutuola's narratives prevents them from being described as unique works of self-expression. And it therefore questions the romantic assumption of originality that informed the opposing sides in his controversial reception. During the 1950s and 1960s Anglo-American reviewers acclaimed Tutuola as the untutored "genius," the innovative "visionary" whose writing bore comparison to "Anna Livia Plurabelle, Alice in Wonderland and the poems of Dylan Thomas" (Moore 1962: 39, 42; Rodman 1953: 5), while African critics dismissed him as an incompetent hack who merely rewrote familiar folk tales. "It is bad enough to attempt an African narrative in 'good English,'" complained one African reader, but "it is worse to attempt it in Mr. Tutuola's strange lingo" (Lindfors 1975:

31, 41; the controversy is summarized in Bishop 1988: 36–37). Tutuola at once achieved and divided an international audience: his work constituted a form of composition that was stigmatized in the hegemonic cultures, but that nonetheless could be assimilated to aesthetic categories and literary traditions that were valued in those cultures. Tutuola's authorship was not self-originating or individualistic but derivative and collective, characterized by an elaboration of the various oral and literary traditions available to an uneducated Nigerian writer under British rule.

Tutuola's translating likewise prevents his narratives from being described as an expression of cultural authenticity, whether from a Eurocentric stand-point that praises them for representing the "true macabre energy of Africa" (Lindfors 1975: 30) or from an Afrocentric one that criticizes their lapse from "folk purity" (Bishop 1988: 75). For despite Tutuola's reliance on Yoruba folklore and literature, the calquing never rendered a specific Yoruba text; no purely indigenous original existed behind Tutuola's eccentric English. In fact, the lexical and syntactical peculiarities indicate that Yoruba was *already* a heterogenous language containing English borrowings. Thus, Tutuola used the neologism "reserve-bush," a rendering of the Yoruba *igbo risafu*, where *risafu* is itself a neologism made from a calque, a loan translation of the English "reserve" (Tutuola 1952: 95; Afolayan 1971: 53). The stylistic peculiarities produced by Tutuola's translating are not metaphors of an ethnic or racial essence, but metonymies of an intercultural difference. They signify that his text stands betweeen English and Yoruba, and they reveal a limit to the colonial imposition of English, a breakdown in the identity-forming process of mimicking British values.

The translingualism that is inadvertent in Tutuola's narratives is deliberately put to political uses in other minority literatures. It is perhaps most typical of Arab francophone writers. Whereas British colonial educators encouraged vernacular literacy (see, for example, East 1936; Cosentino 1978), French policy emphasized assimilation among indigenous elites and "repressed the writing and teaching of African languages" to such an extent that today French remains a powerful literary language in North Africa (Zabus 1991: 19). Still, it is often a French that through translation has been made to absorb Arabic cultural materials, which have themselves been transformed in the process. In the novel *La Nuit sacrée* (*The Holy Night*, 1987), the Moroccan writer Tahar Ben Jelloun incorporates French versions of Islamic prayers, whereby "he renders the French language 'foreign' to its own mono-lingual native speaker and simultaneously commits sacrilege against the very formulas he translates by placing them in a passage that comes very close to black humor" (Mehrez 1992: 130). The translating in Ben Jelloun's French is transgressive, both of the ex-colonial language and culture and of an indigenous religious orthodoxy.

In West Africa, the Nigerian Gabriel Okara's novel *The Voice* (1964) is unique in cultivating a similar linguistic experiment. Describing himself "as a writer who believes in the utilisation of African ideas, African philosophy and African folklore and imagery to the fullest extent possible," Okara declared that "the only way to use them effectively is to translate them almost literally from the African language native to the writer into whatever European language he is using as his medium of expression" (Okara 1963: 15). In practice this meant a highly selective use of translation in which the stylistic peculiarities of Okara's English reproduce lexical and syntactical features of the Ijo language.

Here is a range of representative excerpts:

> Okolo had no chest, they said. His chest was not strong and he had no shadow.

> Shuffling feet turned Okolo's head to the door. He saw three men standing silent, opening not their mouths. "Who are you people be?" Okolo asked. The people opened not their mouths. "If you are coming-in people be, then come in." The people opened not their mouths. "Who are you?" Okolo again asked, walking to the men. As Okolo closer to the men walked, the men quickly turned and ran out.

> He had himself in politics mixed and stood for election.

> The engine man Okolo's said things heard and started the engine and the canoe once more, like an old man up a slope walking, moved slowly forward until making-people-handsome day appeared.

> He was lying on a cold floor, on a cold cold floor lying. He opened his eyes to see but nothing he saw, nothing he saw.
> (Okara 1964: 23, 26–27, 61, 70, 76)

Not only did Okara closely render Ijo idioms ("had no chest," "had no shadow"), but he imitated its inverted word order, its serialized verb phrases ("Who are your people be?"), its recourse to repetition for intensification ("cold cold floor"), and its compound formations ("coming-in people") (Okara 1963: 15–16; Scott 1990; Zabus 1991: 123–126). At the same time, some of Okara's choices, even those that reproduce features of Ijo, resonate within the English literary tradition. The syntactical inversions, along with such early modern forms as "changeth," give an archaic quality to the prose that suggests the King James Bible: "Tell them how great things the Lord hath done" (Okara 1964: 24–25; Mark 5: 19). And the compounds recall modern poets such as Gerard Manley Hopkins and Dylan Thomas, both of whom fascinated Okara, a poet himself (Scott 1990: 80; Zabus 1991: 125).

This translating was much more calculated than Tutuola's and so more disruptive of the hegemonic language. In approximating Ijo, Okara defamiliarized

English by resituating English literary traditions in a postcolonial context, including such traditions as the missionaries' use of canonical texts to promote indigenous literacy. Okara's ideal readership can be seen as bilingual, an Ijo-speaking elite with an advanced English education. But since Ijo is spoken by a relatively small minority, he was mainly addressing English-language readers without any knowledge of Ijo who could nonetheless appreciate the poetic hybridity of his prose. For this audience Okara exploited the global hegemony of English to call attention to an urgent local issue: political dictatorship in Nigeria after independence. In *The Voice*, Okolo challenges a village leader who rules by fostering a personality cult and who follows the counsel of an elder educated in England, the United States, and Germany.

Translating modernity

The hybridity released by translation in colonial and postcolonial situations does indeed transgress hegemonic values, submitting them to a range of local variations. But the cultural and social effects of such translating are necessarily limited by other factors, notably the genres of the translated texts and their reception. Pinpin's language textbook offered the Tagalog reader less an incentive to learn Castilian for anticolonial purposes than an imaginary compensation for the repressiveness of Spanish rule, a subtle reshuffling of the language hegemony for "pleasure and protection." Neither Tutuola's nor Okara's translingual prose initiated any important trends in the West African novel; novelists who draw on African oral traditions or otherwise use African languages have rather followed the example of Chinua Achebe's code-switching in narratives written mostly in standard English (see Bandia 1996).

Translating that hybridizes hegemonic values can stimulate cultural innovation and change only when it redirects indigenous traditions and refashions identities, not just of elite intellectuals, but of other constituencies as well. Ben Jelloun's use of Arabic materials in his francophone novels typifies a recent movement in North African fiction, and his work in particular has earned the acclaim of French intellectuals: *La Nuit sacrée* won the Prix Goncourt in 1987. Yet whether these developments constitute a reformation of the French literary canon, as opposed to a containment of change, is not yet clear. President François Mitterand viewed Ben Jelloun's award as "an homage to the universality of the French language," not as a restoration of a francophone literature excluded because of its postcolonial heterogeneity (Mehrez 1992: 128).

In subordinate cultures, perhaps the most consequential changes wrought by translation occur with the importation of new concepts and paradigms, especially those that have set going the transition from ancient traditions, whether oral or literary, to modern notions of time and space, of self and nation. China at the turn of the twentieth century, when the last imperial dynasty – the Qing – was coming to an end, presents a rich instance of translators intent on building a national culture by importing foreign literatures. Chinese translators pursued a program of modernization by introducing numerous Western works of fiction and philosophy.

Between 1882 and 1913 the quantity of fiction issued by Chinese publishers increased dramatically, and translations constituted almost two-thirds of the total, 628 out of 1,170 books (Zhao 1995: 17, 228). The most influential translator was the prolific Lin Shu (1852–1924), credited with rendering as many as 180 Western literary texts, including the novels of Daniel Defoe, Victor Hugo, Sir Walter Scott, Robert Louis Stevenson, and Sir Arthur Conan Doyle (Lee 1973: 44).

Lin himself knew no Western languages. As was customary in late Qing publishing, he worked with proficient collaborators whose oral versions he quickly turned into classical Chinese prose (*wenyan*) (Zhao 1995: 230 n. 9). His translation practice was thoroughly domesticating: he chose foreign texts that could be easily Sinicized, assimilated to traditional Chinese values, notably the archaic literary language and family-centered Confucian ethics. Lin read Dickens's *The Old Curiosity Shop* as an exemplum of the Confucian reverence for filial piety, so he retitled his 1908 version, *The Story of the Filial Daughter Nell* (Lee 1973: 47; Hu 1995: 81–82; Zhao 1995: 231).

The foreign text that initiated his career in 1899 was Dumas fils's sentimental romance, *La Dame aux camélias*, which he much appreciated because he believed it treated the Confucian theme of loyalty with extravagant emotion. Lin drew a startling analogy between Dumas's heroine, the courtesan Marguerite, and two Chinese ministers distinguished by their legendary devotion, revealing that the values he inscribed in foreign texts were not simply traditional, but imperial, expressing loyalty to the Qing emperor:

> While translating [. . .] thrice I threw down my brush and shed bitter tears. Strong are the women of this world, more so than our scholar-officials, among whom only the extremely devoted ones such as Long Jiang and Bi Gan could compare with Marguerite, those who would die a hundred deaths rather than deviate from their devotion. Because the way Marguerite served Armant is the same way Long and Bi served their emperors Jie and Zhou. As Long and Bi had no regrets even though the emperors killed them, Marguerite had none when Armant killed her. Thus I say, in this world, only the like of Long and Bi could compare with Marguerite.
>
> (Hu 1995: 71)

Lin's sentimental glorification of a female prostitute, so far removed from the misogyny of the *Analects*, was nonetheless underwritten by the passage (18.1) where Master Kong mentions Bi Gan's death and praises him as one of the "humane" ministers under the tyrannical Zhou, the last emperor of the Yin dynasty (Confucius 1993: 74).

Lin Shu's identity as a scholar–translator was formed through a Confucian sympathy with Dumas's character that reflected his own deep investment in serving the emperor more effectively than current scholar–officials. This was a service that Lin chose to perform as a writer instead of a minister because his failure to attain the highest academic degree prevented him from seeking a court appointment (Lee 1973: 42, 57). The *wenyan* and Confucianism of his translations show that they were intended to strengthen imperial culture just as its authority was being severely eroded by political and institutional developments. Although China had been subject to Western military and commercial invasion since the early nineteenth century, Lin's translations began appearing just after the Chinese were decisively defeated in the first Sino-Japanese War (1894–95) and the Boxer Uprising against the foreign presence was repressed by an international force (1898–1900). Perhaps most importantly, Lin continued translating long after 1905, when the abolition of the civil service examination removed the main institutional support for using classical Chinese in official and educated discourse (Gunn 1991: 32–33). Late Qing translators such as Lin Shu and his associate Yan Fu (1853–1921) considered their role to be "that of a guardian of the language rather than simply a contributor to the classical language and by extension, therefore, a guardian of classical civilization" (Hu 1995: 79).

Interestingly, the domestic cultural and political agenda that guided the work of these translators did not entirely efface the differences of the foreign texts. On the contrary, the drive to domesticate was also intended to introduce rather different Western ideas and forms into China so that it would be able to compete internationally and struggle against the hegemonic countries. As a result, the recurrent analogies between classical Chinese culture and modern Western values usually involved a transformation of both.

Between 1907 and 1921, for instance, Lin Shu translated twenty-five novels by Rider Haggard because he found them consistent with Confucian ethics and supportive of his aim to reform the Chinese nation. Lin retitled his version of Haggard's *Montezuma's Daughter* as *The Story of an English Filial Son's Revenge on the Volcano* since he read it as another Confucian exemplum, proof that "he who knows how to fulfill filial obligations by avenging the murder of his mother certainly knows how to be loyal and to avenge the shame of his mother country" (Lee 1973: 51). Lin was very much aware that British colonialism provided the subtext to Haggard's adventure fiction, but he nonetheless believed that representations of colonial aggression could move Chinese readers both to emulate and to resist their foreign invaders. In the preface to his version of Haggard's *The Spirit of Bambatse*, he provocatively adopted the racist stereotyping in such novels to explain that

> they encourage the white man's spirit of exploration. The blueprint has already been drawn by Columbus and Robinson Crusoe.

In order to seek almost unobtainable material interests in the barbarian regions, white men are willing to brave a hundred deaths. But our nation, on the contrary, disregards its own interests and yields them to foreigners. We have invited the guests to humiliate the hosts and to subject a multitude of 400 million to the mercy of a few whites. What an ugly shame!

(ibid.: 54)

The racism of this passage reflected not only the stereotypes of colonial discourse embedded in British adventure fiction, but also the Social Darwinism that Yan Fu's translations of T.H. Huxley and Herbert Spencer disseminated in China to serve a similarly nationalist purpose. Yan Fu rationalized his 1898 version of Huxley's *Evolution and Ethics* precisely by asserting its relevance to "self-strengthening and the preservation of the race" (Schwartz 1964: 100). And yet the racism in these translators' thinking was contradicted by their very reliance on translation as a means of national reform. They both admired Western individualism and aggressiveness, but in resorting to a literary practice to encourage the Chinese imitation of these values, they effectively assumed that the asymmetry between the West and China wasn't determined biologically, but culturally: it derived from the differences in their ethical traditions, which unlike racial differences could be revised.

Lin Shu seems subsequently to have come to this realization. And in moving away from the biologism that underlay his earlier concept of nation, he urged the Chinese to abandon the Confucian virtue of "yielding," or deference, now transmogrified into "humiliation" by imperialism:

The Westerners' consciousness of shame and advocacy of force do not stem entirely from their own nature but are also an accumulated custom. [. . .] In China, this is not so. Suffering humiliation is regarded as yielding; saving one's own life is called wisdom. Thus after thousands of years of encroachments by foreign races, we still do not feel ashamed. Could it also be called our national character?

(Lee 1973: 54)

The traditional "wisdom" preempted thinking about "national character" by discouraging patriotic feelings such as a collective sense of "shame." Yan Fu's translations in turn revised the liberal individualism articulated by such British writers as John Stuart Mill and Adam Smith so that it might better address the Chinese situation, the decline of the imperial state amid foreign invasion. His 1903 version of Mill's *On Liberty* pushed the concept of personal freedom into much more collective and nationalist directions. "If liberty of the individual is often treated in Mill as an end in itself, in Yan Fu it becomes a means to the advancement of 'the people's virtue and intellect,' and beyond this to the purposes of the state" (Schwartz 1964: 141).

The practices of late Qing translators like Lin Shu and Yan Fu demonstrate that domesticating strategies, especially when used in situations of cultural and political subordination, can still result in a powerful hybridity that initiates unanticipated changes. The drive to domesticate was inexorable, given the insularity of traditional Chinese culture and its centuries-long entrenchment in imperial institutions. Consequently, Lin Shu and Yan Fu saw themselves as reformists, not revolutionaries: they used the classical literary language to appeal to the academic and official elite, and they submitted foreign texts to revision, abridgement, and interpolated comment so that Western values and their own nationalist agenda might become acceptable to that elite. In their translating, they were more faithful to *wenyan* than to Western ideas and forms.

Yet this very practice of assimilating foreign texts to the dominant domestic style was at once domestic and foreign, Chinese and Western. Yan Fu's criteria for good translation – fidelity (*xin*), clarity or comprehensibility (*da*), and elegance or fluency (*ya*) – appear in ancient Chinese translation theory, in monarch-sponsored translations of Buddhist scripture during the third century A.D. (Chen 1992: 14–17, 124; correspondence with Chang Nam Fung, 2 September 1997). Yan no doubt revived these ancient criteria because he found them consistent with his use of translating to advance an imperial cultural politics. But the Sinicizing practices of late Qing translation also bear a striking resemblance to the domestication favored by translators during the French and English Enlightenment, a period that Yan studied during a trip to England in the 1870s, and that provided texts he would later translate, not only Smith's *Wealth of Nations* (1901–2), but Montesquieu's *Spirit of Laws* (1904–9). It has been suggested that Yan was influenced by the first systematic translation treatise in English, Alexander Tytler's *Essay on the Principles of Translation* (1789), which similarly advocated sufficient freedom to produce eminently readable versions in the target language (Gunn 1991: 33 n. 5). Tytler's domestications carried a similar ideological significance as well. His ideal translation was endowed with the "ease of original composition" because it appeared familiar to his equally elite readers, invisibly inscribed with the aesthetic and moral values of the Hanoverian bourgeoisie (Tytler 1978: 15; Venuti 1995a: 68–73).

The domestication favored by late Qing translators made their work more accessible than they planned and not always in terms they would have endorsed. Lin Shu and Yan Fu not only cultivated highly elegant styles, but added illuminating prefaces, marginal comments and, in Lin's case, marks of punctuation to clarify the *wenyan* (Link 1981: 136). Their translations of *La Dame aux camélias* and *Evolution and Ethics* were enormously popular well into the 1930s, reaching an educated readership that included officials as well as academics, secondary school students as well as independent intellectuals (Schwartz 1964: 259 n. 14; Lee 1973: 34–35). Lin Shu's versions of sentimental romances didn't consistently transform filial piety into patriotism: they also fed into the craze for escapist novels of tragic love, the so-called Mandarin Ducks and Butterfly fiction that dominated Chinese publishing at the start of the twentieth century, providing a compensatory comfort for conservative readers faced with disruptive cultural and political events – Westernization, the 1911 revolution against the emperor, the institution of the republican government (Link 1981: 54, 196–235). Yan Fu's versions of scientific and sociological texts imported evolutionary theories of history that ran counter to the synchronism of the *Yijing* (*Book of Changes*), establishing "foreign discourse as more powerful than the Sinocentric tradition" (Gunn 1991: 35). And the wide circulation enabled the translations, despite their classical language, to contribute to the emergence of a cultural discourse in the northern Mandarin vernacular (*baihua*). Inadvertently, Lin's and Yan Fu's work questioned the authority of *wenyan*: "their techniques of rewriting and abridging the foreign-language texts served eventually to promote the idea that the classical Chinese they employed was inadequate to the task of understanding and absorbing foreign knowledge" (ibid.: 33).

These late Qing translators also inspired the Chinese writers who came after them to enlist translation in a nationalist cultural politics. The great modernist innovator in Chinese fiction, Lu Xun (1881–1936), enthusiastically read their versions of Haggard and Huxley in his youth and then began translating Western literature, including two novels by Jules Verne. He chose science fiction because it was missing from the Western genres currently available in Chinese and because he believed that popularizations of science could prove useful "to move the Chinese masses forward" (Semanov 1980: 14). Lu Xun thought of the Chinese "national character" in the evolutionary and Orientalist terms that circulated in scientific and missionary texts – Spencer spliced together with Arthur Smith's *Chinese Characteristics* (1894) – which led him to raise questions at once physiological and humanist: "What were the roots of [China's] sickness?" "What was the best ideal of human nature?" (Liu 1995: 60–61). And although he was proficient in several foreign languages (English, German, and Japanese), his view of translation as popularization led him to adopt late Qing strategies of domestication: he translated into the classical language and edited the foreign text for accessibility. In his 1903 version of Verne's *De la terre à la lune* (*From Earth to the Moon*), Lu Xun reduced the number of chapters, gave them summary titles, and, as he explained, "where the wording was dull or not suited to the [experience] of my fellow countrymen, I have made a few changes and deletions" (Lyell 1975: 65).

Yet the late Qing approach soon revealed its limitations. Since neither Lu Xun nor his brother and collaborator Zhou Zuoren (1885–1967) shared their predecessors' investment in the imperial dynasty, their translating quickly assumed the revolutionary aim of displacing traditional Chinese culture. They wanted to build a vernacular literature that was modern, not simply Westernized, earning the acceptance and esteem of modern writers in Western literatures. And to initiate this new literary tradition they came to reject the example set by translators like Lin Shu who, Zhou complained, "did not want to learn from foreigners, so they busied themselves in making foreign works resemble the Chinese" (Zhao 1995: 231). In 1909 Lu Xun and Zhou Zuoren published a pioneering anthology of translations that sought to register rather than remove the linguistic and cultural differences of foreign fiction.

This they did by deviating from late Qing practices in the selection of Western texts and in the development of discursive strategies to translate them. Instead of sentimental romances and adventure novels, instead of fiction governed by the popular aesthetic of immediate intelligibility and sympathetic identification, they chose the more distancing narrative experiments of romanticism, fiction governed by the elite aesthetic of oblique signification and critical detachment. Since they saw literary translation as a means of altering China's subordinate position in geopolitical relations, they gravitated toward foreign countries that occupied a similar position, but whose literatures threw off their minority status to achieve international recognition (Eber 1980: 10; Lee 1987: 22–23). Their anthology contained mostly Russian and Eastern European short stories, including several by the Russian symbolists Leonid Andreyev and Vsevolod Garshin and the Polish historical novelist Henryk Sienkiewicz.

And instead of the fluency that characterized the free domesticating strategies of late Qing translators, Lu Xun and Zhou Zuoren pursued greater stylistic resistance by closely adhering to the foreign texts, which were often German or Japanese intermediate versions. Hence, they created a translation discourse so heterogenous that, despite such aids as annotations, the anthology "still impressed readers as something foreign" (Semanov 1980: 23). Their translations were written in *wenyan* combined with Europeanized lexical and syntactical features, transliterations of Western names, and Japanese loan words (Lyell 1975: 96; Gunn 1991: 36). Here the foreign consisted of what answered to the current Chinese situation while differing from dominant translation practices. In opposition to the comforting Confucian familiarity offered by many late Qing translations, Lu Xun and Zhou Zuoren's strategies were designed to convey the unsettling strangeness of modern ideas and forms.

They produced this effect by deriving their translation discourse from another Western literary tradition which, however, they revised according to their rather different concept of national identity. Instead of the domestication favored by a British theorist like Tytler, Lu Xun and Zhou Zuoren followed the foreignizing strategies favored by German theorists like Goethe and Schleiermacher, whose writings they encountered while studying in Japan. "The more closely the translation follows the turns taken by the original," argued Schleiermacher in his lecture "On the Different Methods of Translating" (1813), "the more foreign it will seem to the reader" (Lefevere 1977: 78).

Schleiermacher also wanted foreignizing translation to serve a nationalist agenda, to issue a Prussian challenge to French cultural and political hegemony during the Napoleonic wars by contributing to the creation of a German literature. Yet his nationalism was grounded in a belief of racial superiority which ultimately devolved into a vision of global domination: he asserted that the German people, "because of its respect for what is foreign and its mediating nature," was "destined" to preserve the canon of world literature in German, so that

> with the help of our language, whatever beauty the most different times have brought forth can be enjoyed by all people, as purely and perfectly as is possible for a foreigner.
>
> (Lefevere 1977: 88)

This is just the sort of naive cultural chauvinism that Lu Xun questioned in Chinese contemporaries who supported the imperial dynasty. His turn to foreignizing translation was intended to build a modern literature that interrogated traditional Chinese culture by exposing its contradictory conditions. In a key 1907 essay about the revolutionary potential of romantic literature, he skewered the self-congratulatory songs in which Chinese soldiers "rebuke[d] the servility of India and Poland," reading these "martial airs" as a compensation for the oppression endured by their own country:

> China, in spite of her present situation, is always anxious to jump at any chance to cite at length her past glories, yet now she feels deprived of the capacity to do so, and can only resort to comparisons of herself with captive neighbors that have either fallen under the yoke of servitude or ceased to exist, hoping thereby to show off her own superiority.
>
> (translated by Jon Kowallis in Liu 1995: 31–32)

In resorting to translation to precipitate stylistic innovations, Lu Xun aimed to revise the self-image of conservative Chinese readers by forcing them, somewhat unpleasurably, to examine their complacencies and confront their dependence on foreign cultural resources – which is to say their reliance on translingual practices (cf. Liu 1995: 32). When critics later derided his translations because the mix of classical and Europeanized language was difficult to read, he made his aim explicit: "instead of translating to give people 'pleasure,'" he responded, "I often try to make them uncomfortable, or even exasperated, furious and bitter" (Lu Xun 1956: 68).

The far-reaching consequences of the 1909 anthology indicate that Lu Xun and Zhou Zuoren's foreignizing strategies made a difference in Chinese literature, but not without introducing a new set of cultural contradictions. Initially, the heterogenous *wenyan* of their translations proved to be too alienating to the elite readers who constituted their primary audience, so that although the anthology was issued in a printing of 1,500 copies, it evidently sold little more than 40 (Lyell 1975: 95–96). A second edition was published in 1920, however, and by that point their translation practices had shifted from the margin to the center of Chinese culture, influencing a number of younger writers to pursue the same stylistic innovations – although *in the vernacular.*

Called the May Fourth movement, after the day in 1919 when thousands of students protested against the foreign presence, these writers associated Euro-Japanized *baihua* with "liberation of the individual from all sorts of institutions and conventions" (Gunn 1991: 107). And so this was the language they used to translate a suitable range of Western texts, including *The Communist Manifesto* (1920), *The Sorrows of Young Werther* (1922), *Thus Spake Zarathustra* (1923), and *Faust* (1928). Lu Xun himself began exploring nationalist themes in vernacular narratives whose formal inventiveness was inspired by foreign writers like Gogol and Sienkiewicz (Hanan 1974). Because the translation of romantic literature imported a number of psychological terms, mostly through Japanese loan renderings, the first Chinese novel of socialist realism, Ye Shengtao's *Ni Huanzhi* (1928–29), "portray[ed] its schoolteacher's passionate commitment to social change in terms unmistakably reminiscent of Goethe's Werther" (Gunn 1991: 107–108).

The 1909 anthology began as a translation addressed to an elite readership so as to mobilize them against rearguard trends, like the residual authority of the Confucian tradition and the popular fascination offered by Butterfly romances. Lu Xun and Zhou Zuoren risked not only deepening the divisions among the various constituencies in Chinese culture, but imposing on them the values of a minority. Yet their influence, however decisive, was neither sufficient nor total in promoting change. Their anthology was in fact joined by such other translation projects as the Union Version of the Bible (1919) in fostering the development of a literary discourse in *baihua*, which subsequently evolved into the national language of China (Wickeri 1995).

The ethics of location

The roles played by translation in subordinate cultures, whether colonial or postcolonial, deepen the scandal of its current marginality in the hegemonic English-language countries. Translation has long been implemented in diverse imperialist projects in Africa, Asia, the Caribbean, and South America, whose very subordination has compelled them in turn to use it against or on behalf of foreign presences. The asymmetries in these international relations are cultural, as well as political and economic, and they project different and competing uses of translation.

Today, in the United States and the United Kingdom, the overwhelming commercial value assigned to books leads publishers to focus on the sale of foreign rights while limiting their investments to foreign bestsellers, trying to repeat at home a profitable performance abroad. This commercialism inevitably represses thinking about the cultural functions and effects of translation, which tend to be reduced to the vaguely defined pro bono book, an object of aesthetic appreciation that more often than not ratifies prevailing canons and identities in English-language cultures. Rare is the publishing program that aims to create both a readership and a market for foreign literatures while remaining critical of the stereotyping that is potentially involved in representing any foreign culture.

The same commercialism certainly shapes the interest in translation shown by many publishers in developing countries. Thriving book markets in South America, the Pacific Rim, and Eastern Europe support competing translations of the canonical works in the major literatures (British, American, Western European). And the translation rights to international bestsellers are avidly pursued, often in response to a book's success in another foreign country.

At decisive historical moments, however, especially during the collapse of an imperial or colonial regime, subordinate cultures have taken another tack. They have valued translation as a practice, not of capital accumulation, but of identity formation, active in the construction of authors and nations, readers and citizens. As a result, translation projects have been promoted by leading intellectuals and academic institutions. And publishing industries, whether established or fledgling, whether private or government-owned, have made significant investments in translation.

Thus, the cultural authority and impact of translation vary according to the position of a particular country in the geopolitical economy. In the hegemonic countries, metaphysical concepts of authorial originality and cultural authenticity denigrate translation as second-order writing, derivative and adulterated, so that especially in the United States and the United Kingdom it receives relatively little attention from writers and critics, scholars and teachers. In developing countries, translation accrues cultural as well as economic capital. The need to communicate between major and minor languages has spawned translation industries and training programs. Translation is seen as a significant intervention into the polylingualism and cultural hybridity that characterize colonial and postcolonial situations, a source of linguistic innovation useful in building national literatures and in resisting the dominance of hegemonic languages and cultures.

These diverse effects and functions bring a new complexity to a translation ethics that takes as its ideal the recognition of cultural difference. If domesticating strategies of choosing and translating foreign texts are considered ethically questionable – a narcissistic dismissal of foreignness in favor of dominant domestic values – minority situations redefine what constitutes the "domestic" and the "foreign." These two categories are variable, always reconstructed in a translation project vis-à-vis the local scene.

In 1957, for example, a year after Ghana's independence, the *Odyssey* was translated into the indigenous Twi language to promote literacy. Not only did it resort to various freedoms to achieve intelligibility in a different ecology, but its domesticating strategies were modelled on E.V. Rieu's prose version for the Penguin Classics (Ofosu-Appiah 1960). Aimed at a mass readership just like Rieu's, the Twi translation sought to be immediately accessible by avoiding scholarly annotations and by producing a discourse so fluent as to cast the realist illusion and solicit the reader's identification. "The work should be read as a novel," wrote the translator, "and the reader's interest should not be diverted unnecessarily from the story" (ibid.: 45).

The dominant domestic values in Ghana after decolonization were British, and English remains the official language of the country. The Twi translator chose a canonical work in a major literature and rendered it according to a domesticating strategy that prevails in a hegemonic culture, in the major language. Rieu's *Odyssey* can indeed be taken as a standard of English-language translation: it inaugurated the Penguin Classics series in 1947 and has sold over two and a half million copies (*Economist* 1996: 85). Yet the Twi Penguinification of Homer can hardly be judged as an exercise in cultural narcissism, an identity formed in the mirror of the imperial culture. The translation could not but be assimilationist: it had to rewrite celebrated Homeric epithets like "the rosy-fingered dawn" because "there is no Twi word for a rose" (Ofosu-Appiah 1960: 42). But the cultural differences bridged in this project were so great that some domesticating revisions were nonetheless alienating. The Homeric phrase "winged words" was expanded into the Twi equivalent of "words which fly into the air like birds," a simile that "struck one reader as unusual" and thereby allowed a glimpse of a different culture (ibid.: 43).

For a translation ethics grounded in such differences, the key issue is not simply a discursive strategy (fluent or resistant), but always its intention and effect as well – i.e., whether the translating realizes an aim to promote cultural innovation and change. It can best signal the foreignness of the foreign text by revising the hierarchy of cultural discourses that pre-exist that text in the target language, by crossing the boundaries between domestic cultural constituencies, and by altering the reproduction of institutional values and practices. A translation ethics of sameness that hews to dominant domestic values and consolidates institutions limits these effects, usually to avoid any loss of cultural authority and to accumulate capital.

Colonial and postcolonial situations complicate this distinction between sameness and difference. There translating moves between multiple differences, not just cultural but economic and political inequalities, so that it forms domestic identities that participate in the hegemonic cultures while submitting those cultures to an indigenous heterogeneity. A publishing industry that repeatedly issues fluent, domesticating translations of the latest American bestsellers – written in the standard dialect of the official language – encourages uncritical consumption of hegemonic values while maintaining current asymmetries in cross-cultural exchange. Publishers that issue more extensively domesticated translations of hegemonic literatures, assimilating them to local values through revision (the Twi *Odyssey*), may facilitate the transition from oral traditions to modern literatures, clearly a momentous cultural change. Yet in subordinate cultures with rich literary traditions, translation that pursues an extreme localization risks a homogenizing emphasis that may reflect and encourage ethnic or religious fundamentalisms while eliminating the cultural differences of foreign texts.

Since the domestic in developing countries tends to be a hybrid of global and local trends, translation can revise hegemonic values even when it seems to employ the most conservatively domesticating strategies – strategies, in other words, that are designed to reinforce dominant indigenous traditions in the translating culture. Recall Lin Shu's remarkable transvaluation of the imperialist subtexts in Rider Haggard's novels: Sinicizing translations on behalf of the emperor eventually eroded the authority of imperial culture. And translation discourses that are radically foreignizing, that pursue linguistic and literary heterogeneity to promote cultural change, can reach beyond the narrow elite for which they were initially intended and exert a wider influence on vernaculars and popular forms. Recall Lu Xun and Zhou Zuoren's reliance on the German romantic translation tradition, which ultimately contributed to the emergence of a Chinese vernacular literature that was both modernist and socialist.

Because developing countries are notable sites of contest between cultural sameness and difference, they can teach their hegemonic others an important lesson about the functionality of translation. The value of any translated text depends on effects and functions that can't be entirely predicted or controlled. Yet this element of contingency increases rather than lessens the translator's responsibility to estimate the impact of a project by reconstructing the hierarchy of domestic values that inform the translation and its likely reception. Colonial and postcolonial situations show that translating is best done with a critical resourcefulness attuned to the linguistic and cultural differences that comprise the local scene. Only these differences offer the means of registering the foreignness of foreign cultures in translation.

ACKNOWLEDGEMENTS

This book was written over the past three years largely in response to invitations to speak at conferences and seminars in England, Canada, Brazil, Ireland, Argentina, and the United States. At several of the English venues my hosts were Peter Bush and Terry Hale, who subsequently recommended the project to Routledge. Without their encouraging support of the polemic I was developing, my research would have taken much longer to complete. Marilyn Gaddis Rose wrote a helpful evaluation.

A great many people offered similar opportunities and encouragement, and a list of names and affiliations can hardly suffice as an expression of my gratitude for their generous interest in my work: Rosemary Arrojo (Universidade Estadual de Campinas); João Azenha Jr., Andrea Lombardi, and John Milton (Universidade de São Paulo); Maria Isabel Badaracco (Colegio de Traductores Públicos de la Ciudad de Buenos Aires); Mona Baker (University of Manchester Institute of Science and Technology); Heloisa Gonçalves Barbosa and Aurora Nieves (Universidade Federal do Rio de Janiero); Susan Bassnett (University of Warwick); Charles Bernheimer (University of Pennsylvania); Maria Candida Bordenave, Paulo Henriques Britto, Maria Paula Frota, Marcia Martins, and Lia Wyler (Pontíficia Universidade Católica do Rio de Janiero); Robert Caserio (Temple University); Angela Chambers (University of Limerick); Deisa Chamahum Chaves and Edson J. Martins Lopes (Universidade Federal de Ouro Preto); Luiz Angélico da Costa (Universidade Federal da Bahia); Michael Cronin (Dublin City University); Sean Golden and Marisa Presas (Universitat Autonoma, Barcelona); Manuel Gomes da Torre and Rui Carvalho Homem (Instituto Superior de Assistentes e Intérpres, Oporto); Freeman Henry (University of South Carolina); Michael Hoey (University of Liverpool); Christine Klein-Lataud and Agnès Whitfield (York University); Edith McMorran (Oxford University); Jeffrey Mehlman (Boston University); Arthur Nestrovsky (Pontíficia Universidade Católica de São Paulo); Jonathan Rée (Middlesex University); Christina Schäffner (Aston University); Martha Tennent Hamilton (Universitat de Vic); Maria Tymoczko and Edwin Gentzler (University of Massachusetts at Amherst); Patrick Zabalbeascoa (Universitat Pompeu Fabra); and Juan Jesus Zaro (Universidad de Málaga). The audiences at these diverse sites were both appreciative and challenging, and my subsequent revisions were shaped by their questions and remarks.

Individual chapters benefited from the incisive comments of numerous readers: Lionel Bently, Peter Clive, Steven Cole, Deirdre David, Basil Hatim, David Kornacker, André Lefevere, Carol Maier, Ian Mason, Daniel O'Hara, Ewald Osers, Jeffrey Pence, Douglas Robinson, Richard Sieburth, Alan Singer, Susan Stewart, Robert Storey, and William Van Wert. Several chapters were rigorously scrutinized by Peter Hitchcock. Michael Henry Heim carefully read the final draft, making several valuable suggestions – including a revision in the title.

Amy Dooling allowed me to draw on her expertise in Chinese literary history. George Economou and Daniel Tompkins gave me indispensable help with classical Greek, especially with the transcriptions that appear here. Martin Reichert translated Ulrich von Wilamowitz's review of Pierre Louÿs's *Les Chansons de Bilitis*, providing the source of my English quotations. Useful information was provided by Susan Bernofsky, Antonia Fusco (of the Book-of-the-Month Club), Edward Gunn, Thomas McAuley, Candace Séguinot, Mary Wardle, Eliot Weinberger, and Donald and Freda Wright. Hannah Hyam copyedited the typescript with her customary precision.

Selections from the Farrar, Straus and Giroux Archive. Copyright © 1998 by Farrar, Straus and Giroux, Inc. Reprinted by permission of Farrar, Straus and Giroux, Inc. I am grateful to the librarians of the Rare Books and Manuscripts Division, New York Public Library, for facilitating my work in this archive; to Timothy Gillen of Farrar, Straus and Giroux, for his help in processing my permission request; and to Sheila Cudahy, for her gracious comments on my use of quotations from her correspondence concerning the Guareschi translations.

Grateful acknowledgement is made to the following journals, where some of this material appeared in earlier versions and different languages: *Il cannochiale*, *Circuit*, *Comparative Literature*, *Current Issues in Language and Society* (Multilingual Matters Ltd), *French Literature Series* (Editions Rodopi), *Radical Philosophy*, *The Translator* (St. Jerome Publishing), *TradTerm*, *Trans*, *TTR Traduction, Terminologie, Rédaction: Études sur le texte et ses transformations*, *Vasos Comunicantes*, and *Voces*. A version of chapter 5 initially appeared in *College English*, © 1996 by the National Council of Teachers of English. Reprinted with permission. My work was supported in part by a Research and Study Leave and a Summer Research Fellowship from Temple University.

The Italian verse in the dedication is drawn from Milo De Angelis's poem "Remo in gennaio conosciuto" in *Distante un padre* (Milano: Mondadori, 1989). The calligraphy is the work of Professor Sadako Ohki of the Institute for Medieval Japanese Studies at Columbia University. Chris Behnam's computer skills helped assemble the dedication page.

All unattributed translations in the foregoing pages are mine.

ACKNOWLEDGEMENTS

Lindsay Davies, who created the space in which I wrote this book, is at once the most deeply complicit and the least responsible.

L.V.
New York City
December 1997

BIBLIOGRAPHY

Abrams, M.H. (1953) *The Mirror and the Lamp: Romantic Theory and the Critical Tradition*, New York and Oxford: Oxford University Press.

Adams, R. (1946) "Efik Translation Bureau," *Africa* 16: 120.

Afolayan, A. (1971) "Language and Sources of Amos Tutuola," in C. Heywood (ed.) *Perspectives on African Literature*, London, Ibadan, and Nairobi: Heinemann.

Altbach, P.G. (1987) *The Knowledge Context: Comparative Perspectives on the Distribution of Knowledge*, Albany: State University of New York Press.

—— (1994) "Publishing in the Third World: Issues and Trends for the Twenty-First Century," in P.G. Altbach and E.S. Hoshino (eds) *International Book Publishing: An Encyclopedia*, New York: Garland.

Althusser, L. (1971) "Ideology and Ideological State Apparatuses," in *Lenin and Philosophy and Other Essays*, trans. B. Brewster, New York: Monthly Review Press.

Ambrose, A. (1954) Review of L. Wittgenstein, *Philosophical Investigations*, *Philosophy and Phenomenological Research* 15: 111–115.

Anderson, D. (ed.) (1983) *Pounds's Cavalcanti: An Edition of the Translations, Notes, and Essays*, Princeton: Princeton University Press.

Appadurai, A. (1996) *Modernity at Large: Cultural Dimensions of Globalization*, Minneapolis: University of Minnesota Press.

Arber, E. (1875–94) *A Transcript of the Register of the Company of Stationers of London: 1554–1640*, vol. 3, London and Birmingham: Privately printed.

Arnold, M. (1960) *On the Classical Tradition*, ed. R.H. Super, Ann Arbor: University of Michigan Press.

Arrojo, R. (1997) "The Ambivalent Translation of an Apple into an Orange: Love and Power in Hélène Cixous's and Clarice Lispector's Textual Affair," unpublished manuscript.

Ashcroft, B., G. Griffiths, and H. Tiffin (1989) *The Empire Writes Back: Theory and Practice in Postcolonial Literatures*, London and New York: Routledge.

Babalolá, A. (1971) "A Survey of Modern Literature in the Yoruba, Efik and Hausa Languages," in B. King (ed.) *Introduction to Nigerian Literature*, Lagos: University of Lagos and Evans Brothers Ltd.

Bacon, H. (1963) Review of J. Jones, *On Aristotle and Greek Tragedy*, *Classical World* 57: 56.

Baker, G.P., and P.M.S. Hacker (1980) *An Analytical Commentary on the Philosophical Investigations: Wittgenstein, Understanding and Meaning*, Chicago: University of Chicago Press.

Baker, M. (1992) *In Other Words: A Coursebook on Translation*, London and New York: Routledge.

—— (1996) "Linguistics and Cultural Studies: Complementary or Competing Paradigms in Translation Studies?" in A. Lauer, H. Gerzymisch-Arbogast, J. Haller, and E. Steiner (eds) *Übersetzungswissenschaft im Umbrach. Festschrift für Wolfram Wilss*, Tübingen: Gunter Narr.

Bandia, P. (1996) "Code-Switching and Code-Mixing in African Creative Writing: Some Insights for Translation Studies," *TTR Traduction, Terminologie, Rédaction: Études sur le texte et ses transformations* 9(1): 139–154.

Barbosa, H.G. (1993) "Brazilian Literature in English Translation," in C. Picken (ed.) *Translation: The Vital Link*, London: Institute of Translation and Interpreting.

—— (1994) *The Virtual Image: Brazilian Literature in English Translation*, unpublished dissertation, University of Warwick.

Barrett, W. (1947) *What is Existentialism?*, New York: Partisan Review.

—— (1953) "Everyman's Family," *New York Times Book Review*, 25 October, pp. 3, 49.

Barthes, R. (1986) "The Reality Effect," in *The Rustle of Language*, trans. R. Howard, Berkeley and Los Angeles: University of California Press.

Bassnett, S. (1993) *Comparative Literature: A Critical Introduction*, Oxford: Blackwell.

—— and A. Lefevere (1992) "General Editors' Preface," in A. Lefevere (ed. and trans.) *Translation/History/Culture: A Sourcebook*, London and New York: Routledge.

Baudrillard, J. (1983) *In the Shadow of the Silent Majorities*, trans. P. Foss, P. Patton, and J. Johnston, New York: Semiotext(e).

Beaugrande, R. de, and W.U. Dressler (1981) *Introduction to Text Linguistics*, London and New York: Longman.

Benjamin, A. (1989) *Translation and the Nature of Philosophy: A New Theory of Words*, London and New York: Routledge.

Bennett, W. (1984) "To Reclaim a Legacy: Text of Report on Humanities in Education," *Chronicle of Higher Education*, 28 November, pp. 16–21.

Bently, L. (1993) "Copyright and Translations in the English-speaking World," *Translatio* 12: 491–559.

Berman, A. (1985) "La Traduction et la lettre, or l'auberge du lointain," in *Les Tours de Babel: Essais sur la traduction*, Mauvezin: Trans-Europ-Repress.

—— (1992) *The Experience of the Foreign: Culture and Translation in Romantic Germany*, trans. S. Heyvaert, Albany: State University of New York Press.

—— (1995) *Pour une critique des traductions: John Donne*, Paris: Gallimard.

Bernheimer, C. (ed.) (1995) *Comparative Literature in the Age of Multiculturalism*, Baltimore: Johns Hopkins University Press.

Bhabha, H. (1994) *The Location of Culture*, London and New York: Routledge.

Birnbaum, A.(ed.) (1991) *Monkey Brain Sushi: New Tastes in Japanese Fiction*, Tokyo and New York: Kodansha International.

Bishop, R. (1988) *African Literature, African Critics: The Forming of Critical Standards, 1947–1966*, Westport, Conn.: Greenwood.

Book-of-the-Month Club News (1950) "Giovanni Guareschi," August, pp. 6, 8.

Bourdieu, P. (1984) *Distinction: A Social Critique of the Judgement of Taste*, trans. R. Nice, Cambridge: Harvard University Press.

Braithwaite, W. (1982) "Derivative Works in Canadian Copyright Law," *Osgoode Hall Law Journal* 20: 192–231.

Brisset, A. (1990) *Sociocritique de la traduction: Théâtre et altérité au Québec (1968–1988)*, Longueuil, Canada: Le Préambule.

Buck, T. (1995) "Neither the letter nor the spirit: Why most English translations of Thomas Mann are so inadequate," *Times Literary Supplement*, 13 October, p. 17.

Burnet, J. (ed.) (1903) *Platonis Opera*, Oxford: Clarendon Press.

Burnett, A.P. (1963) Review of J. Jones, *On Aristotle and Greek Tragedy*, *Classical Philology*, 58: 176–178.

Buxton, R.G.A. (1984) *Sophocles*, New Surveys in the Classics No. 16, Oxford: Clarendon Press.

Bywater, I. (ed. and trans.) (1909) *Aristotle on the Art of Poetry*, Oxford: Clarendon Press.

Calder, W.M. (1985) "Ecce Homo: The Autobiographical in Wilamowitz's Scholarly Writings," in W.M. Calder, H. Flashar, and T. Lindken (eds) *Wilamowitz Nach 50 Jahren*, Darmstadt, Germany: Wissenschaftliche Buchgesellschaft.

Caminade, M., and A. Pym (1995) *Les formations en traduction et interprétation: Essai de recensement mondial*, Paris: Société Française des Traducteurs.

Caputo, J.D. (1979) Review of M. Heidegger, *Early Greek Thinking*, *Review of Metaphysics* 32: 759–760.

Castro-Klarén, S., and H. Campos (1983) "Traducciones, Tirajes, Ventas y Estrellas: El 'Boom'," *Ideologies and Literature* 4: 319–338.

Caute, D. (1978) *The Great Fear: The Anti-Communist Purge under Truman and Eisenhower*, New York: Simon and Schuster.

Cawelti, J. (1976) *Adventure, Mystery, and Romance: Formula Stories as Art and Popular Culture*, Chicago: University of Chicago Press.

Chakava, H. (1988) "A Decade of Publishing in Kenya: 1977–1987. One Man's Involvement," *African Book Publishing Record* 14: 235–241.

Chamosa, J.L., and J.C. Santoyo (1993) "Dall'italiano all'inglese: scelte motivate e immotivate di 100 soppressioni in *The Name of the Rose*," in L. Avirovic and J. Dodds (eds) *Umberto Eco, Claudio Magris, autori e traduttori a confronto*, Udine: Campanotto.

Chapman, G. (1957) *Chapman's Homer*, ed. A. Nicoll, Princeton: Princeton University Press.

Chen Fukang (1992) *Zhongguo yixue lilun shigao* (A History of Chinese Translation Theory), Shanghai: Shanghai Foreign Languages Educational Press.

Cheyfitz, E. (1991) *The Poetics of Imperialism: Translation and Colonization from The Tempest to Tarzan*, New York and London: Oxford University Press.

Chisum, D.S., and M.A. Jacobs (1992) *Understanding Intellectual Property Law*, New York and Oakland: Matthew Bender.

Clark, H.M. (1950) "Talk with Giovanni Guareschi," *New York Times Book Review*, 17 December, p. 13.

Clive, H.P. (1978) *Pierre Louÿs (1870–1925): A Biography*, Oxford: Clarendon Press.

Collins, M.L. (1975) Review of M. Heidegger, *Early Greek Thinking*, *Library Journal* 100: 2056.

Confucius (1993) *The Analects*, trans. R. Dawson, Oxford and New York: Oxford University Press.

Cooperman, S. (1952) "Catholic vs. Communist," *New Republic*, 15 September, pp. 22–23.

Cosentino, D.J. (1978) "An Experiment in Inducing the Novel among the Hausa," *Research in African Literatures* 9: 19–30.

Cronin, M. (1996) *Translating Ireland: Translation, Languages, Cultures*, Cork: Cork University Press.

Currey, J. (1979) "Interview," *African Book Publishing Record* 5: 237–239.

—— (1985) "African Writers Series – 21 Years On," *African Book Publishing Record* 11: 11.

Dallal, J. (1998) "The perils of occidentalism: How Arab novelists are driven to write for Western readers," *Times Literary Supplement*, 24 April, pp. 8–9.

Davenport, G. (1968) "Another Odyssey," *Arion* 7(1) (Spring): 135–153.

David, D. (1995) *Rule Britannia: Women, Empire, and Victorian Writing*, Ithaca, N.Y.: Cornell University Press.

DeJean, J. (1989) *Fictions of Sappho 1546–1937*, Chicago: University of Chicago Press.

Delacampagne, C. (1983) *L'Invention de Racisme: Antiquité et Moyen Age*, Paris: Fayard.

Deleuze, G., and F. Guattari (1987) *A Thousand Plateaus: Capitalism and Schizophrenia*, trans. B. Massumi, Minneapolis: University of Minnesota Press.

—— (1994) *What is Philosophy?*, trans. G. Burchell and H. Tomlinson, London and New York: Verso.

Derrida, J. (1979) "Living On/Border Lines," trans. J. Hulbert, in *Deconstruction and Criticism*, New York: Continuum.

—— (1985) "Des Tours de Babel," in J. Graham (ed.) *Difference in Translation*, Ithaca, N.Y.: Cornell University Press.

Dudovitz, R. (1990) *The Myth of Superwoman: Women's Bestsellers in France and the United States*, London and New York: Routledge.

East, R.M. (1936) "A First Essay in Imaginative African Literature," *Africa* 9: 350–357.

—— (1937) "Modern Tendencies in the Languages of Northern Nigeria: The Problem of European Words," *Africa* 10: 97–105.

Eber, I. (1980) *Voices from Afar: Modern Chinese Writers on Oppressed Peoples and Their Literature*, Ann Arbor: University of Michigan Center for Chinese Studies.

Eco, U. (1980) *Il nome della rosa*, Milan: Bompiani.

—— (1983) *The Name of the Rose*, trans. W. Weaver, San Diego: Harcourt Brace Jovanovich.

Economist (1996) "Back to the Classics," 18 May, pp. 85–87.

Edelman, L. (1993) "Tearooms and Sympathy, or, The Epistemology of the Water Closet," in H. Abelove, M.A. Barale, and D.M. Halperin (eds) *The Lesbian and Gay Studies Reader*, New York and London: Routledge.

Else, G. (ed. and trans.) (1957) *Aristotle's Poetics: The Argument*, Cambridge: Harvard University Press.

Fagles, R. (trans.) (1990) Homer, *The Iliad*, New York: Viking.

Fernández Retamar, R. (1989) *Caliban and Other Essays*, trans. Edward Baker, Minneapolis: University of Minnesota Press.

Feyerabend, P. (1955) Review of L. Wittgenstein, *Philosophical Investigations*, *Philosophical Review* 64: 449–483.

Findlay, J.N. (1955) Review of L. Wittgenstein, *Philosophical Investigations*, *Philosophy* 30: 173–179.

Fowler, E. (1992) "Rendering Words, Traversing Cultures: On the Art and Politics of Translating Modern Japanese Fiction," *Journal of Japanese Studies* 18: 1–44.

Fowler, H.W. (1965) *Modern English Usage*, 2nd edition, ed. E. Gowers, Oxford: Oxford University Press.

Fried, R.M. (1974) "Electoral Politics and McCarthyism: The 1950 Campaign," in R. Griffith and A. Theoharis (eds) *The Specter: Original Essays on the Cold War and the Origins of McCarthyism*, New York: New Viewpoints.

Gable, Sr. M. (1952) "That Same Little World," *Commonweal*, 22 August, p. 492.

Gallagher, F.X. (1952) "Militant Don Camillo Returns," *Baltimore Sun*, 3 September, p. 30.

Gardiner, H.C. (1952) "Skirmishes of Red and Black," *America*, 23 August, p. 503.

Gedin, P. (1984) "Publishing in Africa – Autonomous and Transnational: A View from the Outside," *Development Dialogue* 1–2: 98–112.

Gellie, G.H. (1963) Review of J. Jones, *On Aristotle and Greek Tragedy*, *Journal of the Australasian Language and Literature Association* 20: 353–354.

Gentzler, E. (1993) *Contemporary Translation Theories*, London and New York: Routledge.

Giaccardi, C. (1995) *I luoghi del quotidiano: pubblicità e costruzione della realtà sociale*, Milan: FrancoAngeli.

Ginsborg, P. (1990) *A History of Contemporary Italy: Society and Politics, 1943–1988*, Harmondsworth, England: Penguin.

Ginsburg, J.C. (1990) "Creation and Commercial Value: Copyright Protection of Works of Information," *Columbia Law Review* 90: 1865–1938.

Giroux, H. (1992) *Border Crossings: Cultural Workers and the Politics of Education*, New York and London: Routledge.

Gleason, P. (1994) "International Copyright," in P.G. Altbach and E.S. Hoshino (eds) *International Book Publishing: An Encyclopedia*, New York: Garland.

Glenny, M. (1983) "Professional Prospects," *Times Literary Supplement*, 14 October, p. 1118.

Goldhill, S. (1986) *Reading Greek Tragedy*, Cambridge: Cambridge University Press.

Goldstein, P. (1983) "Derivative Rights and Derivative Works in Copyright," *Journal of the Copyright Society of the U.S.A.* 30: 209–252.

Goulden, J. (1976) *The Best Years, 1945–1950*, New York: Atheneum.

Grannis, C.B. (1991) "Balancing the Books, 1990," *Publishers Weekly*, 5 July, pp. 21–23.

—— (1993) "Book Title Output and Average Prices: 1992 Preliminary Figures" and "U.S. Book Exports and Imports, 1990–1991," in C. Barr (ed.) *The Bowker Annual Library and Book Trade Almanac*, New Providence, N.J.: Bowker.

Greene, R. (1995) "Their Generation," in C. Bernheimer (ed.) *Comparative Literature in the Age of Multiculturalism*, Baltimore: Johns Hopkins University Press.

Greene, T. (1982) *The Light in Troy: Imitation and Discovery in Renaissance Poetry*, New Haven: Yale University Press.

Greenhouse, L. (1994) "Ruling on Rap Song, High Court Frees Parody from Copyright Law," *New York Times*, 8 March, pp. A1, A18.

Grice, P. (1989) *Studies in the Way of Words*, Cambridge: Harvard University Press.

Guareschi, G. (1948) *Mondo Piccolo: Don Camillo*, Milan: Rizzoli.

—— (1950) *The Little World of Don Camillo*, trans. U.V. Troubridge, New York: Pellegrini and Cudahy.

—— (1951) *The Little World of Don Camillo*, trans. U.V. Troubridge, London: Victor Gollancz.

—— (1952) *Don Camillo and His Flock*, trans. F. Frenaye, New York: Pellegrini and Cudahy.

—— (1953a) *The House That Nino Built*, trans. F. Frenaye, New York: Farrar, Straus and Young.

—— (1953b) *Mondo Piccolo: Don Camillo e il suo gregge*, Milan: Rizzoli.

—— (1954) *Don Camillo's Dilemma*, trans. F. Frenaye, New York: Farrar, Straus and Young.

—— (1957) *Don Camillo Takes the Devil by the Tail*, trans. F. Frenaye, New York: Farrar, Straus and Cudahy.

—— (1962) *The Little World of Don Camillo*, trans. U.V. Troubridge, Harmondsworth, England: Penguin.

—— (1964) *Comrade Don Camillo*, trans. F. Frenaye, New York: Farrar, Straus.

—— (1966) *My Home, Sweet Home*, trans. J. Green, New York: Farrar, Straus and Giroux.

—— (1967) *A Husband in Boarding School*, New York: Farrar, Straus and Giroux.

—— (1981) *Gente così: Mondo Piccolo*, Milan: Rizzoli.

Guillory, J. (1993) *Cultural Capital: The Problem of Literary Canon Formation*, Chicago: University of Chicago Press.

Gunn, E. (1991) *Rewriting Chinese: Style and Innovation in Twentieth-Century Chinese Prose*, Stanford, Calif.: Stanford University Press.

Gutt, E. (1991) *Translation and Relevance: Cognition and Context*, Oxford: Blackwell.

Habermas, J. (1989) *The Structural Transformation of the Public Sphere: An Inquiry into a Category of Bourgeois Society*, trans. T. Burger with F. Lawrence, Cambridge: MIT Press.

Hacker, P.M.S. (1986) *Insight and Illusion: Themes in the Philosophy of Wittgenstein*, Oxford and New York: Oxford University Press.

Hallett, G. (1971) "The Bottle and the Fly," *Thought* 46: 83–104.
—— (1977) *A Companion to Wittgenstein's Philosophical Investigations*, Ithaca, N.Y.: Cornell University Press.
Hallewell, L. (1994) "Brazil," in P.G. Altbach and E.S. Hoshino (eds) *International Book Publishing: An Encyclopedia*, New York: Garland.
Hamilton, R. (1954) Review of L. Wittgenstein, *Philosophical Investigations*, *Month* 11: 116–117.
Hampshire, S. (1953) Review of L. Wittgenstein, *Philosophical Investigations*, *Spectator* 22 May: 682–683.
Hanan, P. (1974) "The Technique of Lu Hsün's Fiction," *Harvard Journal of Asiatic Studies* 34: 53–96.
Hanfling, O. (1989) *Wittgenstein's Later Philosophy*, Albany: State University of New York Press.
—— (1991) "'I heard a plaintive melody' (*Philosophical Investigations*, p. 209)," in A.P. Griffiths (ed.) *Wittgenstein Centenary Essays*, Cambridge: Cambridge University Press.
Hanson, E. (1993) "Hold the Tofu," *New York Times Book Review*, 17 January, p. 18.
Harker, J. (1994) "'You Can't Sell Culture': *Kitchen* and Middlebrow Translation Strategies," unpublished manuscript.
Harrison, B. G. (1994) "Once in Love with Giorgio," *New York Times Book Review*, 21 August, p. 8.
Harvey, K. (1995) "A Descriptive Framework for Compensation," *Translator* 1: 65–86.
Hatim, B., and I. Mason (1990) *Discourse and the Translator*, London: Longman.
—— (1997) *The Translator as Communicator*, London and New York: Routledge.
Heidegger, M. (1962) *Being and Time*, ed. and trans. J. Macquarrie and E. Robinson, New York: Harper and Row.
—— (1972) *Holzwege*, 5th edition, Frankfurt am Main: Vittorio Klostermann.
—— (1975) *Early Greek Thinking*, ed. and trans. D.F. Krell and F.A. Capuzzi, New York: Harper and Row.
Heinbockel, M. (1995) Letter to Mercury House, 9 February.
Heiney, D. (1964) *America in Modern Italian Literature*, New Brunswick, N.J.: Rutgers University Press.
Hill, A. (1988) *In Pursuit of Publishing*, London: John Murray.
Hintikka, J., and M.B. Hintikka (1986) *Investigating Wittgenstein*, Oxford and New York: Blackwell.
Høeg, P. (1993) *Miss Smilla's Feeling for Snow*, trans. F. David, London: Harvill.
Hook, S. (1962) Review of M. Heidegger, *Being and Time*, *New York Times Book Review*, 11 November, pp. 6, 42.
Howard, M. (1997) "Stranger Than Ficción," *Lingua Franca*, June/July, pp. 41–49.
Hu Ying (1995) "The Translator Transfigured: Lin Shu and the Cultural Logic of Writing in the Late Qing," *Positions* 3: 69–96.
Hughes, S. (1950) Review of G. Guareschi, *The Little World of Don Camillo*, *Commonweal*, 8 September, p. 540.
Iannucci, A. (1982) "Teaching Dante's *Divine Comedy* in Translation," in C. Slade (ed.) *Approaches to Teaching Dante's Divine Comedy*, New York: Modern Language Association of America.
Ink, G. (1997) "Book Title Output and Average Prices: 1995 Final and 1996 Preliminary Figures," in D. Bogart (ed.) *The Bowker Annual Library and Book Trade Almanac*, New Providence, N.J.: Bowker.
Jameson, F. (1981) *The Political Unconscious: Narrative as a Socially Symbolic Act*, Ithaca, N.Y.: Cornell University Press.

Jaszi, P. (1994) "On the Author Effect: Contemporary Copyright and Collective Creativity," in M. Woodmansee and P. Jaszi (eds) *The Construction of Authorship: Textual Appropriation in Law and Literature*, Durham, N.C.: Duke University Press.

Jones, J. (1962) *On Aristotle and Greek Tragedy*, London: Chatto and Windus.

Jones, Sir W. (1970) *The Letters of Sir William Jones*, ed. G. Cannon, Oxford: Oxford University Press.

Jowett, B. (ed. and trans.) (1892) *The Dialogues of Plato*, 3rd edition, Oxford: Clarendon Press.

Kakutani, M. (1993) "Very Japanese, Very American and Very Popular," *New York Times*, 12 January, p. C15.

Kamesar, A. (1993) *Jerome, Greek Scholarship, and the Hebrew Bible: A Study of the Quaestiones Hebraicae in Genesim*, Oxford: Clarendon Press.

Kaplan, B. (1967) *An Unhurried View of Copyright*, New York and London: Columbia University Press.

Katan, D. (1993) "The English Translation of *Il nome della Rosa* and the Cultural Filter," in L. Avirovic and J. Dodds (eds) *Umberto Eco, Claudio Magris, autori e traduttori a confronto*, Udine: Campanotto.

Keeley, E. (1990) "The Commerce of Translation," *PEN American Center Newsletter* 73: 10–12.

Keene, D. (ed.) (1956) *Modern Japanese Literature: An Anthology*, New York: Grove Press.

—— (1984) *Dawn to the West: Japanese Literature of the Modern Era*, New York: Holt, Rinehart and Winston.

Kelly, J.N.D. (1975) *Jerome: His Life, Writings, and Controversies*, New York: Harper and Row.

Kermode, F. (1983) "Institutional Control of Interpretation," in *The Art of Telling: Essays on Fiction*, Cambridge: Harvard University Press.

Kirkus Reviews (1994) Review of I.U. Tarchetti, *Passion*, 1 June.

Kizer, C. (1988) "Donald Keene and Japanese Fiction, Part II," *Delos*, 1(3): 73–94.

Kripke, S. (1982) *Wittgenstein on Rules and Private Language: An Elementary Exposition*, Cambridge: Harvard University Press.

Kundera, M. (1969) *The Joke*, trans. D. Hamblyn and O. Stallybrass, London: Macdonald.

—— (1982) *The Joke*, trans. M.H. Heim, New York: Harper and Row.

—— (1988) *The Art of the Novel*, trans. L. Asher, New York: Grove.

—— (1992) *The Joke*, New York: HarperCollins.

—— (1995) *Testaments Betrayed: An Essay in Nine Parts*, trans. L. Asher, New York: HarperCollins.

Laclau, E., and C. Mouffe (1985) *Hegemony and Socialist Strategy: Toward a Radical Democratic Politics*, trans. W. Moore and P. Cammack, London: Verso.

Lahr, J. (1994) "Love in Gloom," *New Yorker*, 23 May, p. 92.

Lattimore, R. (trans.) (1951) *The Iliad of Homer*, Chicago: University of Chicago Press.

Lecercle, J.-J. (1988) "The Misprison of Pragmatics: Conceptions of Language in Contemporary French Philosophy," in A.P. Griffiths (ed.) *Contemporary French Philosophy*, Cambridge: Cambridge University Press.

—— (1990) *The Violence of Language*, London and New York: Routledge.

Lee, C. (1958) *The Hidden Public: The Story of the Book-of-the-Month Club*, Garden City, N.Y.: Doubleday.

Lee, L.O. (1973) *The Romantic Generation of Modern Chinese Writers*, Cambridge: Harvard University Press.

—— (1987) *Voices from the Iron House: A Study of Lu Xun*, Bloomington: Indiana University Press.

Lefevere, A. (ed. and trans.) (1977) *Translating Literature: The German Tradition from Luther to Rosenzweig*, Assen, Netherlands: Van Gorcum.

—— (1992a) *Translation, Rewriting, and the Manipulation of Literary Fame*, London and New York: Routledge.

—— (ed. and trans.) (1992b) *Translation/History/Culture: A Sourcebook*, London and New York: Routledge.

Leithauser, B. (1989) "An Ear for the Unspoken," *New Yorker*, 6 March, pp. 105–111.

Liddell, H.G., and R. Scott (1882) *A Greek-English Lexicon*, 8th edition, New York: American Book Company.

Lindfors, B. (ed.) (1975) *Critical Perspectives on Amos Tutuola*, Washington, D.C.: Three Continents Press.

Link, E.P., Jr. (1981) *Mandarin Ducks and Butterflies: Popular Fiction in Early Twentieth-Century Chinese Cities*, Berkeley and Los Angeles: University of California Press.

Liu, L.H. (1995) *Translingual Practice: Literature, National Culture, and Translated Modernity – China, 1900–1937*, Stanford, Calif.: Stanford University Press.

Locke, J. (1960) *Two Treatises of Government*, ed. P. Laslett, Cambridge: Cambridge University Press.

Lofquist. W. (1996) "International Book Title Output: 1990–1993," in D. Bogart (ed.) *The Bowker Annual Library and Book Trade Almanac*, New Providence, N.J.: Bowker.

Louÿs, P. (1990) *Les Chansons de Bilitis*, ed. J.-P. Goujon, Paris: Gallimard.

—— (1992) *Journal de Meryem*, ed. J.-P. Goujon, Paris: Librairie A.-G. Nizet.

Lu Xun (1956) *Selected Works*, vol. 3, ed. and trans. Yang X. and G. Yang, Beijing: Foreign Languages Press.

Lucas, D.W. (1963) Review of J. Jones, *On Aristotle and Greek Tragedy*, *Classical Review* 13: 270–272.

Luke, D. (ed. and trans.) (1970) "Introduction," in T. Mann, *Tonio Kröger and Other Stories*, New York: Bantam.

—— (1995) "Translating Thomas Mann," *Times Literary Supplement*, 8 December, p. 15.

Lyell, W.A., Jr. (1975) *Lu Hsün's Vision of Reality*, Berkeley and Los Angeles: University of California Press.

Macaulay, T.B. (1952) *Selected Prose and Poetry*, ed. G.M. Young, Cambridge: Harvard University Press.

McDowell, E. (1983) "Publishing: Notes from Frankfurt," *New York Times*, 21 October, p. C32.

McHale, B. (1992) *Constructing Postmodernism*, London and New York: Routledge.

McMurtrey, L. (1983) "Rose's Success a Mystery," *Hattiesburg American*, 2 October, p. 2D.

Malcolm, N. (1984) *Ludwig Wittgenstein: A Memoir*, 2nd edition, Oxford and New York: Oxford University Press.

Mann, T. (1936) *Stories of Three Decades*, trans. H.T. Lowe-Porter, New York: Knopf.

—— (1960) *Erzählungen*, in *Gesammelte Werke*, vol. 8, Oldenburg: S. Fischer.

—— (1993) *Buddenbrooks*, trans. J.E. Woods, New York: Knopf.

Mason, I. (1994) "Discourse, Ideology and Translation," in R. de Beaugrande, A. Shunnaq, and M. Helmy Heliel (eds) *Language, Discourse and Translation in the West and Middle East*, Amsterdam and Philadelphia: Benjamins.

Mattelart, A. (1979) *Multinational Corporations and the Control of Culture: The Ideological Apparatuses of Imperialism*, trans. M. Chanan, Brighton, England: Harvester.

Mauclair, C. (1895) Review of *Les Chansons de Bilitis*, *Mercure de France*, April, pp. 104–105.

May, E.T. (1988) *Homeward Bound: American Families in the Cold War Era*, New York: Basic Books.

May, R. (1994) *The Translator in the Text: On Reading Russian Literature in English*, Evanston, Ill.: Northwestern University Press.

Mehrez, S. (1992) "Translation and the Postcolonial Experience: The Francophone North African Text," in L. Venuti (ed.) *Rethinking Translation: Discourse, Subjectivity, Ideology*, London and New York: Routledge.

Meiggs, R. (1972) *The Athenian Empire*, Oxford: Oxford University Press.

Miller, A. (1947) *All My Sons*, New York: Reynal and Hitchcock.

Miller, R.A. (1986) *Nihongo: In Defence of Japanese*, London: Athlone Press.

Mitsios, H. (ed.) (1991) *New Japanese Voices: The Best Contemporary Fiction from Japan*, New York: Atlantic Monthly Press.

Miyoshi, M. (1991) *Off Center: Power and Culture Relations between Japan and the United States*, Cambridge: Harvard University Press.

—— (1993) "A Borderless World? From Colonialism to Transnationalism and the Decline of the Nation-State," *Critical Inquiry* 19: 726–751.

Monro, D.B., and T.W. Allen (eds) (1920) *Homeri Opera*, 3rd edition, Oxford: Clarendon Press.

Moore, G. (1962) *Seven African Writers*, London: Oxford University Press.

Moore, J. (1974) "The Dating of Plato's *Ion*," *Greek, Roman and Byzantine Studies* 15: 421–439.

Morris, R. (1995) "The Moral Dilemmas of Court Interpreting," *Translator* 1: 25–46.

Mukherjee, S. (1976) "Role of Translation in Publishing of the Developing World," in *World Publishing in the Eighties*, New Delhi: National Book Trust.

Mundle, C.W.K. (1970) *A Critique of Linguistic Philosophy*, Oxford: Clarendon Press.

Myrsiades, K. (ed.) (1987) *Approaches to Teaching Homer's Iliad and Odyssey*, New York: Modern Language Association of America.

Nakhnikian, G. (1954) Review of L. Wittgenstein, *Philosophical Investigations*, *Philosophy of Science* 21: 353–354.

Neubert, A., and G. Shreve (1992) *Translation as Text*, Kent, Ohio: Kent State University Press.

New Yorker (1952) Review of G. Guareschi, *Don Camillo and His Flock*, 16 August, p. 89.

—— (1992) "Books Briefly Noted," 2 November, p. 119.

Nietzsche, F. (1967) *On the Genealogy of Morals*, trans. W. Kaufmann and R.J. Hollingdale, New York: Random House.

Niranjana, T. (1992) *Siting Translation: History, Poststructuralism, and the Colonial Context*, Berkeley and Los Angeles: University of California Press.

Nord, C. (1991) "Scopos, Loyalty, and Translational Conventions," *Target* 3(1): 91–109.

Ocampo, S. (1988) *Leopoldina's Dream*, trans. D. Balderston, New York: Penguin.

Ofosu-Appiah, L.H. (1960) "On Translating the Homeric Epithet and Simile into Twi," *Africa* 30: 41–45.

Okara, G. (1963) "African Speech . . . English Words." *Transition* 9(10) (September): 15–16.

—— (1964) *The Voice*, London: André Deutsch.

Oversea Education (1931) "Vernacular Text-Book Committees and Translation Bureaux in Nigeria," 3: 30–33.

Ozouf, M. and Ferney, F. (1985) "Et Dieu Créa Le Bestseller: Un Entretien avec Pierre Nora," *Le Nouvel Observateur*, 22 March, pp. 66–68.

Park, W.M. (1993) *Translator and Interpreting Training in the USA: A Survey*, Arlington, Va.: American Translators Association.

Parks, S. (ed.) (1975) *The Literary Property Debate: Six Tracts, 1764–1774*, New York: Garland.

Partridge, E. (1984) *A Dictionary of Slang and Unconventional English*, ed. Paul Beale, 8th edition, London: Routledge.

Paton, W.R. (ed. and trans.) (1956) *The Greek Anthology*, Cambridge: Harvard University Press.

Patterson, L.R. (1968) *Copyright in Historical Perspective*, Nashville: Vanderbilt University Press.

Paulding, G. (1952) "Don Camillo's Fine, Romantic World," *New York Herald Tribune*, 17 August, p. 6.

Payne, J. (1993) *Conquest of the New Word: Experimental Fiction and Translation in the Americas*, Austin: University of Texas Press.

Peresson, G. (1997) *Le cifre dell'editoria 1997*, Milan: Editrice Bibliografica.

Ploman, E.W., and L.C. Hamilton (1980) *Copyright: Intellectual Property in the Information Age*, London: Routledge and Kegan Paul.

Pope, A. (ed. and trans.) (1967) *The Iliad of Homer* (1715–20), in M. Mack (ed.) *The Twickenham Edition of the Poems of Alexander Pope*, vol. 7, London: Methuen, and New Haven, Conn.: Yale University Press.

Pound, E. (1954) *Literary Essays*, ed. T.S. Eliot, New York: New Directions.

Purdy, T.M. (1971) "The Publisher's Dilemma," in *The World of Translation*, New York: PEN American Center.

Pym, A. (1993) "Why Translation Conventions Should Be Intercultural Rather Than Culture-Specific: An Alternative Basic-Link Model," *Paralleles* 15: 60–68.

Quinton, A. (1967) "British Philosophy," in P. Edwards (ed.) *The Encyclopedia of Philosophy*, vol. 1, New York and London: Macmillan.

Radice, W. (1987) "Introduction," in W. Radice and B. Reynolds (eds) *The Translator's Art: Essays in Honour of Betty Radice*, Harmondsworth, England: Penguin.

Radway, J. (1984) *Reading the Romance: Women, Patriarchy, and Popular Literature*, Chapel Hill: University of North Carolina Press.

—— (1989) "The Book-of-the-Month Club and the General Reader: The Uses of 'Serious' Fiction," in C. Davidson (ed.) *Reading in America: Literature and Social History*, Baltimore: Johns Hopkins University Press.

Rafael, V.L. (1988) *Contracting Colonialism: Translation and Christian Conversion in Tagalog Society under Early Spanish Rule*, Ithaca, N.Y.: Cornell University Press.

Rea, J. (1975) "Aspects of African Publishing 1945–74," *African Book Publishing Record* 1: 145–149.

Redfield, J.M. (1975) *Nature and Culture in the Iliad: The Tragedy of Hector*, Chicago: University of Chicago Press.

Reynolds, B. (1989) *The Passionate Intellect: Dorothy Sayers' Encounter with Dante*, Kent, Ohio: Kent State University Press.

Richards, D. (1994) "Sondheim Explores the Heart's Terrain," *New York Times*, 10 May, p. B1.

Ripken, P. (1991) "African Literature in the Literary Market Place Outside Africa," *African Book Publishing Record* 17: 289–291.

Rivers-Smith, S. (1931) Review of R.H. Parry, *Longmans African Geographies: East Africa* (1932), *Oversea Education* 3: 208.

Robyns, C. (1994) "Translation and Discursive Identity," *Poetics Today* 15: 405–428.

Rodman, S. (1953) Review of A. Tutuola, *The Palm-Wine Drinkard*, *New York Times*, 20 September, p. 5.

Rollin, R. (1988) "*The Name of the Rose* as Popular Culture," in M.T. Inge (ed.) *Naming the Rose: Essays on Eco's The Name of the Rose*, Jackson: University Press of Mississippi.

Rorty, R. (1979) *Philosophy and the Mirror of Nature*, Princeton, N.J.: Princeton University Press.

Rose, M. (1993) *Authors and Owners: The Invention of Copyright*, Cambridge: Harvard University Press.

Ross, A. (1989) *No Respect: Intellectuals and Popular Culture*, New York and London: Routledge.

Rostagno, I. (1997) *Searching for Recognition: The Promotion of Latin American Literature in the United States*, Westport, Conn.: Greenwood.

Said, E. (1978) *Orientalism*, New York: Pantheon.

St. John, J. (1990) *William Heinemann: A Century of Publishing, 1890–1990*, London: Heinemann.

Sandrock, M. (1950) "New Novels," *Catholic World*, September, p. 472.

Sargeant, W. (1952) "Anti-Communist Funnyman," *Life*, 10 November, p. 125.

Saunders, D. (1992) *Authorship and Copyright*, London and New York: Routledge.

Saunders, T. (ed. and trans.) (1970) Plato, *The Laws*, Harmondsworth, England: Penguin.

—— (1987a) "The Penguinification of Plato," in W. Radice and B. Reynolds (eds) *The Translator's Art: Essays in Honour of Betty Radice*, Harmondsworth, England: Penguin.

—— (ed. and trans.) (1987b) Plato, *Ion*, in *Early Socratic Dialogues*, Harmondsworth, England: Penguin.

Savran, D. (1992) *Communists, Cowboys, and Queers: The Politics of Masculinity in the Work of Arthur Miller and Tennessee Williams*, Minneapolis: University of Minnesota Press.

Schare, J. (1983) Review of U. Eco, *The Name of the Rose*, *Harper's*, August, p. 75–76.

Schlesinger, A., Jr. (1949) *The Vital Center: The Politics of Freedom*, Boston: Houghton Mifflin.

Schwartz, B. (1964) *In Search of Wealth and Power: Yan Fu and the West*, Cambridge: Harvard University Press.

Scott, P. (1990) "Gabriel Okara's *The Voice*: The Non-Ijo Reader and the Pragmatics of Translingualism," *Research in African Literatures* 21: 75–88.

Sedgwick, E.K. (1985) *Between Men: English Literature and Male Homosocial Desire*, New York: Columbia University Press.

Semanov, V.I. (1980) *Lu Hsün and His Predecessors* (1967), trans. C. Alber, White Plains, N.Y.: M.E. Sharpe.

Shreve, G.M. (1996) "On the Nature of Scientific and Empirical Translation Studies," in M.G. Rose (ed.) *Translation Horizons: Beyond the Boundaries of Translation Spectrum*, Binghamton, N.Y.: Center for Research in Translation.

Shulman, P. (1992) "Faux Poe," *Village Voice*, 20 October, p. 70.

Simon, S. (1996) *Gender in Translation: Cultural Identity and the Politics of Transmission*, London and New York: Routledge.

Singh, T. (1994) "India," in P.G. Altbach and E.S. Hoshino (eds) *International Book Publishing: An Encyclopedia*, New York: Garland.

Skone James, E.P, J.F. Mummery, J.E. Rayner James, and K.M. Garnett (1991) *Copinger and Skone James on Copyright*, 13th edition, London: Sweet and Maxwell.

Slonim, M. (ed.) (1954) *Modern Italian Short Stories*, New York: Simon and Schuster.

Sondheim, S., and J. Lapine (1994) *Passion: A Musical*, New York: Theater Communications Group.

Sparks, H.F.D. (1970) "Jerome as Biblical Scholar," in P. Ackroyd and C.F. Evans (eds) *Cambridge History of the Bible*, vol. 1, Cambridge: Cambridge University Press.

Stableford, B. (1993) "How Modern Horror Was Born," *Necrofile*, Winter, p. 6.

Stanger, A. (1997) "In Search of *The Joke*: An Open Letter to Milan Kundera," *New England Review* 18(1) (Winter): 93–100.

Steiner, G. (1975) *After Babel: Aspects of Language and Translation*, London and New York: Oxford University Press.

Stewart, S. (1991) *Crimes of Writing: Problems in the Containment of Representation*, New York and Oxford: Oxford University Press.

Strawson, P.F. (1954) Review of L. Wittgenstein, *Philosophical Investigations*, *Mind* 63: 70–99.

Sugrue, T. (1950) "A Priest, a Red, and an Unworried Christ," *Saturday Review of Literature*, 19 August, p. 10.

Süskind, P. (1986) *Perfume: The Story of a Murderer*, trans. J.E. Woods, London: Hamish Hamilton.

Tabor, M.B.W. (1995) "Book Deals: Losing Nothing in Translation," *New York Times*, 16 October, pp. D1, D8.

Taplin, O. (1977) *The Stagecraft of Aeschylus: The Dramatic Use of Exits and Entrances in Greek Tragedy*, Oxford: Clarendon Press.

Tarchetti, I.U. (1971) *Fosca*, Turin: Einaudi.

—— (1977) *Racconti fantastici*, ed. N. Bonifazi, Milan: Guanda.

Therborn, G. (1980) *The Ideology of Power and the Power of Ideology*, London: Verso.

Thomson, G. (1982) "An Introduction to Implicature for Translators," *Notes on Translation* 1: 1–28.

Times Literary Supplement (1951) "The Artist and the Real World," 5 January, pp. 1–2.

Toury, G. (1995) *Descriptive Translation Studies and Beyond*, Amsterdam and Philadelphia: John Benjamins.

Troubridge, U.V. (trans.) (1949) Partial Draft of *The Little World of Don Camillo*, unpublished manuscript, Farrar, Straus and Giroux Archive, Rare Books and Manuscripts Division, New York Public Library.

Truman, H. (1963) "A Special Message to the Congress on Greece and Turkey: The Truman Doctrine," in *Public Papers of the Presidents of the United States: Harry S. Truman, 1947*, Washington, D.C.: United States Government Printing Office.

Tutuola, A. (1952) *The Palm-Wine Drinkard*, London: Faber and Faber.

Tytler, A. (1978) *Essay on the Principles of Translation*, ed. J.F. Huntsman, Amsterdam and Philadelphia: John Benjamins.

Vené, G.F. (1977) *Don Camillo, Peppone e il compromesso storico*, Milan: SugarCo.

Venuti, L. (1985–86) "The Ideology of the Individual in Anglo-American Criticism: The Example of Coleridge and Eliot," *Boundary 2* 14: 161–193.

—— (ed. and trans.) (1992) I.U. Tarchetti, *Fantastic Tales*, San Francisco: Mercury House.

—— (trans.) (1994) I.U. Tarchetti, *Passion: A Novel*, San Francisco: Mercury House.

—— (1995a) *The Translator's Invisibility: A History of Translation*, London and New York: Routledge.

—— (1995b) "Translating Thomas Mann," *Times Literary Supplement*, 22 December, p. 17.

Vivien, R. (1986) *Poésies complètes*, ed. J.-P. Goujon, Paris: Régine Desforges.

Walters, R., Jr. (1950) Review of G. Guareschi, *The Little World of Don Camillo*, unpublished article for *Saturday Review of Literature*, Farrar, Straus and Giroux Archive, Rare Books and Manuscripts Division, New York Public Library.

Ward, H. (1962) "'Don Camillo' Instead of 'Silas Marner'," *New York Times Magazine*, 1 April, pp. 18, 76, 79.

Watson, C.W. (1973) "*Salah Asuhan* and the Romantic Tradition in the Early Indonesian Novel," *Modern Asian Studies* 7: 179–192.

Wei Ze, D. (1994) "China," in P.G. Altbach and E.S. Hoshino (eds) *International Book Publishing: An Encyclopedia*, New York: Garland.

Weigel, G. (1983) "Murder in the Dark Ages," *Seattle Weekly*, 17–23 August.

Welty, E. (1952) "When Good Meets Bad," *New York Times Book Review*, 17 August, p. 4.

Wentworth, H., and S.B. Flexner (eds) (1975) *Dictionary of American Slang*, 2nd supplemented edition, New York: Thomas Crowell.

Westbrook, V. (1997) "Richard Taverner Revising Tyndale," *Reformation*, 2: 191–205.

Weyr, T. (1994) "The Foreign Rights Bonanza," *Publishers Weekly* 28 November, pp. 32–38.

White, C. (ed. and trans.) (1990) *The Correspondence between Jerome and Augustine of Hippo*, Lewiston, N.Y.: Edwin Mellen Press.

Whiteside, T. (1981) *The Blockbuster Complex: Conglomerates, Show Business, and Book Publishing*, Middletown, Conn.: Wesleyan University Press.

Wickeri, J. (1995) "The Union Version of the Bible and the New Literature in China," *Translator* 1: 129–152.

Wilamowitz, U. von. (1913) *Sappho und Simonides: Untersuchungen über griechische Lyriker*, Berlin: Weidman.

Williams, A.D. (ed.) (1996) *Fifty Years: A Farrar, Straus and Giroux Reader*, New York: Farrar, Straus and Giroux.

Williams, C.D. (1992) *Pope, Homer, and Manliness: Some Aspects of Eighteenth-Century Classical Learning*, London and New York: Routledge.

Wittgenstein, L. (1953) *Philosophical Investigations*, trans. G.E.M. Anscombe, ed. G.E.M. Anscombe, R. Rhees, and G.H. von Wright, Oxford: Blackwell.

Woodmansee, M. (1984) "The Genius and the Copyright: Economic and Legal Conditions of the Emergence of the 'Author'," *Eighteenth-Century Studies* 14: 425–448.

Workman, A.J. (1955) Review of L. Wittgenstein, *Philosophical Investigations, Personalist* 36: 292–3.

Worsley, P. (1984) *The Three Worlds: Culture and World Development*, Chicago: University of Chicago Press.

Yoshimoto, B. (1993) *Kitchen*, trans. M. Backus, New York: Grove Press.

Zabus, C. (1991) *The African Palimpsest: Indigenization of Language in the West African Europhone Novel*, Amsterdam and Atlanta: Rodopi.

Zell, H., and H. Silver (1971) *A Reader's Guide to African Literature*, London, Ibadan, and Nairobi: Heinemann.

Zhao, H.Y.H. (1995) *The Uneasy Narrator: Chinese Fiction from the Traditional to the Modern*, Oxford and New York: Oxford University Press.

INDEX

Achebe, C. 178; *Things Fall Apart* 168
African Writers Series (Heinemann) 167
Alfred Knopf 71
America 136, 148
American Comparative Literature
  Association 104
American Speech 144
Amis, K. 149
Anaximander 119, 120
Andreyev, L. 184
Anscombe, G.E.M. 110; translation of L.
  Wittgenstein 107–14, 116
Anzaldúa, G. 94
Approaches to Teaching World Literature
  (MLA) 90–1, 103
Aristotle 59, 75, 83, 118, 120; *Poetics*
  69–70
Arnold, M.: *On Translating Homer* 100–1
Associated Press 144
Asterix 26
Atwood, M. 161
Augustine 78–80; *Confessions* 114

Backus, M.: translation of B. Yoshimoto
  85–7
Bacon, F. 114
Balai Pustaka 167
Baltimore Sun 133
Balzac, H. 168
Barnard College Library 134
Barney, N.C.: *Cinq petits dialogues grec* 45
Barrett, W. 135
Barth, J. 169
Barthes, R. 144
Baudelaire, C. 38, 46
Beaugrande, R. de and W. Dressler 30
Beckett, S. 161
Ben Jelloun, T.: *La Nuit Sacrée* 176, 178

Bennett, W. 92–3
Bent Ali, M. 38–9
Bently, L. 52
Berman, A. 11, 77–8, 81, 84
Berne Convention 51–3, 161–2
Bernheimer, C. 104
Bible 78–80, 83–4, 90, 116, 177, 186
Bioy Casares, A. 170
Birnbaum, A.: *Monkey Brain Sushi* 74, 75
Bogart, H. 131
Book-of-the-Month Club 128, 130, 134,
  139, 152
Books on Trial 136
Borges, J.L. 4–5, 169, 170
British Comparative Literature
  Association 104
Brodsky, J. 150
Brontë, E.: *Wuthering Heights* 16
Bunyan, J.: *The Pilgrim's Progress* 166, 174
Burnett, T.: *Archaeologia Philosophica* 55–6,
  59–60
Burnett v. Chetwood 55–7, 59–60, 64
Byrne v. Statist Co. 58–59, 60–1
Bywater, I.: translation of Aristotle 69–70

Cain, J.M.: *Mildred Pierce* 144
Camden, Lord 57
Campbell v. Acuff Rose Music, Inc. 64
Camus, A.: *The Plague* 90
Caputo, J. 121
Cartland, B. 161
Catholic Digest Book Club 128, 152
Catholic World 138, 147
Cavalcanti, G. 76
Cervantes: *Don Quixote* 90
Chapman, G.: translation of the *Iliad*
  101–2
Charles E. Tuttle 73

Chicago Tribune 128, 136
Christie, A. 161
Cixous, H. 170
Collette 149
Colliers 136, 139
Commonweal 130
Companion Book Club 128
comparative literature 8, 89, 96, 99, 104
Conan Doyle, Sir A. 179
Confucianism 179–81, 184, 186
Confucius: *Analects* 179
Copyright Act of 1911 58–9
Cornell Drama Club 134
Cortázar, J. 169
The Courier (UNESCO) 2
Cudahy, S. 136–48

Dangerous Liaisons 153
Dante Alighieri: *Divine Comedy* 90–2, 93
Defoe, D. 179
DeJean, J. 39, 42
Deleuze, G. and F. Guattari 9, 10, 23, 26, 122
Derrida, J. 91–2
Dickens, C. 168; *The Old Curiosity Shop* 179
Diels, H. 120
Di Giovanni, N.T. 4–5
Donaldson v. Beckett 57
Dumas, A.: *La Dame aux camélias* 179, 182
Dryden, J. 31
Dudovitz, R. 126

East India Company 166, 171
Echo de Paris 34
Eco, U.: *The Name of the Rose* 48, 153, 154–6
Eliot, T.S. 150
Else, G.: translation of Aristotle 70
L'Espresso 164
ethics of translation 6, 11, 23–4, 81–87, 115–16, 187–9
Even-Zohar, I. 27, 29
L'Express 164

Faber and Faber 175
Fagles, R.: translation of the *Iliad* 100
Farrar, Straus and Giroux 138, 148, 150–2
Fiat 24
Fiedler, L. 136
Financial Times 60

Flaiano, E. 138
Flaubert, G. 13, 39; *Madame Bovary* 14
Fleming, I. 163
Fowler, E. 71–2, 84
Fowler, H.W. 97
Frechtman, B.: translation of J. Genet 50–1
Frenaye, F. 152; translation of G. Guareschi 147

García Márquez, G.: *One Hundred Years of Solitude* 90, 169
Gardiner, H.C. 136–7, 148
Garshin, V. 184
Gautier, T. 13
Genet, J.: *The Thief's Journal* 50–1
Gide, A. 38
Gil Blas 40
Ginzburg, N.: *The Road to the City* 152
Giroux, H. 94–5
Goethe, J.W. von 77–8, 184; *Faust* 90, 186; *The Sorrows of Young Werther* 186
Gogol, N. 186
Goldsmith, O.: *The Deserted Village* 113
Goldstein, P. 48
Gordon, R. 149
Goren, C.: *The Complete Canasta* 138
Great Books 2, 89, 90, 92, 94
Greek Anthology 35
Green, J. (G. Sager): translation of G. Guareschi 150
Grice, P. 21–4, 30
Grossett and Dunlap 139
Grove Press 50, 71, 74
Grove Press, Inc. v. Greenleaf Publishing Co. 50–1
Guareschi, G. 127, 131, 133–4, 139, 150–2, 155; *Candido* 133; *Comrade Don Camillo* 152; *Don Camillo's Dilemma* 128, 134; *Don Camillo and His Flock* 128, 135, 137, 152; *Don Camillo Takes the Devil by the Tail* 128, 148; *The House That Nino Built* 128, 132, 135–6; *A Husband in Boarding School* 150; *The Little World of Don Camillo* 127–49, 151; *Mondo Piccolo: Don Camillo* 133, 140, 149; *My Home, Sweet Home* 150
Guillory, J. 92, 103
Gutt, E.-A. 26

Haggard, H.R. 167, 183, 188; *Montezuma's Daughter* 180; *The Spirit of Bambatse* 180
Hamilton, E.: *Mythology* 174
Hancock, T. 149
Harker, J. 74–5
HarperCollins 150
Harper's 136, 155
Harrison, B.G. 18–20, 23
Harvey, K. 25–6
The Hattiesburg American 155
Heaney, S. 150
Hedylus 35, 36–7
Heidegger, M. 71, 119; *Being and Time* 119; "The Anaximander Fragment" 119–22
Heineman 167–9
Heiney, D. 135
Henry VIII 83
Hibbett, H. 72
Hill, A. 168–9
Høeg, P.: *Miss Smilla's Feeling for Snow* 153
Hoffmann, E.T.A. 13
Homer 75, 96, 98; *Iliad* 90, 99–102, 104; *Odyssey* 90, 187–8, 189
Hook, S. 119
Hopkins, G.M. 177
Hugo, V. 179; *Les Misérables* 153
Huxley, T.H. 183; *Evolution and Ethics* 181, 182

Ibsen, H.: *A Doll's House* 90

Jeffreys v. Boosey 54
Jerome 78–80, 83
Johnson, S. 26
Jones, J. 69–71, 75, 83
Jones, Sir W. 166, 170
Jowett, B. 100; translation of Plato 96, 116–17

Kafka, F. 5–6
Kakutani, M. 74
Kawabata, Y. 71, 72, 74, 76; *Snow Country* 71
Keene, D. 72, 74
King James Bible 84, 116, 177
King, S. 13, 161
Kirkus Reviews 18
Kodansha International 73, 74
Koran 62

Krell, D.F.: translation of M. Heidegger 119–22
Kripke, S. 107
Kundera, M.: *The Joke* 5–6

Lambert, J. 27
Lattimore, R.: translation of the *Iliad* 99–102, 104
Lecercle, J.-J. 10, 27
Lefevere, A. 27, 73–4
Lenin, V.I. 158
Levi, C.: *Christ Stopped at Eboli* 152
Life 130, 134
linguistics 1–2, 8–9, 21–3, 25, 29–30
Lin Shu 179, 180, 184; translation of C. Dickens 179; translation of A. Dumas 179–80, 182–3; translation of H.R. Haggard 180–1, 189
Lispector, C. 170
Locke, J. 54, 62; *Second Treatise of Civil Government* 54–5
Longmans 163, 165
Loti, P. 167
Louis, G. 37, 39
Louÿs, P.: *Les Chansons de Bilitis* 34–46
Lowe-Porter, H.: translation of T. Mann 32–3
Ludlum, R. 161
Lu Xun 183, 186, 189; translation of J. Verne 183; and Zhou Zuoren: translation anthology 184, 185–6

MacDonald, D. 136
McGrath, P. 13
Macaulay, T. 171
Macquarrie, J. and E. Robinson: translation of M. Heidegger 119
Malcolm, N. 110
Mallarmé, S. 38, 44
Mann, T. 32–3
Manu 166
Manzoni, A.: *I promessi sposi* 13
Marx, K. and F. Engels: *The Communist Manifesto* 186
Mason, I. 3
May, R. 30
Mencken, H.L. 144
Mercure de France 34
Meredith, G. 17
Mill, J.S.: *On Liberty* 181
Millar v. Taylor 54–5, 56, 57
Miller, A.: *All My Sons* 144
Milton, J. 121; *Paradise Lost* 113

Mishima, Y. 71, 72, 74, 76
Mitsios, H.: *New Japanese Voices* 74
Mitterand, F. 178
Miyoshi, M. 84–7
Modern Language Association of America (MLA) 90, 99, 103
Moeis, A. 167
Montaigne: *Essays* 90
Montesquieu: *Spirit of Laws* 182
Moravia, A. 135, 151
More, T. 83
Morris, I. 72
Multilingual Matters Ltd 9

National Endowment for the Humanities 92
Necrofile 16
Neubert, A. and G. Shreve 30
New Directions 71
The New Republic 132
Newsweek 164
The New Yorker 15, 20, 136, 137, 164
The New York Times 18, 20, 74, 128, 131, 134, 135, 147
Nietzsche, F.: *On the Genealogy of Morals* 70–1; *Thus Spake Zarathustra* 186
Nobel Prize for Literature 150, 151
Nora, P. 125
Nord, C. 83

Ocampo, S. 169–70
Okara, G.: *The Voice* 176–8
Orbison, R. 64
Ortese, A.M.: *The Bay Is Not Naples* 152
Our Sunday Visitor 136
The Outer Limits 18

Parker Pen 164
Partisan Review 135
Pellegrini and Cudahy 136–40, 142, 148, 149, 151–2
Pellegrini, G. 138, 152
PEN American Center 47
Penguin 149
Penguin Classics 91, 117, 188
Perrot d'Ablancourt, N. 81
Petrarch 53
The Phantom of the Opera 153
Philodemus 35, 36
Pinpin, T. 171–4, 178
Pirandello, L. 135
Plato 120; *Ion* 96–9; *Laws* 117–18
Pocket Books 139

Poe, E.A. 13, 14
polysystem theory 27, 29, 30
Pope, A.: translation of the *Iliad* 101–2, 104
Pound, E. 76
pragmatics 21, 30
Prix Goncourt 178
Public Lending Right 47

Rabassa, G.: translation of G.G. Márquez 169
Radcliffe, A. 13
Radice, B. 117
Random House 161
Régnier, H. de 38
remainder 10–12, 14, 17–18, 21–3, 25–7, 29–30, 63, 86, 89, 95–6, 98–9, 101–3, 108–16, 122
Rice, A. 13
Rieu, E.V.: translation of the *Odyssey* 188
Robbins, H. 161
Rorty, R. 119
Rosenberg, J. and E. 128
Rossetti, D.G. 76
Rousseau, J.-J. 16
Routledge 8–9
Rushdie, S.: *The Satanic Verses* 62
Russell, B. 114

Sagan, F.: *Bonjour Tristesse* 125
Sager, G. (J. Green): translation of G. Guareschi 150
Said, E. 39
San Francisco Chronicle 136
Sappho 34, 35, 38, 39, 42, 43, 45–6
Sartre, J.-P. 71
Saturday Review of Literature 128–9, 136, 147
Saunders, T.: translation of Plato 96–9, 117–18
Sayers, D.: translation of Dante 91, 92, 93
Schleiermacher, F. 77, 120; "On the Different Methods of Translating" 77, 184–5
Schlesinger, A., Jr. 131
Scola, E.: *Passione d'amore* 20
Scott, Sir W. 17, 179
Seidensticker, E. 72
Sellers, P. 149
Septuagint 78–80
Shakespeare, W. 28, 117; *Hamlet* 121
Sheldon, S. 161

Shelley, M. 14
Sidney, Sir P. 121
Sienkiewicz, H. 184, 186
The Sign 136
Silone, I.: The Seed beneath the Snow 152
Simon and Schuster 150
Singer, I.B. 150
Smith, Adam 181; Wealth of Nations 182
Smith, Arthur: Chinese Characteristics 183
Snyder, R. 150
Sondheim, S. and J. Lapine: Passion 14, 20
Spencer, H. 181, 183
Stationers' Company 53
Statute of Anne 54, 55, 56, 57
Steiner, G. 116
Stevenson, R.L. 179
Stoker, B.: Dracula 16, 17
Stowe, H.B.: Uncle Tom's Cabin 57
Stowe v. Thomas 57–8
Straus, R. 150–1
Süskind, P.: Perfume 153, 154

Tanizaki, J. 71, 72, 74, 76, 84; The Makioka Sisters 72, 84
Tarchetti, I.U.: Fantastic Tales 13–16; Passion 14, 16–20, 23, 25–6
Tati, J. 149
Taverner, R. 83
text linguistics 21, 30
Thackeray, W. 17
Thomas, D. 177
Thomas More Book Club 137–8, 139
tie-ins 14, 48, 152–3, 165
Tottel's Miscellany 53
Toury, G. 27–30
translated advertisements 24, 159, 164
translation studies 1–2, 8–9, 21, 28–30, 46
translators' contracts 47, 151–2
Troubridge, U.V. 151–2; translation of Collette 149; translation of G. Guareschi 142–4, 149
Truman, H. 129
Tutuola, A. 177, 178; The Palm-Wine Drinkard 174–6
2 Live Crew 64
Tyndale, W. 83
Tytler, A.F. 184; Essay on the Principles of Translation 182

UNESCO 2–3, 53, 158, 160, 161, 165
Union Version (Chinese Bible) 186

Veja 164
Venuti, L. 9–11, 21; translation of I.U. Tarchetti 13–20, 23, 25–6
Verga, G. 13, 135
Verne, J. 167; De la terre à la lune 183
Victor Gollancz 138, 148, 149, 152
The Village Voice 15
Vitale, A. 161
Vivien, R.: translation of Sappho 45–6
Voice of America 140
Voltaire: Candide 90
Vursell, H. 150

Walcott, D. 150
Wallace, E. 163
Walt Disney Productions 165
Ward, H. 134
Weaver, W. 48; translation of U. Eco 154–5
Welcker, F.G. 41–3
Welty, E. 13, 135, 137
Wilamowitz-Moellendorf, U. von 40–3
Wittgenstein, L. 110; Philosophical Investigations 107–14, 116
Wodehouse, P.G. 144
Woods, J.E.: translation of T. Mann 33
Wyatt, Sir T. 53
Wyatt v. Barnard 56

Yan Fu 180, 182, 183; translation of T.H. Huxley 181; translation of J.S. Mill 181
Ye Shengtao: Ni Huanzhi 186
Yijing (Book of Changes) 183
Yoshimoto, B. 74; Kitchen 74–5, 82, 84–7
Young, E.: Conjectures on Original Composition 53

Zhou Zuoren 183–4, 189; and Lu Xun: translation anthology 184, 185–6
Zola, E. 13; Thérèse Raquin 14